—————————

THE LOST DI

New Directions in Anthropological Writing
History, Poetics, Cultural Criticism

GEORGE E. MARCUS
Rice University

JAMES CLIFFORD
University of California, Santa Cruz

GENERAL EDITORS

THE LOST DRUM

The Myth of Sexuality in Papua New Guinea and Beyond

JAMES F. WEINER

THE UNIVERSITY OF WISCONSIN PRESS

The University of Wisconsin Press
114 North Murray Street
Madison, Wisconsin 53715

3 Henrietta Street
London WC2E 8LU, England

Library of Congress Cataloging-in-Publication Data
Weiner, James F.
    The lost drum: the myth of sexuality in Papua New Guinea and
beyond / James F. Weiner.
    224 p.   cm. —(New directions in anthropological writing)
    Includes bibliographical references and index.
    ISBN 0-299-14860-2 (alk. paper).
    ISBN 0-299-14864-5 (pbk.: alk. paper)
    1. Ethnology—Papua New Guinea. 2. Rites and ceremonies
—Papua New Guinea. 3. Mythology, Papuan. 4. Sex—Mythology.
5. Foi (Papua New Guinea people)—Rites and ceremonies.
6. Psychoanalysis.
I. Title. II. Series.
GN671.N5W45   1995
306'.089'9912—dc20   95-7739

For Eamon Robert Weiner
the little (br)other

Contents

Illustrations

Figures

Acknowledgments

I wrote a first draft of this book between December 1991 and July 1994 while a member of the Department of Social Anthropology, University of Manchester. I am grateful for the support and stimulation of all my colleagues and of those students in Manchester and Adelaide who first heard segments of this book in my lectures.

Marilyn Strathern and Roy Wagner provided great encouragement and intellectual challenge while I was writing, and in fact this book is an attempt to restate and extend their theories of Melanesian language and sociality in somewhat different terms. Chapters 5 and 6 owe much to Marilyn Strathern's lectures on the aesthetics of form in Melanesia, given at the University of Manchester, Department of Social Anthropology, 1991–92. The following people also read and commented on various parts of the manuscript: Debbora Battaglia, Eytan Bercovitch, Vincent Crapanzano, Tony Crook, Hastings Donnan, Steven Feld, Bernard Juillerat, Penelope Harvey, Bruce Knauft, James Leach, Jadran Mimica, Henrietta Moore, Richard Parmentier, Alan Rumsey, and Margaret Rodman.

Chapter 2 first appeared in *Semiotica* 99(1–2): 81–100 (1994); Chapter 7 first appeared in *Cultural Anthropology* 9(1): 37–57 (1994). I am grateful for permission to reprint those papers here.

Introduction:
The Object(s) of Myth

Coins bearing the imprint of the scallop shell dating from between the 2d and 1st centuries B.C. have been recovered from several southern coastal towns in Spain and Italy. At this time, the scallop was itself an icon of Aphrodite, the goddess of desire, and her cult. The coin which bears the imprint of this fertile iconography must therefore have had inseminating or fertilizing properties, and in fact such coins were considered appropriate offerings at the goddess's shrines. It could also be that these coastal towns preferred to signal their affinity with the sea by such an emblem, and with the sea goddess herself. From Cythera on Crete, where the cult first entered Greece, Aphrodite is depicted with triton shells and sea anemones; the sea urchin and cuttlefish were sacred to her.

Consider, then, that in our antiquity, in some places our money was itself a shell valuable; that it was redolent of all the things associated with the sea and with asexual shell ontogenesis; that it carried a myth with it; and that the myth was about the birth of desire. Would we not think it necessary to know something about the myth and its cult to know how it functioned as a conduit of this desire, as the body of language which gives form to the objects of desire?

Without a doubt, exchange and reciprocity have been the most dominant concepts that have been pressed into the service of describing and analyzing Melanesian societies. The objects of exchange enter into these accounts as tokens of the efficacy, autonomy, and subjectivity of those who give and receive them, and it is in the distribution of such tokens that these characteristics of the person acquire a social impact. In such a view, a person's *relationship to the object* is both the site of sociality and the space within which the actor achieves a perspective on this sociality.

But long before the person recognizes a distinctness between herself

xiii

and the objects which she invests with such social power, there exists a more primordial stage of undifferentiatedness, a stage in which what is interior to the self and what is external to it are not readily distinguishable, where in the sexual-gustatory pleasure obtained through the satisfaction of hunger the person attempts to orally incorporate the object that satisfies that hunger. These objects, which are themselves persons or parts of persons, first circulate within the orbit of the body's drives. Outlining the body's configuration, they comprise a field within which the subject's speech is anchored, and they serve to constitute the history of the subject in bodily form. It is this embodied history of these objects which is repeated and continuously played out later on in life in the arena of public exchange.

But in what form do these primordial objects appear in social life and in the imagery which makes it visible? Is it not the case that we first become aware of them through their loss, their withdrawal from that original incorporative scene? To speak, however, of a *relationship to the object* implies that both the subject and the object preexist the relationship between them, and that the subject is encountering the object for *the first time.* But to encounter the object, to seek it, to desire it, is to *reseek* that part which was detached from one.[1] This act of detachment creates a gap which allows relationality itself to become visible, and to constitute the person and her drives. Instead of a relationship to the object, then, I will speak of *object relations* and ultimately of *relational objects,* to signal that subject and object themselves are defined only by relationship itself; in fact, the object passing between people *is* the relationship itself (cf. LaPlanche and Pontalis 1988 : 275).

Furthermore, both at the level of the development of the human subject and as a generalized image of Melanesian social process, this relationship, constituted through the phenomena of splitting, detachment, and loss, means that subject and object are relationally constituted *internally* as well as with respect to each other. In what form does this internal split appear in the *forms* of our social interaction?

One of Sigmund Freud's (1920 : 14–17) most famous and most analyzed passages was his description of the *fort/da* game invented by his infant grandson. The eighteen-month-old child, often left alone by his mother for long periods, would amuse himself with an empty spool of thread attached to a string. He would throw the spool over the edge of his crib where it would disappear behind the curtain partition of his cot, at which point he would utter the word *"oooh!"* (*fort!* gone!). Pulling it back by the string, he would greet its reappearance with the word *da!* (there!). This game he repeated over and over again.

It could be said that the child succeeded with a substitute object, the spool, in making the lost object of desire, that is, his mother (or at another level, the mother's breast), reappear. But would this alone explain why the child repeated the game of alternating 'gone!' and 'there!' over and over again?

Or was the child detaching precisely that part of himself that was *split off* by the mother's disappearance, that part of himself, that is, his mother and her breast, which constituted the most profound perception of his primordial undifferentiated bodily being? Was he not demonstrating that internally this being was composed of a radical oscillation between himself and the other which was originally a part of him but which was now split from him? That the spool could be no more than a token of the *gap* or *scission* at the very heart of the self, a self-alienation that can never be repaired but whose terms of creation can only be resought and resought and played out over and over again? And finally, could we see the child's accession to language as his first labeling of this gap, in this case modeled by the vacillating spool, the endlessly recycling, empty, unraveled shell, a labeling which tries to insert a substitute object in place of that gap?

The pearl shell origin myth among the Foi of Papua New Guinea details not how shells arrived in Foi, but how they were originally *lost*, and had to be reclaimed through trade. Is this not a commentary on how in Melanesia every wealth object sought is in fact being resought? And is it not precisely this lost object that is, as Ricoeur (1970:379) so perceptively notes, the constant and enduring theme of psychoanalysis?

The Papuan myths I consider in this book deal with lost or detached objects that, although destined to complete the missing parts of persons, instead elude their control, or incorporate the whole person instead of being reincorporated themselves. They parody our Western demand for social inalienability: These objects refuse to make proper connections; they have wills, desires, and voices of their own, but also take over, incorporate, or *become* the owner. Like sexual organs, they have their own embarrassing powers of extensibility, intrude themselves into people's desire, swallow other objects, organs, persons, and discourses.

In the obviational model I employed in *The Heart of the Pearl Shell* (Weiner 1988) and will continue to elaborate here, I depict the movement of a mythical narrative as a series of substitutions. In the myths I examine in this book, these substitutions take the form of certain bodily extensions that move from person to person, reminding us that each person's subjectivity may at any time escape his or her power, may in fact participate in and constitute other subjects. In so doing, these metonymic bodily tokens both expand and expose the limits of and holes within those persons' social extensibility.

Let us now make the following assumption about social life. Let us say that there are gaps or holes in meaning of this kind in any arena of social activity we might care to isolate—exchange, production, ritual, language, and so on. These gaps cannot be exposed with the resources of that particular activity alone—the exposure must come by way of another perspective that is deliberately situated in a relationship of externality to it. We could say that the making visible of social meaning and social knowledge becomes possible when some external perspective is attained on that activity. Social life then becomes the ceaseless attempt to fashion different languages, different analytic perspectives that allow the actor to uncover the concealments of conventional thought and action.

It is significant then that Ricoeur chooses to characterize psychoanalysis in the following manner:

> analytic experience unfolds in the field of speech and . . . within this field, *what comes to light is another language, dissociated from common language* . . . (1970:366–67, my emphasis)

Psychoanalysis works by inventing a new language for the patient, one that replaces or glosses the language that is her symptom. And here I am identifying the following parallel questions for anthropology: What else do people do for their social life when they tell a myth? What else do we attempt as anthropologists when we provide the gloss on those myths or rituals? And if this is so, do not all these glosses play their role in creating the possibility of meaning within myth and social behavior?

We can say that the myth is the body of the object whose orbit and movement it describes; the myth provides an account of how and why the object becomes trapped within human desire. But at the same time, we the listeners become traps for the myth. A myth about an object, for example, the Foi pearl shell, is thus a double trap: the object is trapped in our drives, and the myth that enframes it traps *us*; it becomes the shell of signification which gives birth, Aphrodite-fashion, to the object of desire.

The shell is a good object to begin with, since it has exerted such a fascination for people in diverse traditions, both Western and non-Western. In *The Poetics of Space*, Gaston Bachelard described the shell:

as the clearest proof of life's ability to constitute forms. According to this theory, which was propounded in the eighteenth century by J. B. Robinet, everything that has form has a shell ontogenesis, and life's principal effort is to make shells. (1969:111)

Containers of all sorts—flasks and other earthenware and glass vessels—were also frequently adorned with shell motifs in the classic periods. In *Le bestiaire du Christ*, Charbonneaux-Lassay writes: "Taken as a whole, with both its hard covering and its sentient organism, the shell, for the Ancients, was the symbol of the human being in its entirety, body and soul" (cited in Bachelard 1969:116).

Let me recall what I identified as the crucial insight of psychoanalysis: that to perceive the world as relationally based is to recognize one's own internal relational constitution. And this identification works in reverse: If a person has shell-like qualities, then his/her relationships will model the shell ontogenesis too—they will be embodied.

Jeffrey Clark once showed me a picture that one of his Wiru informants from the Southern Highlands of Papua New Guinea had drawn for him (see Illustration 1). It shows a man standing with his arms outstretched, and every part of his body from head to toe is covered with pearl shells, so that the man himself seems composed of shells. If the shells are tokens for those parts of a person's identity that are donated or formed and then detached by others, then the pearl shell-covered man is what such a person literally looks like. It would function for the Wiru exactly how an X-ray functions for us. The drawing "shows" that what appears as a single body or single skin is constituted by the replicated and repetitive acts of detachment by other bodies, and that these tokens are themselves detachable and returnable; they are the space between the *fort* and the *da*, simultaneously in one and in others.

We will also have to say that the *inside* of the Wiru man's body is an assemblage of shells. And paradoxically, through an appeal to this most organic image, the shell and its living encased creature, we deny the Western appellation of "organic" to the Papuan body. For as each pearl shell bespeaks its own history, so does each organ of the Papuan body have a separate causality, and together they do not constitute an irreducible, individual organic whole.

In Papua New Guinea, the shell is the exemplary product of the hermeneutic of embodiment. In Mt. Hagen, these shells are cemented into a resin board so that they have a visible body (A. Strathern 1968). They are lined up in a single file which ends or begins at the door of the men's house, each line tethered by a "head" shell, each shell standing for a whole man and a line of shells for a line of men and a house of men.

The men are themselves organs of the men's house, each with his own shells.

Among the Foi and other southern-fringe highlands groups, even though "naked" shells are given, they too are embodied. Foi shells are displayed not outside the men's house but within it, so that the house is the body of the pearl shell. The Foi display the "head" pearl shells, the ten or twelve large shells that are the core component of a bridewealth payment, by propping them up against the pillow bar of the sleeping area. The shells are the "heads" of the men who are giving them. The Foi unit of ceremonial payments is one "hand" of shells, that is, thirty-seven, the highest number of the Foi counting system which begins with the fingers of one hand, and traveling up the arm, shoulders, head, face and back down the other hand, delimits the arms and head of a man. A hand of shells is thus a whole man.[2] The shell is the whole person as well as token of the whole person, as the head pearl shells are the whole bridewealth, the whole bride and the entire groom's side.

We are discouraged by such considerations from seeing these transactions in shells and people as the simple detachment of persons or parts of persons. Rather, they are processes in the embodiment and reembodiment of persons and other social actors and the relationships which the shells mediate.

To make appear in this way a form of any kind—a social protocol, a person, a relationship, an image—is thus to create a shell around it so that it stands forth. This is one definition of obviation as Wagner (1978, 1986) and I (Weiner 1988) have described it: the punctuation of imagery implicated by such embodying process, the folding of imagery back on itself so that it comes to have an inside and an outside. In the chapters of this book I will demonstrate how myths keep growing new shells over themselves and within themselves and their constituent images, so that each mythic closure can detach itself and travel independently, fertilizing other myths and providing the enframing skin for further transformative extension. And seeing how such dissemination also contributes to the formation of what we call cultural identity, we can also say that people form a shell of knowledge and speech around their own local reading of this enchaining, form-producing process. How many times in Papua New Guinea have inquirers into myth been told something like "We do not know the story beyond that ridge," or "To find out what happened next, you must go ask the people in the next valley." This is what is parodied in the myth "The Lost Drum": the drum which at the end of the story makes a noise by itself *is* the myth, an enframed speaking, a self-sounding myth, which leaves the human world altogether. In such a case, the final obviation does not just comment on the myth, it *becomes* the myth. And this is why I have chosen the title of this myth for the entire book, to indicate that in the embodying process in Papua New Guinea, something is lost, shed, or discarded. That something is nothing less than what we would identify as the *logos* of myth, for in the collapse of imagery in a myth that obviation makes visible, language as convention and sign disappears. It becomes revealed first and foremost as that which gives shape to the voice, which is lost in intersubjectivity.

It is no surprise then that the objects of the myths of this book are often sound-producing instruments—the bull-roarer, flute, drum, pearl shells (recall that in the Foi myth "The Place of the Pearl Shells" [Weiner 1988] shell fragments made a loud noise like a waterfall or the beating wings of a flock of birds). Such sound-producing objects are metonymic of the fertilizing sound of the myths themselves; they tell their own myth through their sounding. We might think that languages are local and bounded, and that objects travel between such local dialect communities. But I maintain that these objects never traveled without their framing shell of myth. Is it not true that in Papua New Guinea the acquisition of new cult objects, bull-roarers, *sacra* of different varieties, as well as wealth objects, always have to be accompanied by a validating story? In such cases, we might say that the objects bring both place and word with them in their travels and that we cannot appeal to stability in terms of production or territory. It is a matter not of identifying the borders between Melanesian cultures but of tracing the routes of communication and thematic entrapment which have themselves contributed to that differentiation.

Nor can we find such stability in language. As a result of our commitment to the foundational arbitrariness of signification, and the exalting of the conceptual nature of language, we approach language as if words are parasitic on the world, have clearly defined surfaces which faithfully reflect that world's contours. We often mask the displacement our words undergo when they are subject to something as demanding as translating what the Foi or the Marind-anim or the Gimi people say. We instead insist on the distinctiveness of the myth and analytical terminology we bring to bear on it so that we can establish the fixity of the latter and the contingency of the former.

In Jacques Lacan's reformulation of Freud I find an important model for how anthropology can refashion its own relationship to language and its role in the anthropological analysis of myth. The neo-Freudian revision that Lacan identified made language in psychoanalysis a subordinate tool—the nosological orthodoxy stipulated that the lineaments of the psyche were formed in the wordless drama of the Oedipal triangle. Lacan's rejection of this was based on his relocating in Freud the fundamental role of language in the very constitution of the self, the subject, and the ego.

I see myself in the same relation to those anthropologists who would make of language an inventory of meanings, who see subjectivity as prevening speech and thought, who see words as tokens for things in the world, who see our anthropological prose as a tool with which to translate the myths of the X people into decomposable texts, who see language itself as something which only gets in the way between the knower and the knowable world, who see the goal of myth analysis as arriving at the "meaning of the myth," and who thus see the task of the analyst as the identification of a community's conventional meanings. By contrast, I maintain that the task of "analyzing the myth" is subverted from the start if one presumes that the myths are the fixed source of categorical stability and order which have crystallized out of the day-to-day use of language, or a conceptual resource which always mirrors a stable cosmological formula. Although a myth provides a "point of view," it is not necessarily a stabilizing point. A myth strikes obliquely onto any local language, and in so doing displaces it—far from being the source of order, coherence, and correspondence with the world, speech is itself the very source of relativism, contingency, and displacement which makes convention visible.

In the Papuan communities I consider in this book, I maintain that myth is the cause and symptom of a much more fundamental condition of their language, something which Philippe Lacoue-Labarthe calls *desistance*, a term which refers to "the inherent infirmity of the subject" (1990:82). An infirmity in the sense not of an affliction, but of an instability or incompleteness, "without which no relation (either to oneself or to others) could be established and there would be neither consciousness nor sociality" (1990:83). More generally, myth stands outside language and by so doing illuminates the limits of its significatory function, which limits are a mirror for the subject itself: "The subject itself cannot desire without itself dissolving, and without seeing, because of this very fact, the object escaping it, in a series of infinite displacements" (Lacan 1991b:177). And in somewhat more positive terms, Wagner says:

> The cultural person contains implicitly the relationships that
> contain it; where else but in the mirroring dimension of myth can
> this reflexivity be articulated? And if it were not so articulated, then
> sociality could not enter the world of personal meaning, and would
> represent a merely imposed arbitrage. (Wagner 1988:xi)

The focus on the mythical shape and function of objects accentuates their instability and desistance and makes the Melanesian world of objects appear to us to have unmistakably surrealist qualities. At two points in this book, I am going to inspect paintings by Hans Holbein and Salvador Dali. We can say, as did the New Guinea man Yali when he found his community's sacred objects in an Australian museum, "Our myths are there . . ." (Lawrence 1956:191). They do not provide much help in building a theory, but they illustrate a way in which people recognize the *contingency* of language and representation—scientific and otherwise—in the constitution of subjectivity. Holbein and Dali both in their ways, at very different times, mocked the attempts that our culture makes to ensure the fidelity of our perceptions and representations, made it clear that something always eludes our visual and linguistic control, slips away to make unforeseen contacts and connections elsewhere.

What I try to do by juxtaposing different images—Papuan and Western—is not to provide analyses of the myths. I am taking my cue from Marilyn Strathern's observation: that in New Guinea, the task of sociality is not to implement some conventionally agreed upon rules of social engagement but to devise procedures for making the form of social life appear obvious. My task thus is not an exercise in model building or in ethnography narrowly conceived. Nor am I trying to compare Foi, Yafar, Marind-anim, Gimi, and Western cultures, although such a comparison inevitably emerges as a by-product of my intention. I am attempting something more idiosyncratic. I am pretending that each object like the drum, the pearl shell, and the bull-roarer is a myth, and that each myth is like an object. They show the outline of a culture rather than constitute its assumed core; they fragment local significances, paradigms, and classificatory systems, rather than serve as enzyme-like templates for their buildup or synthesis. My task in this book is not to translate New Guinea myths into English but to allow their incorporative, fertilizing, and encompassing properties to gestate a version of New Guinea reproductive life.

PART I

CADUCITY

1

The Little Other Myth

Dehiscence and Caducity

The Yafar and Waina people of the West Sepik Province, Papua New Guinea, say that they perform their Yangis (Ida) ritual in order to ensure the fertility of sago, the palm from which they process one of their staple food items. But since such vegetative vitality is accomplished only through the human agency of ritual, what is more accurately at stake is the reproductive capacity of humans phrased in these terms. The masks used by the Waina and the Yafar in the Yangis are made of the fibrous husk of the coconut, decorated with leaves of different varieties, and festooned with fruit in some cases. These masks cover the whole upper body of the wearer, so that what we see are human beings making themselves over in the image of the vegetative world.

What then is the truth of human reproduction, that it can be found only in the terms of the vegetable realm? Now we might say that botanical reproduction calls to mind hidden processes of growth, and thus the seemingly delayed effects of fertilization; the dualism of surface and core, of tropic responses to light and energy and of growth in the direction of such sources, of maturity and immaturity and of the dangers in allowing things to ripen too slowly or too quickly; the recapitulation of ontogenetical stages; the dropping off of organs after their functions have been performed; the power to regenerate a whole from a part; and in general, the fertility of detached parts and their ability to root themselves.

In the use of botanic and vegetal idioms to refer to the processes of human procreation, the world of West Sepik reproduction and sociality opens itself to what I wish to explore in this book—the possibility of a Lacanian anthropology.

In one of his earliest published essays, Lacan speaks of the "vital dehiscence that is constitutive of man" (1977a:21). Dehiscence refers

3

to the bursting open of a seedpod and the subsequent discharge of its contents. Lacan's view of the human subject is that it is essentially fragmented and disjointed; the prematurity of human birth means that the infant lacks a sense of corporeal integrity and acquires one only from the outside, when it reaches the age at which it can perceive externally the visible unity of the human figure—in others, or in its own reflection. Our corporeality, in other words, "has an alien origin" (Lacan 1991a:153). But this unity will always retain the status of a meconnaissance—an illusion, a boundary made visible and tangible only through the complicity of others. In this view, the ego develops as a product or precipitate of the person's past attachments to other people and to the objects that move between people—attachments that are established and then abandoned. As Freud (1917:243–58) said, our internal self is filled with the introjected specters of these lost objects of desire.

But there is always something left over after a seedpod bursts open. Juillerat appeals to the imagery of *caducity* in his description of the Yangis ritual. This term describes an organ which drops off after its function has been performed: the placenta, or the husk of a seed. The Yangis ritual seems to acquire its momentum from a series of acts of such detachment and discarding—yet such detachment has a transformative rather than a subtractive effect on the bodies involved. What we want to consider is how something can be detached from something else without that thing's being diminished in any way—for does this not capture the essence of what Melanesian sociality is all about, at least in the current formulation of Marilyn Strathern (1988)? But I would also like to make a case for a more expanded use of caducity: the dropping off of lexical meaning in myths through institutionalized secrecy; the way in which such myths *fail* to account for the rituals whose origin they apparently describe; the falling away of our own explanatory glosses of such myths and rituals after descriptive and theoretical fertilizations have been made.

In this chapter, I address the remarkable volume edited by Bernard Juillerat, *Shooting the Sun: Ritual and Meaning in West Sepik* (1992), in which he gathers together the views of anthropologists and psychoanalysts on his and Alfred Gell's (1975) analyses of the Yangis (Ida) fertility ritual of the Border Mountains region of western Papua New Guinea. In the introduction, Juillerat lists the questions with which he proposes to interrogate the Yangis ritual. Among them are:

> Is the ritual to be taken as the reflection, whether faithful or
> inverted, of the social structure, or as the cultural manifestation of

individual, unconscious representations? Should the analytical approach first be sociological or psychoanalytical . . . ? What place should be given to lexical similarities, binary oppositions, or Freudian interpretation in the analysis of ritual metaphors? Do the exegetical commentaries of informants have a heuristic value, or must they be excluded from the scientific model that the anthropologist is trying to construct? (1992:3).

What strikes me about these questions is how indicative they are of the premises of psychological anthropology as it has been conventionally propounded, for the most part in the United States. It remains faithful to the acceptance of the self-evident distinction between culture, society, and individual (the first question) and of the antinomy between sociological and psychological (or psychoanalytical) analysis (the second question); to the contrast between lexical versus interpretive meaning (the third question); and to the three-pronged distinction between behavior, its native exegesis, and the anthropologist's scientific analysis (the fourth question). All of these topographies still play their role in current (psycho)anthropological analyses—they have not fallen away after their fertility has been exhausted—and all of them deserve a systematic critique from other current perspectives that take a more phenomenological, relational approach. This means that we must collapse, at least temporarily, the distinction between psycho logical, cultural, and social-structural analysis—something that one of the earliest proponents of current psychological anthropology, Melford Spiro (1951), advocated more than forty years ago.

I want to widen the scope of such a new psychoanalytic anthropology by creating, in the context of the current formulations of Melanesian sociality, a meeting ground between Sigmund Freud, Jacques Lacan . . . and Marilyn Strathern and Roy Wagner; to point to the very real convergences in the terms created and deployed by all four, to show that Lacan's "relational organs" are like Strathern's "gifts"; that Wagner's obviation is like Freud's *Nachträglichkeit;* that Strathern's "anticipation of completeness" is like Lacan's desire of the desire of the other. What emerges is their separate views on a common set of issues: the constitution of the image out of language and vice versa; the essentially relational constitution of image and symbol; the formation of the relational person and its detachable metonymic extensions; and above all else, the interpretive nature of social perception in the construction of the subject and what we can call, following Freud (1923:28), the ego ideal.

In this chapter I focus on one theme that serves as a meeting point between psychoanalytic theory, as formulated by Freud and reformulated by Lacan, and anthropology: the nexus of language, sexuality, and embodiment in Lacan's formulation of the Imaginary and the Symbolic. A second theme pertains to the general question of interpretation in the behavioral sciences, and this I take up in the final chapter. And although there are other topics—such as the question of scale, the role of the Oedipus configuration—which are also addressed by the contributors to Juillerat's volume and which deserve attention in any full assessment of the possibilities of a psychoanalytical anthropology, these themes bear directly on the issue of Papuan myth and ritual that is my subject matter.

But first let us outline the drama of Yangis.

The Yangis

The Waina and Yafar speak non-Austronesian languages and are culturally and linguistically distinct from both the Upper Sepik plain region to the east and the Yuri and Abau language groups immediately to the south that separate the Border Mountains languages from the body of Mountain Ok groups further south.

The societies of the Border Mountains are characterized by a village organization comprising exogamous hamlets which are named after the clan that resides there. The hamlet is also organized into "hamlet moieties." These moieties are designated male and female. Among the Yafar they are associated with the coconut or *feenaw* sago palm (female) and the *afweeg* sago palm (male). Moreover, these two species, the *afweeg* and the coconut, are the incarnations of the creator deities, the male and female couple who were the progenitors of the human species. Unlike the Ida, which is performed every year in the dry season (July–August), the Yangis is staged only intermittently. Juillerat concludes however that it is "the ritual enactment of the two moiety totems, the embodiment of the society" (1992:16), and while we cannot disagree with this, it in no way satisfies us as an analysis of the Yangis.

Let us look at the sequence of named masked figures that take the stage during the course of the Yangis. First to appear are the *eri sabaga*, the "original couple," the mythical originators of mankind, representing the male and female varieties of sago. The couple are each given a package containing "sago from the male and female totemic clones, respectively, taro and yam flesh from two sexualized clones of these species, and sexual fluids provided by the two moiety priests and their wives" (Juillerat 1992:30). All these items are examples of *hoofuk*, a term in Yafar which refers to the productive, germinal, vital core of anything. At the end of the night, the two secretly eat a bush fowl egg, which Juillerat says represents the single breast of the female originator, and is also *hoofuk*. Juillerat's primary informant offered him the following myth as an explanation of this nourishment of the *eri:*

> Two brothers and two sisters live together. The elder brother has
> married the two sisters. He discovers that his younger brother is
> having sexual intercourse with the younger sister. He then lures
> his brother into the forest on the pretext of collecting [bush fowl]
> eggs and grubs, and kills him in the [bush fowl] nest. Next day,
> the elder brother asks his younger wife to come and help him
> collect [bush fowl] eggs. She discovers her lover's body. Her
> husband compels her to swallow the dead [man]. She sits down on
> the nest (like a fowl) and does so; her husband leaves. She can't
> move and only after a long time is she helped by two little
> birds . . . and she evacuates, as children, her lover's bones. They
> immediately turn into *ogomo* spirits (sago growth spirits . . .) and
> they go to a dance at a (Yangis) festival . . . , the trumpets of which
> are heard from a distant village. Their mother joins the feast later
> and feeds her sons with cooked [bush fowl] eggs (the public
> version talks only of sago jelly). They are very tall now and she is
> quite small. Then the [bush fowl] mother utters her call, thus
> announcing dawn after "a very long night." (1992:31)

Let us defer momentarily a full consideration of the myth and its relation to this particular juncture in the Yangis ritual.

Appearing at the same time as the *eri* are the *rawsu-inaag*, which one of Juillerat's informants translated as "in the blood of the hymen." They are said to represent the blood shed by both the male and female creator couple after their first intercourse. In the associated mythology, this blood is said to have turned into *bana* fish, and in fact, the *rawsu-inaag* wear the fish masks called *ogomo mesoog*. But *raw* was also ambiguously explained to Juillerat as "that part of the vagina which 'falls down' during the first intercourse" (1992:32) or perhaps after the first childbirth.

The next figures to replace the central *eri* figures are the *yis*. *Yis* is coagulated sago jelly, made from a mixture of sago flour and boiling water, and the solidification of this jelly is said to represent "the coagulation of both sexual substances, that is, the formation of the embryo" (1992:34). Semen may strike us as the embodiment of *hoofuk* par excellence. But *yis* is specifically semen in its reproduced form, the fetus; that is, semen in its combinatorial, relational manifestation, its "whole," bound state. The two moiety priests carry a container full of *yis* before the two dancers, and they fling handfuls of the jelly into the air, an operation referred to as the "'breaking-dropping of the sago jelly'" (1992:36).

The *yis* are replaced by the *ware-inaag*, whom Gell's Waina informants call "'firewood of the netbag'" and which the Yafar term "'remains of sago jelly'" (Juillerat 1992:37). They represent the sexual fluids that are left over or discarded in the act of the formation of embryonic *yis*. At this point, Juillerat says:

> The *ware-inaag* are peripheral to the *yis* as the *rawsu-inaag* were to the *eri: eri,* and *yis* appear as the active and productive personages, whereas *rawsu-inaag* and *ware-inaag* are their nonreproductive waste discarded during the reproductive process. (1992:38)

Next to appear are the *sawog,* "fish." Up until the advent of the *yis,* the dancers have appeared in predominantly monochrome color, black for the *eri,* red for the *rawsu-inaag.* With the arrival of the *yis,* the body decoration introduces polychrome patterns. In the *sawog* segment, the transition from black to red and polychrome is emphasized, as is the movement from central to peripheral, or from inside to outside.

The first fish are the *ogomo.* The *ogomo* are spirits from the land of the dead; they exert a deleterious effect of caducity or ripening on those men who don the masks. Juillerat associates them with the maternal realm. They are followed by the *sawog* proper, who wear the same masks but have a polychrome pattern of body paint. An important piece of exegetical information was provided by Juillerat's informants: some generations ago, the *sawog* wore not masks but instead string bags over their heads. Their penes were not covered with a phallocrypt but were naked, "decorated only with a thin tie made of the *fut* vine, a young sago shoot leaf . . . , and a ginger leaf" (1992:42). Juillerat's conclusion, based on the appearance of the sago shoot in their genital decoration, is that the *sawog* "seem to be the *ifege* [that is, the bowmen who will appear in the final stage of the ritual] in their fetal state" (1992:42). The enclosing tightness of the string bags was said to be harmful to the wearers, especially as the bags were anointed with semen or some symbolic substitute, and many deaths were attributed to them in the past (which is why the Yafar say they abandoned their use in favor of the fish masks).

What we see in these early stages of the Yangis is that the focus of *hoofuk* is shifting from detachable substances and foods (the contents of the packages, *abi* egg, *yis*), to the specific organ of caducity of males, the

penis, and finally to the whole body of the dancer. It is the act of caducity which is being revealed as the form of regeneration.

The young fish dancers are like fetuses, and the women attempt to
trap them in their net bags as the boys dance along the periphery of the
ritual ground. Both the *ogomo* and the *sawog* performances are referred
to as the work of *hoofuk;* let us note the equivalence being established
between the net- (or mask-)enclosed head and the sheathed penis of the
dancers, as well as the intimate connection drawn between fetus, fish,
head, and penis: all acquire their conventional appearance by virtue of
a container which outlines them, traps them, and allows their *hoofuk* to
detach itself and achieve independent growth.

While the fish are dancing their game of attempted capture and escape from their mothers' net bags / uteri, the *kwoor* enter the arena.
Painted monochrome red, Juillerat states that they represent something
"rotten," something associated with the menstrual capacity of
women—but the *kwoor* are also good hunters. They portray, according
to Juillerat, "an extremely marginal product in the procreative process.
Something that urgently needs to be discarded in order to proceed toward the end of pregnancy (*amof*)" (1992:47–49).

The *amof* figures who then appear are the "termites," and they mark,
according to Juillerat, the end of pregnancy. The work of *hoofuk* is over,
and the sago babies are about to be born. Along the circumference of
their masks are ranged *boof* fruit, semicultivated, inedible orange fruits
which characteristically fall down before they achieve full ripeness.
Juillerat explains:

> In short, they are a perfect symbol of *ripeness* and *caducity*. This
> concept is a crucial one in Yafar and Waina symbolism: the self . . .
> of any human being may be endangered by early ripening through
> contamination during sleep with the maternal underworld. . . . The
> purpose of some aspects of hunting ritual is to let 'ripen' the game's
> [self] to accelerate its death when wounded . . . (1992:49)

What ripens and falls off belongs to the domain of *roofuk* (skin, bark,
outer layer, debris), as opposed to *hoofuk* (core, heart, egg, seed, germinal portion, the portion that grows and develops). But the Yafar also
say that an especially thick and abundant *roofuk* is a sign of an equally
fecund and abundant *hoofuk*. Once again, Juillerat is able to provide a
more or less complete myth which concerns the *amof* figure:

> Wefroog [the culture hero] catches sight of a *boof* tree. He asks its
> fruits: "Will you stay, or will you fall? I need you to make a man."

Nothing moves; he goes away, but hears a big noise. He turns back; all the *boof* fruits are on the ground. Wefroog uses sticks and roots from the *afweeg* sago palm to make limbs; then he decorates his new creature with fruits. He utters spells *"kikikiki"* and the man comes to life. Wefroog gives him two names: *Boof* and *Amof.* Then he orders him to go to the [Yangis] festival: "You must dance at the periphery of the place, with the women." (1992:51)

While the *amof* dance around the periphery, the *eri, yis, ware-inaag* and *sawog* appear again. They leave only after the *ifege* make their exit.

Ifege refers to the pronged bird (and fish?) arrow that these bowmen carry and will ultimately use to "shoot the sun," but "the true etymology of *ifege* is *ifeeg eri*, literally 'original human being'" (Juillerat 1992:53). The treatment of these figures' penes is elaborate:

the foreskin is pulled back, the glans covered with strips of *keg* leaves concealing a little piece of . . . red sago shoot and decorated with caudal plumes . . . of the bird of paradise . . . a female symbol for the women's skirts [which are called by the same name, *nay*] . . . and the whole thing is tied up with strips from the *fut* vine. (1992:56)

The arrows of the *ifege* bowman are also bound with a sago shoot, and according to Juillerat the Yafar clearly recognize the equivalence between arrow and penis. But furthermore, the penis and arrow are themselves like the masks which cover the entire body of the dancer; they all partake of the material and imagery of the new red sago shoot, so that the expansion of arrow → penis → whole body is also revealed in this instance. In other words, the *ifege* retain the fetalized penis, bound with sago shoot and women's skirt fiber, that was introduced in the *sawog* phase.

Short mythical paraphrases are also provided for the fish figures (*sawog*), the *ogomo*, the *ware-inaag*, the *yis*, the *rawsu-inaag*—evidently, every phase of the Yangis has an associated mythology. What are we to make of these myths and mythic fragments—for due to the secrecy which surrounds the revealing of these myths and the hidden names of certain ritual elements they contain, Juillerat, as much as any Yafar, can never be sure whether any mythic material related to him is complete or not. Moreover, the ritual is assumed by us to be a complete thing, with a beginning, a middle, and end; not one contributor to Juillerat's volume assumes otherwise, though they differ as to what the actual starting and ending points are. But by the same token, the associated myths and mythic fragments do not make a whole, do not relate to one another, do not build any analogous complete thing.

Is the function of myth then to pull apart the body of the ritual by means of language? I turn once again to the metaphors of dehiscence and caducity with which I began. How do the myths take root in the ritual and vice versa? What vital part of the ritual is encased within them? Why does the secrecy which regulates their transmission cause them to drop away from the ritual, and our analysis of it? What, in more general terms, is the relation between the essentially visual display of ritual, of whose completeness we are in no doubt, and what is hidden and fragmented by the verbal constitution of mythic language? I wish to substitute such questions for the ones that Juillerat posed.

The Relational Subject

To address them, let us begin by first admitting that psychoanalysis, as opposed to *psychology*, is a *social science*, perhaps even "the human science par excellence" (Lacan 1977a:144–45; Macey 1988: 88). And by this do we mean that it recognizes some central, foundational social arrangement: the nuclear family and its Oedipal configuration, say? No. This no more defines what is distinctive about psychoanalysis than descent groups and reciprocity characterize anthropology's subject matter. Rather, to call it a social science is to recognize that *its procedure makes use of the social relationships that are its subject matter*—the phenomena of repetition, deferral, repression that Freud first identified are at once items of analysis and characteristics of the mode of inquiry. Like ethnography or linguistics, it uses its own subject of study as the medium of that study. And the realization of this reflexivity is found specifically in its technique, what Freud (e.g., 1912: 104; 1914:154) called the transference, and in the resistance to transference. The language of psychoanalysis is also the language of its theory, which is to say that its technique, theory, and object of analysis are all given simultaneously.[1]

Anthropology until recently has always struggled against the relativization of the transference through an appeal to a methodological objectivism and to a variety of descriptive and analytical languages that allowed the anthropologist the privilege of outside observer. As Wagner (1981) puts it, we attempted to study the social relations of our hosts as if our own were not also implicated. In an analogous fashion, what the revisionist ego psychology as it developed in the United States accomplished was to repress or repudiate the radically anti-Cartesian view of the subject toward which Freud had labored. Neo-Freudian doxa stipulated that the analyst always acts as a point of stability and rationality; that there is a corresponding core of rationality hidden within the disturbed patient that it is the analyst's duty to make contact with and draw out, so that it can overpower the pathological part of the patient's personality; that the transference procedure that effects this struggle goes one way, from patient to analyst, but not back again.[2] This was made possible, as was the case in anthropology, by a view of the self and its origin as distinct from the relations into which it entered.

But Lacan wished to take a much more radical view of Freud, one which he felt was more faithful to the subversiveness of Freud's original message. The autonomous ego which is thought to preexist all psychological defenses is itself a defense. There are only defenses played off against each other to give particular ones the illusion of preexistent personality. There is not the ego and his/her alter, only types of alter—the subject and the ego are, after all, constituted from the same acts of speech and perception as all other objects and relations, and the subject takes its place amongst these things, in the space created between them rather than prior to them.

Freud (see 1914) found that his patients inevitably came to act toward him in the same way they acted toward the persons who were the focus of their anxiety and who were the sources and subjects of their self-narrative. He noticed that the analytical dialogue did not just stand as external commentary on the patient's relational history, but was playing a constitutive role in it. Freud called this the transference—in effect, the analytic encounter came to model the person's own relational topography. For psychoanalysis, then, *transference occurs when the model* becomes *or takes over* *the thing modeled.* This to me is the most crucial difference between what has passed for psychoanalytic anthropology up until now, and the possibility of a rapprochement between psychoanalysis and anthropology with which Lacan's reformulations provide us. For Lacan has reinserted the radical intersubjectivity, the essential relational constitution of all the components of the self—the ego, the drives, object attachments, the subject—and in so doing, restored psychoanalysis as the study of the history of a subject's *relations.*

We should then be cautious of our common contrast between *subjectivity* and *intersubjectivity.* The addition of the prefix *inter* to the noun stem *subjectivity* makes it appear as if the latter were a derivatory form of the former, that subjectivity comes first and intersubjectivity is dependent upon it. But from the perspective I am taking here, the opposite is more nearly the case: we should call subjectivity *intrasubjectivity,* to signal the way in which our relational encounters are deposited in the identity structure of the speaking subject. Let us then proceed as if intersubjectivity is the semantic primitive, the fundamental orientation toward others that is primordial and originary, and *intrasubjectivity*[3] is a derivative, analytic isolate.

Like other social sciences, psychoanalysis constitutes its image of such relationships by an inspection of their effects as well as of those relationships themselves. But what it offers social science, what it makes prominent, is the necessity to contemplate what the *limits* of those effects are and to make such limits part of the technique. And we find these limits in the language that persons use to both describe and enter into such relationships. If we see the subject as constituted by his/ her relationships, then Lacan's psychoanalysis views social relationships as themselves limited by the language and the repression of language available to the subject.

> What I seek in the Word is the response of the other. What constitutes me as subject is my question . . .
> I identify myself in Language, but only by losing myself in it like an object. (Lacan 1977a:86)

It is the speech of the interlocutor, whether analyst or other, that constitutes us as subjects. All this is summed up in Lacan's now famous dictum: The unconscious is the discourse of the other. Insofar as we are inclined to see the unconscious as a space within our mental terrain, it is a space made possible by the euphemizing, concealing properties of language, for what is characteristically hidden from us within our unconscious is the meaning of our acts to which only language can give us access.

But we would be ill-advised to reduce subjectivity to language's pure semiological properties. For as Lacan also reminds us, "Language is not immaterial. It is a subtle body . . . Words are trapped in all the corporeal images that captivate the subject . . ." (1977a:87). And since that language and the material, corporeal tokens that embody it are enabled and presented to us by our interlocutors, what we find at the heart of the person is not some inviolable self-identity but the deposited or introjected traces, both semiological and imagistic, of the others who constitute that person.

The Subject of Gender in Melanesia

Like Lacan, Marilyn Strathern too begins her analysis of the Melanesian person with a critique of the Western theory of the ego:

> The center is where the twentieth-century Western imagination puts the self, the personality, the ego. For the "person" in this latter day Western view is an agent, a subject, the author of thought and action, and thus "at the center" of relationships. (1988:269)

Strathern wishes to substitute for this Western theory a more properly Melanesian one: that the person is distributively and excentrically constituted, a sum of its relations with others without necessarily centering itself within them. In Melanesia, "social relations are the objects of people's dealings with one another" (1988:172), and hence any objects that move between people are efficacious insofar as they personify relationships themselves. Thus, people use ceremonial objects of different kinds (such as pearl shells, pigs, masks) to make certain aspects of relationality visible and manipulable. "Persons or things may be transferred as 'standing for' (in our terms) parts of persons" (1988:178).

As a result of being caught in such relationships, where the very stuff of relationality is objectified and detachable in the form of such objects and parts of persons, Melanesians are forced to make their bodily capacities visible and available to others. And "if it is the body's capacities which are made known, then the evidence for these must lie in the effectiveness of action. In Melanesian terms, this implies interaction" (1988:123).

Now in Melanesia, gender is made visible by what people perceive as a complementary set of "capabilities of people's bodies and minds, what they contain within themselves and their effects on others" (1988: 182). It follows, says Strathern, that since people constitute themselves relationally through such capabilities, then gender is an intrinsic component of such interaction. The objects that move between people and which tether them relationally to each other are also gendered. While persons themselves contain both male and female capacities and hence are not intrinsically either one sex or another, specific acts and relational modalities are gendered, depending upon which capacities they elicit from persons. They temporarily make persons appear as wholly male or female by concealing or detaching the relational, androgynous base of Melanesian personhood.

Detachment, and the object relations made possible by such acts of detachment, are thus the engine of both gender and personhood in Melanesia. And here Strathern goes beyond the Western terms of psychoanalytic theory. Freud and Klein, despite their understanding of the fragmented nature of the ego, of the primal processes of attachment and loss that split the ego, nevertheless remained committed to the view

that to be whole was satisfying (e.g., Klein 1986). What Lacan introduced was the idea that to make this whole, something must be detached from it. For him, the critical act of perception was the making of
a cut, of which the model was the specular image, the cutting off of the
scopic field by the operation of that most relational of organs, the eye.
And what Melanesians present us with, according to Strathern, is
merely the practical, productive consequence of such an understanding: they strive to detach parts of themselves, they aspire to a partiality
and excentricity of perspective, to maintain the externality of the various sources of the self, to *not* introject them, to maintain the multiplicity
of compositional influences on the self. And recognizing that this too
constitutes a critique of Lacan, Deleuze and Guattari say, "To withdraw
a part from the whole, to detach, to 'have something left over,' is to
produce, and to carry out real operations of desire in the material
world" (1983:41), a statement that could very well serve as a summation of the Melanesian theory of action.

But recall what I said about psychoanalysis: it becomes visible as
technique and theory at the point when the model takes over the thing
modeled. A relational view of the world means a relational view of the
perceiving self. Freud and Klein understood that in entering into object
relations, in separating itself from objects, the ego itself becomes split
(Klein 1986:168). And because Melanesians constitute themselves as
gendered persons through analogous operations of detachment and incorporation of objects, Strathern also says of them that "Gender refers
to the internal relations between parts of persons, as well as to their
externalization as relations between persons" (1988:185). The Yangis
begins with the *eri* figures, who represent this original couple, and ends
with the bowmen, the *ifege*, who are the "totemic mothers' sons in their
transformation into men" (1988:24). In the masked images of Yangis,
male and female are never presented in, so to speak, a monolithic way:
they are always appresented in the context of the ritual and its associated mythology in relations of encompassment with each other. The
procedures of detachment in the ritual and in the myths make male and
female capacities appear momentarily, only to allow them to collapse
back into their essentially mediatory, relational constitution.

Relational organs, as Lacan termed them, are what Yafar physiology
and procreative theory are all about. Everything has a *hoofuk* and a *roofuk*, everything has a detachable part and a left-behind part. The corner-
stone of Strathern's analysis in *The Gender of the Gift*, these operations
constitute the gendered person in New Guinea. *Hoofuk* and *roofuk* are
relational terms; they concern how the capacities of entities are drawn
out in confrontation with desiring beings.

In this relational view of human life advocated by Lacan, Strathern, and Wagner, we do not speak, therefore, of the ways in which the body replicates, or acts as a small version of, the cosmos. Instead, we take our cue from the Yafar and the Waina themselves. They ask of things, what is its *roofuk*? How does a thing's *hoofuk* manifest itself? In other words, they speak of relations as if they always have a body and are always embodied.

The Imaginary and the Symbolic

What Strathern makes clear, and what the Yangis dancers make evident, is that insofar as such relational modalities are imaged in terms of the body's compositional features and appearances, then we can say that external sensory triggers are necessary to the elicitation and formation of such relations in their conventional manifestation. In the same way, Lacan's paper on the mirror stage (in Lacan 1977a) was an attempt to demonstrate how such a conceptualization was dependent on the image, and that since the image arises only within the confrontation with an other, then it itself is relationally constituted at its inception (see Muller and Richardson 1982:29):

> the total form of the body by which the subject anticipates in a mirage the maturation of his power is given to him only as *Gestalt*, that is to say, in an exteriority in which this form is certainly more constituent than constituted . . . this *Gestalt* . . . symbolizes the mental permanence of the *I*, at the same time as it prefigures its alienating destination; it is still pregnant with the correspondences that unite the *I* with the statue in which man projects himself . . . (Lacan 1977a:2–3)

Lacan saw the bounding function of this *Gestalt* as having extremely important implications in early life. The mirror image is an everted pregnancy, where the child recognizes the *contingency*, that is, the social origin, of its corporeal boundary.

> The identification of oneself with another being is the very process by which a continuing sense of selfhood becomes possible, and it is from successive assimilations of other people's attributes that what is familiarly called the ego or the personality is construed. (Bowie 1991:30–31)

In much the same vein, Wagner has said:

> The self is an effect that we perceive indirectly in the reactions of persons, creatures, or objects around us . . . We become a self

through the mediation of things other than that acting, perceiving self. (1977:147)

We first identify our self only in another person who him/herself is also a desiring subject. And hence our relation to all others and objects is mediated by such desire. Marilyn Strathern's observation of Melanesian personhood can thus be read in more general terms: "Intention and motivation have physiological consequences. The person is vulnerable, so to speak, both to the bodily disposition of others toward him or her and to their wills and desires" (1988:131–32).

What Lacan referred to as the *Imaginary* refers not just to the imaginative capacity, but to the *image* of one's body that grows out of the subject's visual confrontation with an encountered other. In the Imaginary, one draws forth the limits of the body, an image of the body's outline, a projection of a body schema in imaginary space. As Wilden puts it, "the Imaginary is the area of the biological maturation through perception" (1968:175). Insofar as Lacan seizes upon the common biological phenomenon whereby physiological and hormonal changes are set off by a sensory stimulus, he recognizes, as does Marilyn Strathern (1988), the role of form and of the aesthetic contours of the image as elicitory trigger. "I use 'image' to refer both to the sense impression of perception and to the conceived, elicited forms of sense impressions such as 'a figure' or 'a pattern'" (Strathern 1991b:129 n. 49).

But as Wagner has suggested, the notion of embodiment finds its most organic expression only in the actual human body, and should be broadened to include any perception which calls forth its own external bounding, any articulation which calls forth the whole of which it is part.[4] It includes the ways in which we assemble a framing "skin" around the things we isolate, the way in which a space or frame is constructed-in-anticipation of certain events, acts, performances whose effects are also anticipated. We can recall the words of another thinker for whom the elicitation of its own limits was the core feature of human being: "form, *forma*, corresponds to the Greek *morphē*. It is the enclosing limit and boundary, what brings and stations a being into that which it is . . ." (Heidegger 1979:119).[5]

In other words, the delimitation of these relational processes does not proceed solely within the domain of the body image, the specular image of the other. For Lacan, the accession to language, which in his view ontogenetically follows the acquisition of body image, introduces an entirely different relational register to the subject. It is language, the domain of the *Symbolic* as Lacan terms it, that provides this more encompassing embodiment, for it brings to the specular field of body im-

age the expansive properties of metaphor, and the enchainment of signifiers that metaphor makes possible.

What language affords is the possibility of labeling the gaps and detachments that constitute object loss as the first experience of embodied
relationality. The loss of the maternal breast, its absence, becomes,
through the act of signification, as much a positivity as its presence.
Words and signs come to fill the spaces that are created through the
detachments that make relationality possible.

What results is a hermeneutic of the embodiment of language, and
this is what is captured by Lacan's contrast between the Imaginary and
the Symbolic. If language has hitherto been seen as exclusively part of
the conceptual function, then Lacan's reformulation means that we
have to come to terms with the embodiment of linguistic and cultural
meaning—that is, the fact that in the realm of the Symbolic, it is language itself which is revealed as the outer limits or skin of the subject,
as the boundary within which a subjective history can unfold as a discourse, a discourse between, for example, patient and analyst, or between informant and anthropologist. Through language, the Imaginary
becomes recast as a myth of origin of the body, and in fact, as Wagner
puts it, "This is the fractality of the Melanesian person: the talk formed
through the person that is the person formed through talk" (1991:166).

Wagner and Lacan thus make a case for the embodiment of the visual
image as a vital constitutive process of *language*. They phrase this embodiment of language in sexual terms through what Wagner calls the
trope of embodiment: language is the figure-ground reversal of
thought, and the reproductive body becomes the microcosmic embodiment of the socialized body:

> The counterpart of the brain's synthesis of collective cultural image
> through language is the body's reproductive synthesis of another
> body. As the brain contains the microcosm of the mind within the
> macrocosm of the body, so the loins—particularly the uterus—
> contain the macrocosm of the body, as fetus, within a reproductive
> microcosm. (Wagner 1986:138)

Relationality is thus a capacity shaped by the body's spatial, motile, and
sensorial contours, all of which are themselves aspects of something
analogous to the "total social fact" and which Freud called "*die ganze
Sexualstrebung*," the "total sexual tendency" (Lacan 1977b:199). And by
this we mean not some narrowly defined range of erotogenic drives or
posited instincts but a consideration of how body schema, language,
desire, and world emerge together within a total cultural order (cf.
Bourdieu 1977).[6]

Because we depend upon our presence in a social field for the making visible of conventional meaning, and because, as we have seen, this social field is delimited by the domain of body image and its perceptual register, we must understand that for Freud, Lacan, and Wagner, meaning is itself a function of perception. The sensoriness of the sexual capacity, its functioning at the superficies of the body, is already embodied by the conceptual capacity of the brain. Freud himself made a phylogenetic argument for the evolution of conceptualization out of imagistic sensation:

> the central nervous system originates from the ectoderm. The grey matter of the cortex remains a derivative of the primitive superficial layer of the organism and may have inherited some of its essential properties. (1920:26)

The symbolic capacity is as much a part of our *perceptual* apparatus as our eyes, ears, and voice. Hence, without the symbolic limits that language places on the world, there would be no body, in the sense of an encompassing limit, to our actions or thoughts. We are forced to conclude that in order to make these limits visible, the function of bodies of language such as myths is more to cut off or obviate explanatory expansion than to facilitate it. What productive actions ensue from such a discursive bounding?

The Melanesian *Objet Petit A*

Let us repeat what Lacan said about the mirror stage: that the vision of corporeal unity that a subject acquires always comes from an external, alien source—the image of another's body or of one's own body in a mirror. It is an effect of the specular capacity, primarily, that is, of vision as it competes with other sensory modalities—synesthesia, kinesthesia, and so forth.

But the subject *anticipates* this unity, this completeness. To be human is to be temporal, which is to say that we look forward to the completion of our acts, to the bounding and finishing of our intentions and the effectiveness of such acts and intentions. And this temporality inflects the visual sense itself, makes of vision and of the body image a moment of resolution into form. Because this anticipation of form precedes its visual confirmation, there are always parts or regions of the body that escape the mirror, that are not retained by the subject in the formation of its ego ideal.

Those parts of the body that escape are destined to become what Lacan called *objets a*, or *objets petit a*, the "little other objects." For the most part, they occur at the body's margins, where the specular boundaries or limits are most pronounced: the lips, the nipple, the phallus, excreta. But they also include those *functions* of the body's borders: "the phoneme, the gaze, the voice . . . the nothing" (Lacan 1977a:315). These are "the 'stuff,' or rather the lining, though not in any sense the reverse, of the very subject that one takes to be the subject of consciousness" (1977a:315). The subject him/herself is included in this, being precipitated by all the leftover bits of discourse that cannot be attributed to others. And because language comes to designate this subject, the subject so referred to by such designations is also "no more than such an object" (1977a:315). The *objet a* designates all these bits which do not ordinarily surface in discourse, but which impinge upon its domain of representation. They appear as a result of the inherent caducity which inevitably accompanies vision and perception. Lacan notes:

> The imaginary function is that which Freud formulated to govern the investment of the object as narcissistic object . . . the specular image is the channel taken by the transfusion of the body's libido towards the object. But even though part of it remains preserved from this immersion, concentrating within the most intimate aspect of auto-eroticism, its position at the "tip" of the form predisposes it to the phantasy of *caducity* in which is completed its exclusion from the specular image and from the prototype that it constitutes for the world of objects. (1977a:319)

Caducity here is made to serve a function in every sense opposite to that of the vegetable realm: it is the discarded bit that serves as the marker of the body, that makes it visible. We might say that the *objets a* are the elicited ground that allows the body to stand forth as an ideal unity. The outline of what we recognize as the elements of the perceivable world—the object, the eye, the cortex, the ego—are provided by all those "little other objects" that escape perception, that drop off or are discarded by the focusedness of perception. The *objets a* are *refractions* of the subject, or we might say they are distortions of it; although they maintain the shape of the body's geography, they do so in a perspectival, nonproportional way, as an anamorphic projection distorts the proportions of the depicted object.

Since the *objets a* are those things which complete the person, they become the means by which the relations between persons can be objectified in the manner we have become acquainted with in Melanesia. Strathern observes that it is this anticipation of completeness that is such a crucial component of the Melanesian person.

The creation of a same-sex state seems a symbolic prerequisite for separating gift from giver, the transacted from the transactor. Only this separation allows the detachment of an object which can then be exchanged between persons and signifies the relation between them. Detachment makes the person incomplete . . . and therefore seek completion with another. Completion is inevitably anticipated . . . (1988:222)

What we see in the progression of masked dancers in the Yangis is the movement by which the unspecularized *objet a* becomes a whole figure. The thing detached comes to model the whole from which it was separated. And ultimately, in the Melanesian world, *"these objects are apprehended as both cause and effect of the relations"* (Strathern 1988: 221).

The gaze, the phoneme, the voice, the nothing—to this list we add the relationship. A relational view of the person always implies a refraction of the subject, because for a relationship to be perceptible between persons or objects, some space or gap must be created between them, some limit on their respective bodies and subjectivities must be established. Through the imposition of such a limit, the subject is anamorphized, for his/her subjectivity is dependent upon the external triangulated perspective of others.

To the extent that the *objets a* are a residue of the perception of a whole figure, then they must retain the shape of that whole figure, despite their partial, *roofuk*-like status. The decorated or phallocrypt-encased penis, the *abi* egg, the mask, the string bag—and elsewhere in New Guinea, the pearl shell, the drum, the bull-roarer, the flute, the magic fertility stone—paradoxically, these objects mirror back a condition of completeness to the multiply composed Melanesian person. They are the opposite of what psychoanalysis calls "partial objects."

We return to the vegetal images with which we started this exercise. Our intuition would be, as Werbner has suggested in his chapter in *Shooting the Sun,* to see the *roofuk* as the "sterile, discardable part" (Juillerat 1992:232) and the *hoofuk* as the vital, reproductive core. But in terms of both Lacan's and Strathern's understanding of the analogic nature of sexual differentiation, it is as much the other way around. As Juillerat notes:

the opposition seems to be between a discarded part, which is the object of transformation . . . and the owner, who proceeds toward sexuation and individuation and thus is propelled toward a more socialized, and also a more sterile, destiny. (1992:271)

But in fact in the Yangis we cannot identify anything which is purely *hoofuk* or purely *roofuk*. The bundles that the *eri* dancers hold contain sago, taro, and yam flesh, and sexual fluids collected by the moiety priests with the aid of their wives. These are all manifestations of *hoofuk*, but they function in a *roofuk*-like way. And this is true for the other bits of *hoofuk* we find being passed from one masked figure to another: the *abi* egg, the sago jelly. *Hoofuk* becomes reproductive only when it is detachable, when it becomes *roofuk* itself. Thus in the Yangis, it is the discardable, leftover, detachable bits that are passed from one masked dancer to the other and which thus keep the reproductive imagery flowing in the ritual. It is these which temporarily acquire the status of the "whole thing." If we were to focus on these little bits, if we were to keep our eye on the little peas in this elaborate shell game, rather than on the diversion provided by the masked figures themselves, we would see the leftover bits gradually transforming themselves from semen, to egg, to homuncular fish and termite, to fetalized penis, and finally to whole man.

The Limit of Myth and Ritual

But without the competing register of language, the imagery of such detachments can only oscillate within the metonymic field of part and whole. What language provides, as a gloss on this alternating current of embodiment, is its constituting dimension in the history of the subject. And the unfolding of such a history is an exercise in the judgment of the proper proportions of such imagery.

Those analysts whom Juillerat gathered together do not disagree on what is being symbolized in the Yangis. The Yangis is about sexuality, procreation, fertility, maternity, hunting. But we do not need to be told this. What each analyst offers is a variable assessment of the proportions between images in the Yangis.

Let us return to the two myths which Juillerat provides as glosses on different images of the Yangis. The first myth appears to draw an analogy between a woman and a bush fowl, by equating the bush fowl egg with semen: a man's semen deposited in the nest of his wife's uterine cavity is like an egg incubated within a bush fowl nest. The elder brother responds to his younger brother's adulterous appropriation of his wife by treating *him* as an egg, killing him and depositing him in the bush fowl's mounded, uterine nest. This analogy leads to the next image: the younger sister now is forced to swallow the dead body/egg and sit on the nest like a bush fowl. She incubates the younger brother in an alimentary fashion; it is as if his whole body has orally fertilized the bush fowl/sister. She evacuates—gives birth to as a fowl—the brother's bones as two *ogomo* spirits. Now Juillerat says that the "self" (*sungwaag* in Yafar) of the *ogomo* dancer may be threatened by the proximity of these spirits, "and thus become ripe (*abuk*), that is weakened and ill" (1992:40), and further, that they are depictions of "the male principle at work in the growth of the fetus" (1992:40). The *ogomo* have become the egg, the dancers, and the masks all at the same time. What are we to make of this most vividly parthenogenic image, that of an avian mother giving birth to sons by having swallowed a "father," and then nourishing them on the "semen"/fetus (eggs) she herself produces?[7] We should sense that consumption remains the most socially regnant manifestation of gendered acts in these societies. And we could thus confirm one of Marilyn Strathern's observations that throughout Melanesia, becoming socially effective turns on being forced to consume or forcing others to consume. It follows that the act of bringing something that is inside to the outside (whether it be through childbirth, bleeding, the removal of tubers from the earth, the unwrapping of a pearl shell prior to its transaction) is how people judge the social nature of the consumptive act which results in such bodily eversion (Strathern 1988:290–91).

The Yafar myth does not just comment on the part of the ritual to which the local exegesis allegedly attaches it: it retroactively serves to explicate the all-important inauguration of the hunting period months before the Yangis ceremony. The two designated *ifege* performers climb two coconut palms. Breaking open the spadix spathe they say, "Break open the possum children, break open the cassowary children" (Juillerat 1992:79–80), and so on, listing other species. Then, shaking the coconut inflorescence, they cause the flowers to fall, which the Yafar say is maternal milk. The men below, including the designated *eri* and *yis* performers, all stand with their hands open and raised. Juillerat explains:

> Men who get a flower into their hands are said to be "in the Mother's net bag" . . . , that is, in her womb, or actually in her net bag like a baby (in both cases, fed by her). Men who do not get any flower will say: . . . Mother abandoned me . . . (1992:80)

The *ogomo* are named by the *ifege* as they cause the flowers to fall, as if they have effected the act of caducity, the dropping of the milk/flowers. In other words, the *ogomo* here are the external cause of hunting caducity, while in the bush fowl myth they are the internal *effect* of alimentary caducity.

The activity of hunting is envisaged in one form by the Yafar as

bringing influence upon the game animal that allows its self to drop
away and cause it to die: "The purpose of some hunting ritual is to
let 'ripen' the game's *sungwaag* [self] to accelerate its death when
wounded" (Juillerat 1992:49). Whereas the coconut ritual sets Yangis
up as a function of the hunting perspective of men, the myth looks at
Yangis from a female perspective which is more inclined to see such
reproduction in terms of avian encompassment and nourishment. The
point is, however, that *each perspective includes the opposite gendered view
within it* as its own internal (hidden) motivation: men become hunters
only when they are encompassed by women's containing function;
women become uterinely reproductive subsequent to an act of killing.
But each act takes an unmistakably consumptive form, and it is in this
sense that consumption models a social aesthetic in New Guinea. To
return to a point made earlier, in New Guinea consumption involves
making the internal (gendered) capacities of the body visible, and "it
rests on techniques of revelation which must also continually external-
ise and thus represent these capacities in new forms" (Strathern 1991a:
199).

The image of the proper time of ripening, and of the danger of too
early ripening, is returned to in the second complete myth, where once
more we see the part become the whole, the item of caducity become
the reproductive core, the fruit/testicle become insect/*imago*/fetus.
Here the hunter reveals the ultimate product of death, which is reproduction itself. Caducity results in the reproduction of the *amof*/fetuses,
and they present themselves in the form of *roofuk*, dancing around the
periphery of the plaza, being "shed" by the action of the central dancers, and captured in a reproductive, bound state by the women's string
bags.

We must note that in both this myth and that of the bush fowl, the
growth of sago is at the center of the image. The *ogomo* are themselves
sago growth spirits; the *boof* fruits are made in the image of the homuncular *amof* by being arranged along a frame of sago sticks and roots;
and the *amof* themselves are the sago babies. But clearly an appeal to
symbolic coding is insufficient in these circumstances; it is not enough
for us to note that they are all "about sago growth," for such a coding
is by definition without context or shape—and it is the shape, the body
that limits the free play of such coding, that we want to make visible.

Here is where Ricoeur makes a vital observation by insisting that
"analytic interpretation" must be distinguished from and supplemented by "genetic interpretation." "[D]reams make use of symbolism," he pointed out, "they do not elaborate it . . . the proper path of
interpretation is the dreamer's associations and not the pregiven con-

nections in the symbols themselves" (1970:101, 102). The mere decoding of symbolism does not constitute an interpretation—of a dream, a myth or ritual, or a culture. And it is only where there is a difference of kind between two things—such as myth and ritual, or two different languages, or language and behavior, or between the Imaginary and the Symbolic—that we are provided with the genuine possibility of interpretation.

It would be a grave error—the error I think that has been at the heart of so-called psychoanalytic anthropology from its beginning to this very day—to take this distinction between the analytic and the genetic as synonymous with an antinomy of culture and individual, or public and private, or collective and personal. We need to replace such antinomies with a consideration of the *differential proportions that meanings take in human life.* In Wagner's terms, contrasts such as that between individual and collective are a function of the variable potential for expansion of various tropic constructions: private and personal versus collective and public become labels for the differential in perceived proportion of social currency a symbol or usage acquires.

What psychoanalysis has always remained faithful to—and what anthropologists continuously waver from—is the idea that it is this *usage* which is the beginning and the end of their subject matter. And I could paraphrase something that Marilyn Strathern said at the end of the Fourth ASA Decennial which would indicate the kind of anthropology that would have a similar focus: what is perceived as individual or collective, or as culture or social life, does not lie outside this dialogic, relational usage—on the contrary, such perceptions are precipitated and produced by it (1993:7; see also Merlan and Rumsey 1991). Ricoeur and Lacan have made a decisive contribution to the human sciences by showing that social process and relationality are interpretive action, and in so doing they have established the grounds by which we recognize the similar goals and technique of psychoanalysis and anthropology.

The chapters that follow do not each add an incremental part to an anticipated whole; they are not parts of the standard monographical jigsaw. They are different attempts to demonstrate, *to show,* the analytic and methodological implications of the anthropology of myth and ritual I have just outlined. In fact, it could be said that each chapter has the same subject matter and it is in the manner in which this subject is repeated that the demonstration itself resides.

In the next chapter, I reintroduce the phenomenon of symbolic obviation that was the analytic theme of *The Heart of the Pearl Shell*, addressing specifically the issue of linguistic conventionality. From a psychoanalytic point of view, I maintain that one cannot consider convention without a simultaneous uncovering of what *resists* convention, for resistances are construed by speakers as motivation for appeals to convention itself, whether this be grammatical, semantic, or cultural.

One of the themes of this book is that language is itself embodied, in the sense both of being an activity of the human body, and of taking different forms, having different bodies itself. The ways in which bodies of discourse relate to each other thus take the same form as processes of bodily detachment, encompassment, insemination, swallowing, and so forth. In Part II, I begin by showing how obviation is itself a phenomenon of the surface of the body of myth. By imposing *pointes de capiton* within the imagery of the myth, it limits the manner in which myths and parts of myths can combine and be used in other stories. The relationship between these "partial organs" of myth is then not semantic or combinatorial, but metonymic: they combine with other stories by altering the resolution of each myth as interpretive whole, rather than through the increment or deletion of individual structural components.

Roy Wagner's glossing of obviation as a "holography of meaning" (1986) identifies a spatial and topographical dimension to meaning itself, and in fact it calls to mind Lacan's phrase: "Let us consider consciousness to occur each time . . . there's a surface such that it can produce what is called *an image*" (1991b:49). It could be said that myth and ritual are the verbal and visual shape of obviation. If this is so, then our appeals to the shell-like properties of myth are not misplaced.

These three-dimensional properties imply more generally that speech always has spatial (and temporal) dimensions. In Chapter 3, I consider a Foi myth in which the space of sexual intercourse is seen as equivalent to the spatial route by which flowers (which represent pearl shells) entered the region of Foi habitation from the outside. Furthermore, the myth has an associated magic spell through which these two spaces are made identical.

The image of sexual intercourse that emerges from the two different Foi mythical treatments in Chapters 2 and 3 is that pearl shells and their movement literally provide the shape and outline of the human organs themselves, rather than (or as well as) the other way around. And since pearl shells are so much more than phallic symbols (whether male or female), since they are the embodiment of productive and consumptive values in general in Foi social life, then the space of sexual intercourse is coeval with the total space of such historically constituted productive acts, considered as a series of movements through space. Furthermore, to so move productively is to leave a trace or imprint upon the path of one's journey. The descriptive and inscriptive functions of speech are united in these myths which accord a marking, place-creating power to certain reproductive organs and acts.

The myths of these two chapters show that a pearl shell is always a whole thing—it is the whole person, the whole clan, the act of sexual intercourse itself, the fetus in a womb. It is neither detachable nor inalienable but rather *the projection of the form that completed acts of productive consumption take in Foi social life.*

To say that it is a whole thing is to imply that it retains the capacity to be a sign not of any one sex but of the relational act of disjunctive synthesis itself. The subtitle of this book, "The Myth of Sexuality," indicates that the myths I have chosen all *appear* to concern in one way or another sexual organs, capacities, substances, acts. But I intend that it should be taken in a more critical sense, as an indication of the manner in which we are all too inclined to accept the sexually monolithic nature of these reproductive organs at face value, and to phrase the ultimate description of their effects solely in procreative and/or erotogenic terms. But is clear from an examination of West Sepik reproductive imagery that whatever libidinal component there is to sexuality, it is vegetative propagation that provides the most compelling image of human reproduction. By an appeal to caducity, the Yafar make reproduction a matter of the disjunctive act of detachment rather than erotic fusion. Furthermore, we find that detachment is paradoxically accomplished through the *encompassment* or containment of the detached thing, which indicates that the relational component of reproduction can be ascertained only through an inspection of the *product* of men's and women's capacities rather than the capacities themselves.

Because these sexual acts are relationally constituted, they are contingent upon social effect: they depend upon people's making available their sexual capacities in specific ways to each other. The organs that are the site of these acts are never merely "partial objects" but are made to be the whole person (temporarily at least, in specific acts of sexual reproduction), and in the context of myth these organs themselves come to caricature the person. The myths seem to pose questions such as: how would a man with a uterus or a woman with a penis reproduce? But to phrase them in this way is already to cut off the possibility of a Papuan view of sexuality, for it is precisely the point that the organs of men and women are always both penile and uterine in our terms.

One of the implications of the psychoanalytic approach to language I am taking is that it is only through language and speech that an appeal to the imaginary partiality and incompleteness of these whole things can be made. Only in language are repression and negation possible.

And we can return to the point made by Deleuze and Guattari: if the act of detachment is a productive act, then the making partial and incomplete of an image through language is also a productive act with respect to social meaning.

In Part III, I examine how myth provides us with evidence for this detachment and reencompassment at all levels of New Guinea social articulation—the body, and the relations sustained through body image, the voice, and language itself. In Chapter 4, I begin, as did Freud at one point, with the image of castration—the detachment of the penis in Marind-anim mythology—and I then trace the consequences of the entrapment of the penis by the female organ. The Lacanian contrast between penis and phallus is affirmed here, for while the former is ever only a part organ, the latter is a label for the differential relationship to detaching and containing functions the organ is made to play as a relational construct.

If at one point the Marind penis becomes a bull-roarer, a sound producing instrument, it is because the realm of the acoustic is the site of social extensibility throughout most of New Guinea—the projection of sound and voice is inseminating and fertilizing, as I mentioned in the Introduction. It would not be unreasonable to speculate that sound itself can become trapped, can become contained, and that the voices which produce sound can also be subject to the corporeal bounding of form. In Chapter 5, the Foi drum and the Gimi flute provide us with images of the containment of voice in New Guinea, and how men and women draw forth different voices from these "relational instruments": in other words, we find that there are men's and women's myths about the same instrument, and that the relationship between such myths is also one of containment. We discover that the men's version is literally surrounded or engulfed within the narrative structure of the women's version. Not only, then, is the voice a little other object of myth—a residue or discard of its imaginal structuring—but insofar as viewpoint and perspective are negotiated through language, then language too becomes subject to this caducity that is the product of the form-engendering process.

If the drum contains man's voice, then the string bag, the "object" of Chapter 6, contains that which attracts and attaches the voices of men: children (who as infants are carried on their mothers' backs in these bags). I say they attach the voices of men inasmuch as children receive patronyms from their father and are also named after places in his territory. Insofar as the child *contains* its father's paternal function in this way, as it does its mother's in a different fashion, the string bag represents the *containment of containment*. But the string bag also holds food, particularly meat, and we might ask ourselves how the Foi imagine a single organ that carries out both alimentary and uterine functions. The two myths of this chapter concern each of these functions, and our answer makes us confront the possibility that these two myths might be the Freudian negation of each other.

These three chapters all deal with the migratory, nomadic potential of what we identify as reproductive organs. Their relational capacities ordain their loss and detachment and confirm that splitting and the social ectasia it makes possible are the first and most important concomitants of relationality, at least in New Guinea. In Chapter 7, I return to the image of flow at the heart of the Foi social world. Procreative fluidity, the movement of fertile bodies across the earth, the coating of men's bodies in decorative tree oil which mythically derives from women's menstrual blood, all make their appearance as flows which are contained, halted, or momentarily encapsulated. And since the late 1980s, another flow, that of crude oil from the ground itself, has added a new vector of reproductivity to this world of fertile movement. But since these flows are all invoked mythically in the speech of Foi persons, we find that the conflict between different kinds of reproductive fluidity is also a conflict between different myths themselves, as new stories emerge which swallow, halt, or encapsulate other ones. Territoriality, as a function of language and its ability to disperse names; procreative fluidity, the emissions of the body's internal reproductive organs; language, in the form of the myths which account for the historical inscription of the ground itself; and speech, as the pragmatic acts through which linguistic imagery is deployed in social encounters, all come together to demonstrate not just how myth contains its own antecedent motivation but how it projects a present and anticipates the future in the discursive events that comprise social life.

PART II

THE TIME OF ANALYSIS

2 _____

Convention and Motivation in Foi Myth

Part I: Convention and Repetition

By what terms are human communicative events established? This is arguably one of the most important questions for an anthropology of language (I prefer this as a rubric to "linguistic anthropology," which presupposes the very thing that is in question, namely, the constitution of language through human sociality and vice versa). As an opening hypothesis, let us say that these terms of reference are the historically specific ways of glossing utterances in different contexts that emerge among a community of speakers. These glosses are the net effect of the repeated use of terms over time; they acquire the sediment of habitual, repetitive confirmation within the arena of intersubjective negotiation, often to such a degree that their connection to the things they gloss seems self-evident, what Bourdieu (1977) calls doxic (see also Benveniste 1971; Eco 1986).

I assume that it is the behavior of such speakers that we are interested in, and that it is chiefly this behavior that has to figure as the subject of any generalization we want to label as "language" or "a language." Included in this behavior are the rhetorical appeals made to the force and felicity (or weakness and infelicity) of conventional meanings or dictionary meanings, which are part and parcel of the speech events themselves. Terms such as "semantic reference" and "metaphorical innovation" are ever only labels for specific social effects that certain utterances are felt to have in given situations. Austin (1975) attempted to catalogue these different social effects of utterances by what he called their illocutionary and perlocutionary properties: the meanings and actions they elicited, which are not always in accord with either the literal meanings of the words that compose them or the intentions of the speakers.

In this respect, semiotic anthropologists such as Richard Parmentier are to be commended for their enrichment of semiology through pragmatics, as outlined by Silverstein. What pragmatics should force us to realize is that there is no such thing as pure, unmediated linguistic reference, hence no such thing as pure conceptual structure (See Weiner 1991b, 1992). All of our utterances, our linguistic representations, are framed by an actual, pragmatic speech situation and do service first and foremost to the practical requirements of such specific communicative situations. At any given time, some meanings seem stable and unproblematic; others seem eccentric, questionable, transient—semiotic parvenus. What is at issue is how we label these contrastive discursive effects and why such an attempt often leads to a distinction between the vehicles that give them shape (language and its component elements) and the rules that govern their use.

It is to this putative contrast among discursive effects that Parmentier (1990) directs himself in his comment on the semiotic grounding of symbolic obviation. Obviation, a term first coined by Roy Wagner (1978), refers to the way symbols act upon each other in certain contexts so as to reveal what I just described above as the relative contrast between conventional and idiosyncratic meanings. At any given time some meanings are held steady by a community. They constitute a conventional ground upon which more incidental figures can emerge. To achieve that innovative effect, the background must be accepted as perfectly self-evident, natural, and innate, when in fact it is just as much a symbolic construct as the figure upon which it is built. Obviation achieves this revelation of the arbitrariness, the historical specificity, of convention.

Parmentier addresses himself to this issue and suggests that we should, however, distinguish between two types of conventionality. The first he calls Peircean convention: "a semiotic ground linking sign and object such that the sign would not stand for the object it does without some further sign, its "interpretant," representing it to be so related" (1990:172). This is arbitrariness in a pure uncontaminated form, the interface between word and world. The other kind of conventionality he calls normative: "the habitual, typical, taken-for-granted, literal or normative quality of cultural symbolization" (1990: 173). This second type of conventionality takes place wholly within the realm of communal, human meanings. In short, leaving aside the status of the shadowy third term, the "interpretant," there is one kind of convention that defines the relationship between linguistic signifiers and their nonlinguistic signifieds, and another kind of convention that is the historical world of standard *cultural* meanings.

But again it is behavior we are interested in. Behaviorally, is there any difference in the way people defer to or invoke one kind of conventionality as opposed to the other? What, in any case, is the primary evidence that linguists and anthropologists have for distinguishing between these types of conventionality? Is it not precisely people's verbal assessments and glosses on particular social encounters? Are the effects which constitute their allegedly distinct status significantly different? I think not. In habitual, unreflective language use, one simply utters the word, unaware of whether the conventionality betokened by such habituality is one of language or of culture.[1] If Parmentier is appealing to a distinction between language and culture, then it must be pointed out that prima facie, there is no way we can read off such a distinction from actual speech events because the distinction itself is an effect, rather than (or as well as) a precondition, of discourse.

When I talk of behavior, however, I talk not of the responses to observable stimuli as defined, for example, by behaviorists; I talk of actions and judgments that emerge within a field of meaning which encompasses an actor's perceptions. This, as I suggested in the previous chapter, is what makes psychoanalysis a social science. Ricoeur thus points out that

> For the analyst . . . behavior is not a dependent variable observable
> from without, but is rather the expression of the changes of
> meaning of the subject's history as they are revealed in the
> analytical situation . . . [Behavioral facts] do not function as
> observables, but as signifiers [*signifiants*] for the history of desire.
> (1970:364)

Using much the same line of reasoning, I would now like to suggest that a subject's own history and the history of his/her "society" or "community" are a product of such accumulated usages, including those we label as myth. They both are products of a hermeneutic recovery of the past using the discursive resources available to one in the present. This hermeneutic recovery takes many forms. The social and historical world of an author needs to be elucidated before a reader can assess the possibilities of interpretation provided by a text; the recorded "facts" of history need to be set side by side with the biographies and reconstructed interests of the recorders so as to determine who are the beneficiaries of a particular reading of such facts; psychoanalysis seeks to recover all that has been censored or repressed by the subject but which is nevertheless implicated in the subject's own causal chain and the story he or she formulates as a gloss for that chain; and the analyst of myth tries to recover the reflexive effect of communal figures of speech that are brought out in myth.[2] In every instance of speech there is both a revealing of the conscious intentions of the speaker and a simultaneous covering over of the origins of those intentions. Any theory of language that privileges one of these movements over the other is bound to be incomplete as such.

Like songs and certain kinds of poetry, and also like dreams and certain kinds of compulsive behavior among Westerners, myths, at least among the Foi people of Papua New Guinea, are told and retold in the same way. They are repeatable, and people know what the ending of the story is.[3] It is not an ingenuous or trivial question to ask why a myth or ritual can be repeated over and over again if people already "know" what the punch line is, what the anticipated effect will be. The problem is that as analysts we can judge the conventionality of an act or an utterance only by its reiterability, the property of being recognizable as the same act or word or utterance. And we do not know on the face of it whether we are responding to the sameness of the isolated act or word or the sameness of the framing conditions that define it, or both at once.[4] Such an anticipation would, on the face of it, work against the motivations and intentions of the actor. We are forced to conclude that conventionality is a bar to communication, and speech acts which fail to deflect or displace conventionality fail to achieve any pragmatic effect at all.

It would seem that any theory of repetition would thus stand as a critique of the temporal nature of speech.[5] Am I then saying that myth is the Foi's own version of repetition compulsion? If so, where does it enter into the hermeneutic of their conventionalized language uses, as a symptom of a Foi community's hidden meanings, or as a cure for the relativization of intention which is an effect of such hidden meanings? In other words, is it a mechanism by which to further conceal and euphemize the causal chain of signification, or a therapy which draws attention to the multiple readings available to any such concealing chain? Or is it both at once?[6]

One of the fundamental starting points of psychoanalysis is that there is a scission between psychic events and their surfacing or emergence in linguistic form. Human subjectivity has as one of its core features the selective and yet methodical repression, forgetting, and denial of key memories (LaPlanche and Leclair 1972). The traces of these events remain in the unconscious to which they are consigned by these repressive mechanisms, and one might say that they constitute the unseen lineaments of our conscious, subjective discourse, shaping it without our being aware of it, resurfacing in our verbal and representational activity in disguised form, for example, as slips of the tongue and dream imagery. It is useful to draw upon one of Lacan's notable assertions: that it is not the unconscious which is the condition of language, but language which is the condition of the unconscious (1977a). It is through language, and the polysemy that is the basic fact of language, that things get hidden from consciousness (Ricoeur 1970, 1981).

Every time we speak, the pragmatic contours of the speech situation narrow down and hide these multiple possibilities. Ultimately, this repression of multiplicity accompanies every sentence and every word, a constant turning away from, a *Verneinung* of the basic polysemy of language. When we utter a sentence, we suspend or defer the significance of its terms until the end, the final term. "In other words, the meaning, suspended to the end of the sentence, must be read backwards into the preceding words once the sentence is finished" (Muller and Richardson 1982:364). But the sentence carries on its crest the intention of the utterer, an intention that looks forward to its own completion, and this too is a meaningful perception. The hermeneutic I am describing is not about how meaning gets apportioned *post festum* over an act but how one kind of perception (that of the speaker's intention) is played off against or used to model another (that of the external resistance to that intention). Meaning flanks the point of the sentence, always one step ahead as well as one step behind it. In the present of the speaking subject two waves ripple in opposite directions, one carrying the subject's anticipation of the future, the other depositing signifiers behind the subject which can be followed and recovered in reverse.

An important part of our subjective posture in the world is the way we strive to create a felicitous context for our speech in the presence of others. We can say that our desire for others motivates us to manage and influence their perceptions. As anthropologists, we are interested in the manner in which people construe the motivation for their actions, the things that emerge as resistance to their actions and intentions, because it is only in terms of such resistance that we measure the limits and range of these intentions in the first place: they achieve their force against what they overcome and displace. It follows that every instance of speech bears the scars of this resistance, some mark of the cutting off of semiotic extension of our words forced on us by the constraints of intersubjectivity.

Part II: Myth and Temporality

I would like to suggest that a myth models this hermeneutic of speech, and that obviation is a disclosure of the possible glosses of this hermeneutic itself. But obviation aims at more than simply the recovery of the background to a sequence of actions, or symbolic actions; it reveals the range of possibilities opened up by symbolic innovation; it projects a future route as well as an antecedent origin. A background always contains this map of the future, always bears the trace of a complementary chain of motivations which shadows the explicit actions and forward-looking intentions of the agent.

In psychoanalysis the concept of motivation is linked to compulsion, the urge to recreate the terms of some early interpersonal conflict in the hopes of resolving it or reliving it in successful or beneficial form. The issue of temporality stands forth prominently here, for what answer can we give to the question, in what time does the compulsion occur? Insofar as there is a time, it is in a certain space of life created by the structure of the compulsion. The compulsion motivates the subject to orient his/her actions so as to recreate this space, the context of the repressed episode.

A motivation is not to be confused with a causal antecedent. A motivation is construed along with the perception of the act and is retrospectively projected backward in time so as to precede and ground the act. In other words, they are not just explanations *post festum* but also interpretations *ante festum;* they are already implicated in the action, having set the terms for its subsequent interpretation.[7]

Because as acting subjects we encounter a world, including the world of other subjects, as one which offers resistance to us, we easily construe these motivations to be at odds with or in opposition to the actions we undertake. As an afterimage shows a reverse color value, so does a motivation often appear as an inverted form of the action itself, since the easiest way to erase a condition or cause it to withdraw is to reverse its terms, its polarity, or set up an antithetical negation to it in order to cancel it.

A myth is a deliberate parody of this process, or perhaps its most highly condensed and compacted form (as poetry is the most condensed form of speech, and dance is the most condensed form of bodily *hexis*), in that it sets up a situation such that the motivation is forced to reveal itself, as it were, and in a particular way. As Wagner and I have explained it in various places (Wagner 1978, 1986; Weiner 1988), a myth relates a sequence of incidents that can be seen as a series of substitutions. These substitutions step by step take an opening initial situation and transform it. The substitutions themselves alternate between those of convention and those counterimages which inevitably displace, distort, or render problematic that convention. By the end of the myth, the displacements have accumulated in such a manner as to cause the conventional premise upon which the opening of the myth was founded to collapse altogether. At this point, some glimpse of the limits of social protocol is achieved. Wagner explained that these substitutions in a myth alternate between what he called the

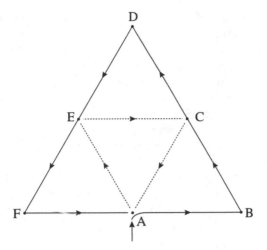

Figure 1. Obviation triangle.

facilitating and the motivating modalities. The substitutions of the facilitating modality—points A, C, and E on the ternary obviational diagram (see Figure 1)—present some conventionalized social situation. The incidents which work to transform or efface these conventionalized images are the substitutions of the motivating modality—points B, D, and F.

It is upon this issue that Parmentier centers his reanalysis of the Foi myth entitled "The Hornbill Husband," which I discuss in Chapter 7 of *The Heart of the Pearl Shell*. I am not going to dispute Parmentier's alternative glossing of the episodes of that myth, because in terms of their status as significant images in the myth they are as valid as any (as is also the case with the patient's discourse in psychoanalysis, or with episodes and images in a dream, there are no unsignificant events in the myth anyway). This does not yet constitute the interpretation of the myth. What I want to do now is make a criticism of both his and my own *interpretations*. And I want to do so by returning to Williams' (1977:313–14) original myth, "The Origin of the Kutubu People," for which I did not actually provide an obviative outline in my earlier treatment.

THE ORIGIN OF THE KUTUBU PEOPLE

A girl was gathering firewood in the bush when she fell in with an ugly old woman. Going on together they came to a *haginamo* tree and decided to gather berries. The girl climbed into the tree when the old woman, who stood underneath, suddenly struck the trunk. The tree sprang up to an enormous height, so that the girl could not possibly get down. She sat there crying in the branches and the old woman went away.

For several days the girl remained without food. But one morning she woke to find a great stock of provisions beside her. She ate and ate and fell asleep. Next morning there was fresh supply, and so on each day—sugar-cane, sago, meat, firewood, etc. (a long enumeration). She now stripped bark from the tree and made herself a new skirt and settled down to a solitary life.

Presently she found herself pregnant. She was very puzzled and angry about it. She could not imagine who had brought her to that condition. But in due time the child was born and nursed in the top of the tree; and after that a second child. Now she had a boy and a girl. Food continued to be supplied each day, and ornaments, *bari* shells, armlets, etc. were sometimes found with it. These she put on her children.

By now they had grown up. The boy had long hair and the girl's breasts were showing. Then one day the mother told her two children to close their eyes together. When they opened them there was no mother, no tree. They were standing on the ground beside a house.

At first they wept for their mother. But there was a supply of sago in the house, so they ate and made themselves comfortable. Then they fashioned a *toio* [stone axe] and a sago scraper and set about getting their own food. While the girl made sago the boy would hunt. One day they found a number of young plants set down near the house, and they proceeded to make a garden. Another day they found two piglets done up in a parcel of leaves; another day two puppies. The brother said, "You look after the pigs, and I will look after the dogs." He gave them medicines and took them out hunting and caught many animals. Brother and sister were very happy.

But the brother noticed that his sister was each day absent a long time at the sago place. He wondered what she was up to, and followed her secretly. He saw that she used to embrace a palm tree, rubbing up and down against it with her legs astride. Next day, while she was elsewhere, he wedged a sharp piece of flint in the tree trunk, and lay in hiding to see what would happen. When the girl came to embrace the tree again she cut herself, and was thus furnished with a vagina. She fell at the foot of the tree bleeding profusely. The boy did his best to stanch the blood, using various leaves (which have ever since been red or autumn-coloured).[a] Finally he thought of applying *bari* shells and pearlshells, and the bleeding stopped.

Thenceforward they lived as man and wife and their children intermarried and populated the whole Kutubu district.[b]

The following were Williams' footnotes to this text:

[a] In another version it was said that the girl's blood was responsible for red colours in nature, the boy's semen for white colours (white leaves, stones, etc.).

A theory of conception or the make-up of the body, is that the mother's menstrual blood makes all the soft fleshy parts (thus, if you cut yourself the blood flows); the father's semen makes the hard "white" parts—bones, teeth, finger- and toe-nails.

[b] This story was one of those given me without names for the characters, my informant only supplying them after the tale was told. The mother (i.e. the girl who climbed the tree) was Saube (she became a *marua* bird on leaving the children). The person who supplied the food, i.e. the father who revealed himself, was Ya Baia, a hawk (the imagery is obvious). The boy was Kanawebe and the girl Karako. These were said to belong to "Paremahugu" *amindoba.*

The first part of the story is one of the *amindoba* myths, representing "Paremahugu" as the original clan. The second part, the story of how the girl cut herself, etc., is a general myth. Other versions of it give the characters different names.

Williams' myth begins when an old woman meets a young woman in the bush and they go off to gather edible tree leaves. I will label this opening substitution *A:* "nonreproductive for reproductive woman." In my version of this myth, it is made clear that the young woman is already married. The old woman, the *ka buru,* the "black woman," as the Foi call this character, traps the young woman by elongating the tree (*B:* lone female in treetop for lone woman on ground). There she finds herself succored by an invisible caretaker, whom we know to be a bird (*C:* avian for human domesticity; the woman is like a nestling). After a time she becomes pregnant, gives birth to a boy and girl, and then sends them back to the surface world (*D:* brother and sister for original pair of women on ground; *D → A:* the brother and sister are successfully complementary in a domestic sense, unlike the two women who opened the tale). But they are without genitals and are not reproductive. This is a consequence of their mother's assumption of avian status, and the egglike way they are provided with domestic animals.

The brother discovers that the sister is in the habit of straddling a palm tree and sliding up and down on it, an image which could suggest her desire for sexual relations (*E:* sexually desirous women for nonsexual woman [B]; the image itself is a figure-ground reversal of B: there the woman stayed still while the tree shot up). The brother seizes upon this opportunity to furnish her with a vagina (F: human female repro-ductive organ for tree; F → C: vagina for "nest"). This allows the pair to engage in sexual relations which leads to the population of the region through sexual reproduction. We find, therefore, that the myth returns to its starting point A in significantly altered form. Sexual reproduction is "not" predatory sexual competitiveness between women (depicted in substitution A). It is also "not" the inverse of A, asexual cross-sex complementarity (depicted in substitution D). It is the negation of the negation of A, or the "not-not" of A, as Wagner puts it: it is the violent striking of a woman by a man, which is one male image of Foi coitus.

This image, which we can label G, incorporates the sequence A → B → C → D → (A). Whereas D provides the obviation of A, G provides an obviation of the entire myth, which yet retains the terms of that original cancellation. The whole of the myth's "structure," should we so wish to describe it, is thus revealed to be of the same scale as a "part" of it.

In the second of the two footnotes to this myth, Williams says that the narrator supplied him with the names of the characters after the story was told. The unseen supplier of food was the hawk, Ya Baia,[8] a meat-eating bird. The mother trapped in the tree turns into the *marua* bird upon her separation from the children. But let us not be misled by Williams' consigning of these glosses by his Foi narrator to footnotes (as I was myself the first time I confronted this myth). To take this at face value is to make an arbitrary distinction between the text of the myth and the particular terms of reference that are calling forth our specific reading of it at that time. Let's assume instead that though they are given as ostensive "explanations" of the myth, they are in fact com-ponents of its antecedent framing conditions, providing clues to the lis-tener as to how certain substitutive images in the story are to be glossed.

The *marua* bird may be the black monarch flycatcher but it is more likely one of the butcher-birds (*Cracticidae*). These birds forage both terrestrially and arboreally (Beehler et al. 1986:218), and as is the case with the related magpies, they annually make their nests, which they defend vigorously. The *marua* figures prominently in many Foi myths. Its cry signals the advent of the Usane ceremony (see Weiner 1988), in which men visit the longhouses where their sisters and daughters have borne children to exchange forest game for pork with their female re-latives' husbands. I have labeled this common Foi mythologic sequence the Usane Transformation (1988:175), and noted that in the context of the myths in which it appears, it replaces the domain of female domestic life with that of male hunting, exchange, and ceremonial life. The bird's cry tells people to cease making gardens, rearing pigs, and other domestic tasks associated with the longhouse and go and find game in the bush. Insofar as it is a bird, an egg-laying creature, which signals this expansion of human sexuality, the identifying of the central female character in the myth as a *marua* bird is a virtual summation of the myth, or at the least the shell within which everything else in it is held in place. The transformation of the woman into a *marua* bird occurs at point *D* of my present analysis, the obviative midpoint of the myth. Hence, sexual reproduction is the "not" as well as the final "effect"—that is, the Hegelian sublation—of the Usane, which is itself the "not" of the image of female gardening and leaf gathering which opens the myth (since the Usane explicitly replaces female subsistence with its male counterpart).

You could say that in the myth, subsistence has become sexualized, or rather, the phallus has overwritten female domesticity, literally: the "surprise" of the myth is that a tree is like a penis upon which women subsist, on top of which they are borne and themselves give birth, which (seasonally) bears them helplessly up and down, and upon which they themselves slide up and down, finally finding themselves puzzlingly pregnant. The woman is a butcher-bird, whose productive life slides up and down between the base of trees and their canopies, who calls out to men to hunt and to copulate, that is, to efface women's own arboreal domestic work. Instead of the penis moving in and out of the vagina, it is the woman who moves across a planted tree turned edged phallus, who deflowers herself on the male implement of the hunt. It is in line with the Lacanian perspective I am taking here that the penis as such is not present as the original sexual organ, and in fact it remains invisible in this myth; like the woman herself, it is equally effaced and overshadowed by the canopy of the phallic-ovarian tree.[9] What is being circumscribed is not the power of the penis but the route of the phallus—the contour of male signification more generally.

Let me repeat what I said in the closing chapter of *The Heart of the Pearl Shell*: the condensed, compacted nature of each metaphoric "turn" in a myth allows of multiple glossings, any of which results in a different perspective on the myth's imagery. In the interpretations that Parmentier and I have presented, we have used the most ostensive social images of the Foi—that of marriage and female siblingship—to gloss the rather "obvious" effects of the myth and the related aspects of the Foi life cycle. But because marriage, gardening, and co-wifehood are themselves part of the total constitution of sexual reproduction, the inversions represented in the myth can themselves have a more literal glossing in these terms, should we so choose to see them. In other words, I am asking the question: Why should the Foi choose to depict such social imagery in terms of trees, birds, vaginas, and shells if these latter images are themselves not meaningful in their own right? Is this not the question of repetition restated?

Now with these initial images and questions in mind, I can return to my original analysis of the myth I collected entitled "The Hornbill Husband."

THE HORNBILL HUSBAND

Once there lived a young woman. She was working in her garden one day when a *ka buru* approached her and said, "Sister, my *hagenamo* leaves are ready to pick and I want to gather them. But since I am too old to climb up the tree and pick them, I have come to ask you to help me." The young woman agreed and they left. When they approached the *hagenamo* tree, the *ka buru* said to the young woman, "Remove all your clothing and leave it at the base of the tree here; take my clothing instead before you climb up." The young woman did so and climbed up the tree. While she was in the top branches picking leaves, she heard the sound of the tree trunk being struck repeatedly. The *ka buru* called out, "I am going to marry your husband. You will stay here and die." And with that, the trunk of the *hagenamo* tree elongated greatly and the branches spread out in all directions and the young woman was marooned in the top of the tree. She looked down at the ground now far below her and thought, "How shall I leave this place?" and she cried. That night she slept. In the morning she awoke and found that someone had built a fireplace and a small house. In this house she lived. At night while she slept, someone had fetched firewood and with this she made a fire.

She lived in this manner and presently she became pregnant and eventually bore a son. Someone had built a small confinement hut for her. The unseen provider also began to bring food for the infant boy. When the child grew up to be a toddler, one night the woman only pretended to sleep. While she waited there in the dark, a man arrived and held the child. The woman quickly arose and grabbed the man's wrist. He said to the woman, "Release me" but she held tight. Finally, the man said to her, "The *ka buru* who trapped you here is married to your husband. But he will soon come to make sago nearby. You must make a length of *hagenamo* rope and tie one end onto the middle of the sago frond. In this manner you may pull yourself and your child onto the top of the palm. When they come to cut down the palm, you can then return to the ground." The woman did as the man instructed, and when her husband cut down the sago palm, accompanied by the *ka buru*, he found to his surprise his first wife and her child. The *ka buru* was full of shame. The two women made sago together and they all returned to the house afterwards and lived together.

The two women began making a garden together, but the *ka buru* would constantly shift the boundary marker between her ground and the younger wife's, making her own bigger. The young woman repeatedly moved the marker back to its proper place and the two women eventually fought. The husband came upon them quarrelling and blaming the younger woman, hit her on the head with a stick, drawing blood. The young woman became very disconsolate and remembered the words of her tree-top husband: "While you live with your husband on the earth, I will be around. If he mistreats you, call out to me. I will be flying in the sky above." For he was really a hornbill and his name was Ayayewego or Yiakamuna. Now the young woman called out to him, "Ayayewego, Yiakamuna, come fetch me!" She heard the cry of the hornbill. It approached her and grabbed the woman by her hair and pulled her along with her child. They returned to their treetop home. The distraught husband cried, "Come back, wife!" but in vain. At the same time, the *ka buru* turned into a cassowary and crying "hoahoa" she departed. That is all (Weiner 1988:158–61; abridged)

I want to address the very reasonable comment by Parmentier concerning the status of the facilitating and motivating modalities within the obviational structuring of a myth. Parmentier questioned whether my assigning of certain episodes in my analysis of "The Hornbill Husband" made sense in these terms: specifically, the point at which the trapped woman is nurtured in her treetop abode by the unseen bird husband seemed to him a clearly conventional image and should have been assigned to the facilitating modality. If Foi myth were only a matter of portraying conventional social meanings, we would expect such an episode to always form the ground against which an innovative event was substituted. How do we resolve this?

Figure 2 shows my original analysis of this myth (Weiner 1988:166). I originally presented the first sequence of this myth as the ironic depiction of co-wifehood: two women who have competed for the

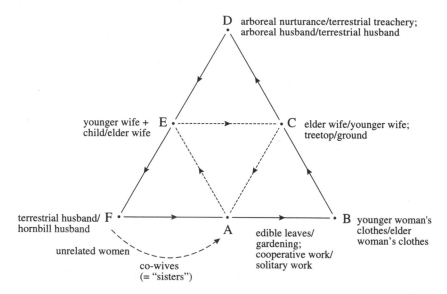

Figure 2.   Obviation of "The Hornbill Husband."

same man wind up as co-wives to each other. Let's focus our attention on the inscribed internal triangle *CAE* that I outlined in my original analysis (Weiner 1988:166), keeping in mind that the plot of the myth, in moving forward, is dropping the traces of its own motivation which will appear to be moving backward against the direction of the plot. This time, in order to preserve the symmetry of the transformation, I am going to label point *E* "younger wife + child for elder wife" instead of "sago palm for *hagenamo*" as I did in my original analysis.

The taking of a second, younger wife by a Foi man usually has depressing consequences for his first, older wife. She no longer receives the bulk of his sexual attention, often finds herself alone, in her own dwelling, her children grown up and no longer needing her. The sequence seems to be saying that there is no way that an older woman can keep a younger rival co-wife from bearing children and ultimately displacing her as the source of the husband's attention. This itself works out as an inverted image of what the Foi see male and female capacities to comprise. A woman's reproductive capacity is spontaneous, *repetitive,* and regular, while a man's is contingent and external. Once seen in the context of polygyny, however, a woman's reproductive capacity is bounded by the natural term of her fertility and sexual attractiveness, while the reproductive life of a man spans the fertile periods of more than one woman. The sequence $A \rightarrow E \rightarrow C$ (older woman $\rightarrow$ younger woman $\rightarrow$ "phallic" separation of women) unfolds this conventional image against the direction of the plot of the myth. But in the novel context of this myth, it becomes a consequence of a woman's acts, rather than a man's—does it not strike one how passive the first husband is in this story, letting his wives slide back and forth past him? We can say therefore that the internal sequence AEC is a "novel conventional image" and that one of the effects of myth is precisely to render situational and contingent any assessment of conventionality.

If this is true *within* a myth, then it is also true *between* myths that are perceived to be in a narrative relationship to each other. We can now address the fundamental issue: Since "The Hornbill Husband" includes in its integral plot the original story collected by Williams, how are these two images related?

In my first analysis, I described how the plot of "The Hornbill Husband" kept moving beyond the first obviative closure, and that this was a retrograde movement against the direction of the plot. Let us now turn to this inverted sequence which I claim is represented by the story I heard as "The First Married Couple" and which is also the second half of Williams' original story.

THE FIRST MARRIED COUPLE

There once lived a man and his sister. Each day, the woman went out to make sago, but she would be gone an inordinately long time and would not return until late at night. "What is my sister doing?" the man wondered. One day he followed her. He watched as she approached a *tamo* palm [an areca species]. He watched her climb up the tree and slide down, climb up, and slide down, doing this repeatedly. She finished doing this and left. When she was gone, the man took a stone blade and inserted it into the middle of the trunk. The next time she tried to slide down the tree, she cut herself on the blade, and this created her vagina. Before this she had no sexual organ. Her brother came upon her and saw she was bleeding heavily and unconscious. He gathered all manner of leaves and tried to stop the bleeding but was unable to. The leaves he used in this way became colored red, and all the present day trees with red leaves were the ones the brother first used to stop his sister's bleeding. He then rubbed the tip of a pearl shell on the wound and the bleeding stopped a little. He then used the tail of a marsupial and it stopped a little more. Finally he tried a pig's rope and the bleeding ceased. He tied a pearl shell to the wound with a piece of bark cloth. When the woman recovered, they became husband and wife and had sexual intercourse. From their offspring the Foi people originated. That is all. (Weiner 1988:161; abridged)

Figure 3 depicts my original obviational analysis of this myth, and Figure 4 shows it in inverted relation to the myth "The Hornbill Husband" (see Weiner 1988:169). In a figure-ground reversal, the internal points CAE are now the external triangle of the inverted myth. Instead of two women being separated by vertical zones (one trapped in the treetop, the other free on the ground), there is a single woman sliding up and down the vertical tree (C). Instead of two women coming together, there is a single woman being split down the middle (A). Instead of avian reproduction, there is human sexual reproduction (E). The whole mythic complex ends with the old woman turning into a (female) cassowary, the inverse in every way of the (male) hornbill.[10]

But it is not enough merely to demonstrate the relation of inversion—the question remains, what kind of gloss can we put on its *social effect*, its effect on the perceptions of the myth tellers and hearers? Notice how in contrast to the first sequence, the brother, the man, takes an active role in effecting the transformation of his sister. Triangle BDF as a retroactive grounding of the inverted myth is the manner in which a brother splits his sister off from himself and thereby gains wealth for her. But since the implicit substitution of point F in relation to C, which it obviates, is "wealth for tree," the pearl shell which stops

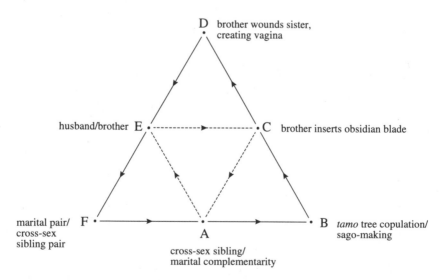

Figure 3.   Obviation of "The First Married Couple."

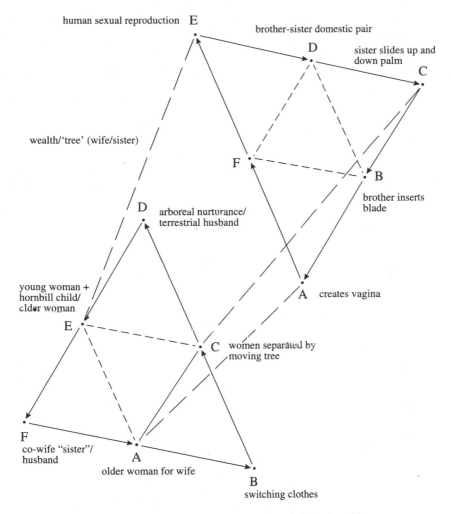

Figure 4. Inversion of plot in "The Hornbill Husband."

the flow of blood is the "other end" of the phallic tree which initiated it. Once again, the penis is very much retracted in this myth, replaced by the pearl shell as the effective organ of male extensibility.

It is important to emphasize that the obviation sequences themselves are not "the meaning of the myth." Like the myth itself, and the image of life which it retroactively makes visible, these sequences are data: the way its images fit together is data, and obviation as a basic characteristic of metaphor and image themselves is data. What is *interpre-*

tive is the alternatives we find in social imagery for glossing these sequences, and the alternatives that the Foi employ for doing the same.
What is *interpretive* is narrowing down the extensive implications of a
particular sequence to this or that particular social effect, which is always a pragmatic issue, as Parmentier understands the term.

The mistake Parmentier makes is in assessing the assignment of any
particular episode of the myth as either conventional or innovative
(nonconventional) in isolation, apart from the resolutions and counter-
traces set up by the sequence of episodes themselves. This is equivalent
to saying that the semantic meaning of a word precedes (and hence is
independent of) its pragmatic effect. But just as, according to Saussure,
the lexical meaning of a word is demarcated by its oppositional relations with all other similar words, so can the identification of any particular episode in the myth be assigned to one or the other of the two
obviating modes only when they are considered in their totality against
each other. As I said in the beginning of this chapter, we are trying to
gloss not isolated events in the myth but the effect of a whole sequence
of images. But more than this, it is the innovative act which antejects, as
it were, its own conventional ground. From this perspective, there are
no purely conventional acts, only acts that are more or less creative of
the total context of meanings in relation to each other.[11]

Another way of commenting on this is to reconsider a point that
Wagner made in *Lethal Speech:* the opening substitutive event of the
myth is always somewhat arbitrary. What in fact is the conventional
situation being commented upon? Before the myth as a story opens,
the speaker has already shifted the conventional contextualization of
the speech event, announcing, if nothing else, that a myth is about to
be narrated, warning listeners that an alternative mode of glossing
words and descriptions is called for. The speech event has already
shifted to a different mode. But who can say whether it is a more or
less conventional mode? And further, what is to be gained—other
than a rigidification and routinization of pragmatic effect—by deciding either way? The narrator is like the *marua* bird, announcing that in
the myth the signifiers are going to slide back and forth and cut themselves on the blade of obviation.

Part of the problem is that Parmentier stipulates an isomorphy between two contrasts, that between conventional and innovative usages
in general on the one hand, and that between facilitating and motivating modalities within an obviation sequence on the other. But points
A, C, and *E* are conventional only *in the context of the myth,* and in the
context of the total speech situation which elicits the narration of the
myth. Although these images are "conventional" in regard to the mo-

tivating substitutions which alter them, they are clearly not conventional in the "everyday" sense. In fact, Foi myths usually open with some unusual or bizarre version of conventionality—an old woman and a young boy living alone together; two brothers, one with two wives and the other with none; a man and his sister who have no genitals; and so forth. In fact, it is only when the motivating substitutions eventually invert this bizarre conventionality that some focus on what "everyday" conventionality is all about is achieved.

One might respond that I am merely replacing Parmentier's antinomy of Peircean and normative convention with my own more Durkheimian one—that between "mythical" and normative convention. But it would be a mistake to think that these points of relative conventionality are "there" in the myth, anchoring the transformations that the plot focuses on, constraining the myth teller. These points are themselves created as a result of the combination of two discursive moments: the speaker weaving the elements of the story together and the analyst trailing behind, so to speak, and identifying the points at which these conventional images emerge as a consequence of the plot's forward movement.

The obviating inversion of the myth then is accomplished through the setting up of a counterseries of pseudoconventional images which move against the direction of the plot, that is, in the opposite direction. What this counterplot traces is the shadow of a life situation or life movement, a parodying of life's motivational resistance to human intention, will, and desire. And this is what brings obviation into contact with psychoanalysis. Forrester thus observes that

> Psychoanalysis starts with, and always works within, an original intersubjectivity; it then works *backwards,* to earlier states, whose reality and significance is only conferred on them retrospectively. (1990:203)

This countermovement, this reversibility of perceived cause and effect is a fundamental feature of human temporality, and what an obviation sequence foregrounds is this reversibility of human perception and meaning. This is why an obviation sequence makes visible the nodes of meaning that arise within what we might call a discursive form of life and why it is therefore iconic of that discursive form. Myth so envisioned cannot then be a matter of component semantic parallelisms, as Parmentier suggests. To focus on parallelism suggests that meaning is only a conceptual structure, rather than a by-product or an accompaniment, so to speak, of human action and intention and their temporal character.[12]

Again, I would point out that a myth does not represent social reality but only models a specific way of making it visible. In fact, it was to avoid just this collapsing of symbolic anthropology into a foundationalism of the normative that Wagner (1981) first stipulated the use of the terms collectivizing and differentiating constructions. Hence, though I accept Parmentier's elucidation of the Durkheimian resonances in a term that seems to invoke a sense of normative collectivity, I must reiterate that a collectivizing trope is a label for a certain moment in the perception of meaning rather than a tool for the building of normative orders.

The point I am making thus is a Nietzschean one, you might say. Nietzsche denied that there were such things as moral principles—there were only moral judgments. Likewise, in spite of my early appeals to such things, there are no conventional acts per se, no rules of conduct that comprise something as characterizable as Foi culture, only temporary and situational assessments or judgments of what is conventional. And a myth and its resolution, and the message it either does or does not get across to its audience, are no less a situated and particular moment of conventionality than the performance of a ceremony, the handing over of a marriage payment, or the success with which a Foi man argues his particular view of current events. The tropic potential of any of these actions is much the same. The attention we pay to the use a community of speakers makes of these forms of life and speech is what makes the study of language and speech historical.

3

The Space and Time
of Sexuality

I

In Lévi-Strauss' famous article "The Effectiveness of Symbols" (1963), he discusses a curing ritual of the Cuna Indians of Central America which was employed by the shaman in the case of a difficult childbirth. The first task of the shaman is to contact certain spirit helpers who will guide him to the abode of Muu, the power responsible for the fetus's *in utero* development. For the Cuna, difficult childbirth occurs because Muu has captured the *purba* "soul" of the mother-to-be. The shaman's task is to recapture the lost *purba* soul. The treatment consists in the shaman's chanting of a song which tells the story of his journey to Muu's domain in the supernatural world in order to recover the *purba* soul.

But the abode of Muu is not merely some mythical place where the spirits live. According to the song, it represents literally the space of the vaginal and uterine anatomy of the pregnant woman, which are reconnoitered by the shaman and his guardian spirit or *nuchu*, and which represents the battleground on which the struggle to regain the *purba* is waged.

To reach Muu, the shaman and his spirit helpers, the *nelegan*, must follow the road called "Muu's Way," which is the birth canal of the afflicted woman. The uterus is described as "the dark inner place," and there are detailed descriptions of the increased flow of blood caused by the difficult birth. The trip itself is phrased in terms of a fantastic landscape—it is, as Lévi-Strauss says, "a complicated mythical anatomy, corresponding less to the real structure of the genital organs than to a kind of emotional geography" (1963:195). So, at one point, the shaman chants:

> The *nelegan* set out, the *nelegan* march in single file along
> Muu's Road, as far as the Low Mountain,

> The *nelegan* set out . . . as far as the Short Mountain,
> The *nelegan* set out . . . as far as the Long Mountain,
> The *nelegan* . . . (to) [the place] Yala Pokuna Yala . . . ,
> The *nelegan* . . . (to) Yala Akkwatallekun Yala . . . ,
> The *nelegan* . . . (to) Yala Ilamalisuikun Yala . . . ,
> The *nelegan* . . . into the center of the Flat Mountain.
> The *nelegan* set out, the *nelegan* march in a single file
> among Muu's road . . .
>
> (1963:195)

The route of the *nelegan* and the shaman becomes a movement between various named places in this cosmized female anatomy. This movement, moreover, is given a specifically sexual character: The *nelegan* at the outset "take on the appearance and the motions of the erect penis" in effecting this entry onto Muu's Way:

> The *nelegan*'s hats are shining white, the *nelegan*'s hats are whitish.
> The *nelegan* are becoming flat and low (?), all like bits, all straight.
>
> (1963:195)

According to Lévi-Strauss, the shaman is actually attempting to make the afflicted woman feel the entry of the shaman and his helpers, so that she can trace their progress to the site of the difficulty in her uterus. It could very well be that the route followed by the phallic *nelegan* is an inseminating, fertilizing one: that is, a mark or trace, in the form of the mythical named "places," is left behind which can be read as a record or imprint of their journey and its efficacy. Thus, from the point of view of the afflicted woman, "Not only does she feel them [i.e., the *nelegan*], but they 'light up' the route they are preparing to follow—for their sake, no doubt, and to find the way, but also to make the center of her inexpressible and painful sensations 'clear' for her and accessible to her consciousness" (1963:195). We could say that into an inchoate sensation of pain and anxiety is placed a series of spacings, in the form of a felt succession of named points along the painful internal route of her birth canal.

Now let us turn to another part of the world, to Northeast Arnhem Land, Australia. Here, instead of having a sexualized geography inscribed in the interior of a human body, we have various phallicized bodies inscribing the earth itself, an everted form of the very same Cuna process. Once again, a highly formal speech form gives shape to these inscriptive acts. In the Djanggawul song cycle of the Yolngu people (formerly known as Murngin), the journey of the Djanggawul brother and his two sisters is detailed. They move across the land creating sacred objects, which are metonyms of their sexual organs, and also creating named features of the landscape. In part 3 of the cycle, each song begins with the phrase: "We walk along, *waridj*,[1] step by step, with the aid of the *mauwalan*, plunging in its point . . ." (Berndt 1952:119–30). The *mauwalan* is the sacred walking stick carried by the Djanggawul brother and which was also described by Ronald Berndt's Yolngu informants as the brother's penis. At each spot, the stick is inserted in the ground to create a well from which water gushes forth, which is said to be the refluxive flow of semen out of the vagina subsequent to coitus.

In other songs from the Arnhem Land area, we find variations on this sexualized discursive landscape. From song 2 of the Rose River song cycle:

The sound drifts over towards the place of the Snake . . .
Always there, the speech of those people, talking slowly together
    drifting towards the place of the Snake:
People talking together quickly, speech of the barramundi
    clans . . .
Barramundi people belonging to Laindjung, talking slowly; and
    others quickly.
Talking together slowly, moving their lips in speech. They are
    always there . . .

(Berndt 1976:87).

Here, the landscape is differentiated by being populated by different groups of people who speak in different ways, some "talking slowly; and others quickly." They are coming together, however, for the purposes of ritual defloration of maidens and a period of continual sexual intercourse, traditionally an integral part of the Kunapipi ceremonies (Berndt 1976: chapter 5). The speech itself, however, is fecund, lush, variegated, polyrhythmic; it is clear that it too is the sperm that is aiding in this regional fertilization. Finally, the image of a marking, speaking, spatialized sexual organ is succinctly evoked in this phrase from song 13:

The penis moves slowly, "talking," as he ejaculates:
Erect penis copulating, moving forward.

It should also be noted that in the Roper River area to the south of Arnhem Land, a ritual boomerang was traditionally used to perform this defloration of maidens' hymens. The boomerang, its shape so elusively suggestive of both phallus and vagina, each imperceptibly turning into the other as a result of the obtuse open curves of the boomerang, curved lines that never suggest closure but only parabolic approximation and outline, was inscribed with markings that portrayed the journey of the Wawilak beings who named and created the topographical features of the landscape.

What I want to point out is how literally people like the Yolngu and the Cuna are apt to interpret the relationship between movement, space, language, and sexuality.[2] Insofar as time and space are being demarcated in these practices, they are a specifically embodied time and space, which convey the limits and capacities of the intentionality, the forward-lookingness of human consciousness and of the human body, the shape and contours of the body's productive movement and sexual and intersexual configurations. But it is not simply the body's own space that I wish to discuss, but the relationship between such space and the discursive acts that make them appear for the Cuna and Yolngu. The discursive form is not something which merely expresses this space, but with its own linguistic and conceptual tempos puts limits and intervals onto the body itself, in an ongoing dialectic of embodiment and objectification. It is on the sexual, embodied characteristics and hermeneutic implications of such spacing that I wish to focus.

When I speak of embodied time, as does Roy Wagner (1986), I automatically oppose it to a notion of external, natural time, a conventional Western time measured by our instruments, and in a parallel fashion, I oppose the space of sexuality, desire, and the body to the similarly conceived natural space of Cartesian dimensions. I oppose them for didactic purposes only, however, because the world of external conventional time and space presupposes and controls the time and space of the body and of human intention (Bourdieu 1977; cf. also Gell 1992).

But under what conditions could embodied space and time come to be distinct from conventional space and time in Western thought? It is within Kant's *Critique of Pure Reason* that our modern conceptions of space and time as analytical categories originated, and it is to the Kantian critique of pure reason that anthropology traces its own roots. Although we are possessed of a priori categories of sensible intuition—most important, the awareness of spatial and temporal relations—Kant insisted on our capacity to differentiate between our inner experiences on the one hand and the external disposition of the objects of such experience on the other. Temporality then described the inner sense of the succession of sensations that are brought to our consciousness, while spatiality referred to the outer sense, the awareness of the external disposition of the objects responsible for such intuitions. Here Kant seemed to reverse the fundamental Cartesian postulate: it is because we are aware of the spacing and differentiation of external objects that we become aware of a corresponding temporal differentiation of *internal* sensations.[3] But Kant in the end privileged temporal over spatial relations. There is no realistic way, he maintained, that we can speak of the "space" of inner sense, or of the intuition of a spatial *relationship* between our sensibility and outer experience. While there are states of mind that cannot possibly have a spatial form—moods, desires, drives—every inner sensation or representation can be intuited in terms of a succession of states, of one sensation following or preceding another. Kant said therefore that "Time . . . cannot be a determination of outer appearances; it has to do neither with shape nor positions, but with the relation of representations in our inner state" (1990:B49–50). As Heidegger put it, "time dwells in the subject in a more original way than space" (1990:93). But for the Cuna and Yolngu, it is the internal *spatial* inscription of the body that makes time concrete, and the progress of the Cuna shaman lights up or illuminates Kant for us in an altogether different way. Their internal sensations always follow the contours of the body rather than the conduits of the Western cognitive terrain.

Ernst Cassirer turned these Kantian forms of intuition into what we as anthropologists would identify as linguistic and cultural categories. Drawing on the late-nineteenth-century linguists Jespersen, Wundt, and Humboldt, he demonstrated in his *Philosophy of Symbolic Forms* (first published in 1921) how different ideas of spatial and temporal perception were expressed in the grammatical, semantic, and syntactic forms of different languages, an exercise that Jakobson and Whorf were to repeat later on in the century with extremely important ramifications for cultural anthropology. Temporality and spatiality were seen as encoded in the grammatical and semantic categories of language. Drawing upon Boas' description of Native American languages, Cassirer observed that

> The American Indian languages use . . . suffixes to indicate whether the motion occurs within or outside of a certain space, particularly inside or outside of the house, whether over the sea or over land . . . whether from inland toward the coast, or from the coast inland, whether from the fire site toward the house or from the house to fire site. (1955:211)

This Whorfian position is still very much at the foundation of North American cultural and linguistic anthropology (see for example Witherspoon 1977; Sherzer 1990). But it is evident that in languages such as

Haida alluded to by Cassirer in the above quote, *all* speech is about "space." To use language is to automatically situate oneself spatially in any number of dimensions—quotidian, mythical, cosmological, political. From this point of view, it is difficult to separate the creation of places from the verbal or narrative procedures which often are most responsible for their creation.

Adhering to the Whorfian view of the world encourages us to think that the world is the way it is because our language is structured in a particular way. We then might see this Whorfian position as North American anthropology's attempt to hang on to the Kantian distinction between the analytic and the synthetic a priori. But on the other hand, if we start with the time and space of the body, we argue for a more porous and pragmatic view of the relationship between language and the world, and hence a less radical scission between space and time themselves. In considering narratives of place, as does Rodman (1994), for example, we are not dealing with a set of predefined places that are subsequently given discursive recognition and elaboration. This would be analogous to saying that human sexual reproduction always creates a predefined set of genealogical relatives which different "cultures" subsequently draw connections between in different ways. If we go this route, we make the relationship between places something that is ontologically dependent upon an antecedent creation of places themselves. But we would not want to deny that when the places are created in the first place (if, indeed, we can ever appeal to such an unrecoverable and hypothetical event as the creation of a place), they come about as a result of human movement and language—history, if you will—so that they already exist as a set of patterned connections, a patterned region of human intention, language, and meaning. *It is within the very horizons created by these human actions that the most "real" human space is created.* And, hence, different modalities of intention and signification, all of which have discursive properties, whether it be productive activity, sexuality and desire, speech, or art, create different kinds of spaces and lend a differential value to places identified within those discourses. I say they are all discursive because human desire, intention, and action are the source of the forms through which we create the world, including the differentiation between places within it. A large proportion of this process is not conscious or deliberate but habitual and unfocused, so that while it seems we are encountering pristine external states of affairs, they have already been placed in a perceivable potential by the prior deposition of human interest. Ultimately, these actions are describable as certain patterns of movement, whether it be the movement of the body creating a garden on the land or the movement of the vocal apparatus creating the gestures of speech that mark out that activity. And it is movement which creates the temporal and spatial intervals within which we deposit, again, for the most part, unconsciously, the results and effects of our perception and understanding.

What kinds of spaces exist between our words? In gross physical terms, none. If we were all connected to oscilloscopes, our speech would be depicted as a constant jangle of sound, a continuous stream of buzzes and whistles. Whatever spaces there are between words and sentences, they are marked by the insertion of intervals of absence arising from within our perceptual faculty. The spacing itself creates the perceived temporality and linearity of speech, turns it into a succession of vocalized instants, the resolution of which we look forward to as we seek to communicate with others.

But the spaces are not put there as an equivalent act of consciousness; they emerge instead as a by-product of our focus on the limits of communicable nodes of sound, or writing, nodes which are made to have a beginning and an end to them. We focus on the nodes, then, and see the spaces between them as naturally occurring background. But, in fact, they are equally the product of a human imposition of form. They are the holes in the donut of language. And as we do when we make a donut, what we do when we speak, hear, write, read—and move, produce, procreate—is to create such a boundary between something and nothing. Lacan thus said, "If linguistics enables us to see the signifier as the determinant of the signified, [psycho]analysis reveals the truth of this relation by making 'holes' in meaning the determinants of its discourse" (Muller and Richardson 1982:359).[4]

"The signifier is thus the difference of places, the very possibility of localization . . . it does not divide itself into places, it divides places—that is to say, it institutes them" (Nancy and Lacoue-Labarthe 1992:43). *Hence, it is not different places that lend different voices to people, it is different kinds of voice that create the space within which different places emerge.* By "voice," however, I do not mean merely the attribution of subjectivity. Subjectivity itself happens within what we might call the clearing (another spatial term) of human agency and intention, an effect that owes much to the conventionally defined forms of grammar and language, as, for example, Wittgenstein (1953) and Benveniste (1971) have suggested. But while retaining this non-Cartesian view of subjectivity, others like Hanks (1990) and Friedrich (1979) have invoked Merleau-Ponty's phenomonology of the body (1962) and remind us that language meets the world along the contours and within the time of the human body.

What kind of time is this embodied time? Let us first look for it within a Foi myth.

II

In an early analysis I made of Foi spatiality (Weiner 1984), I described how the dimensions of the Foi cosmos are created as a result of a perceived collection of distinct though related movements: the rivers which flow from northwest to southeast and which create the space of habitation and travel; the seasonal appearance of various edible plants and animals which creates the temporal rhythms of the productive year; the regular flow of women's menstrual fluid which demarcates the times and spaces of reproductive work.

A theme that I have repeatedly articulated in my analysis of the Foi lifeworld (cf. Weiner 1988, 1991a) is that the Foi perceive these movements, and the various spaces they create—geographical, productive, sexual/reproductive—as the source of life itself. But these movements do no real human work, acquire no real moral valence, until people impose some redirection on them, until they cause them to start and stop for their own purposes. In other words, it is only when people insert spacing and interval into these movements that they acquire potential for human productivity. They divert the flow of water by constructing dams, which allows them to fish; they set traps at specific points in the bush to trap moving animals; they seek to bind women's menstrual blood in their uteri so that fetuses can gestate and be born as children.

The following myth describes how the most common red- and yellow-colored flowers and crotons in the Foi region originated in the distant "upstream" (i.e., westerly) direction. The Foi refer to *me ga kore,* "place source upstream," as the source of water, pearl shells, flowers, and life itself, in contrast to *haisureri,* the afterworld, located in the opposite direction, where presumably the rivers end and where movement and hence life itself cease.

THE ORIGIN OF FLOWERS AND CROTONS

There once lived two brothers. The elder brother had two wives but the younger brother was unmarried. One time, they heard the cry of the *marua* bird: "go'oro goai, go'oro goai, dorefe, dorefe." The elder man said, "My wives, what is that bird saying?" And they answered, "It is saying, 'garden vegetables will ripen, bamboo shoots, *hagenamo* leaves and *kōya* shoots will ripen, children and pigs will grow.'" The elder brother replied, "No, it is saying 'There

will be an Usane. Go find game.'"' The elder brother and his elder
wife went to the Usane exchange ceremony and left the younger
brother and younger wife behind at the house.

While they were gone, the young woman visited their garden.
She returned and said to her husband's brother, "A pig has been
rooting around in the garden; go and shoot it." The young man
took his brother's *baduane* arrow and his bow and with it he shot
a very large pig. When he shot it, the tip of the arrow had broken
off inside the pig. But he did not find the point in the pig when he
butchered the animal. So he carved a new arrow head, fastened it,
and wrapped it as his elder brother had left it and replaced it. The
young man didn't eat the pork, he cut the liver in half and ate half
of it. He wrapped other portions in leaves and set the meat aside for
his brother.

The elder brother returned and saw all the pork in the house. The
younger brother explained, "Yesterday I shot a pig with your arrow.
The tip broke off but I repaired it." The elder brother inspected his
arrow and saw that it had been mended poorly. So he struck his
brother on the head and hit his wife also. The younger brother in
shame returned to the garden. He noticed that the pig had arrived
from the upstream [westward] direction. Taking some pork with
him, he followed the footprint of the pig upstream. He traveled a
long distance and finally came upon a longhouse. There was a
young man like himself there, and he said to him, "I've come
seeking my brother's *baduane* arrow." The man replied, "We have
no knowledge of this arrow. But here is some meat for you." He
offered a large amount of pork and other meat to the younger
brother, but he only took a small amount. He slept and the next day
continued upstream. The same thing happened at several other
longhouses along the way, until he came to a longhouse where the
man there said, "This is the last house of people. Beyond, no people
live." The younger brother asked again for his arrow, but the people
there denied any knowledge of it and gave him meat to eat instead.
The next day, the young man set off into the uninhabited bush
beyond. "Don't go," the other man said, but he went. He broke off
small twigs and branches along the way so that he would be able to
find his way back again.

Presently, he came upon a valley and he heard the sound of sago
being pounded. Following the sound, he came upon a young
woman making sago. At first she was afraid that he was a ghost, but
he assured her that he was a real man. After she finished her sago
making, he said to her, "Let us go to your house." But she replied,

"My father is a cannibal—he will eat you." He responded, "Let him eat me if he wishes; we will go to your house." She cooked food for him there and he ate. He lay down and she covered him with a cloak so that her father wouldn't see him.

After a while, her father and mother arrived. As they approached the house, her father called out, "Ah! I smell something!" and going inside he said, "Have you brought something back?" But the woman replied, "No, I have brought nothing." The father, however, quickly discovered the hidden man. He said to him, "Thank you! Why didn't you show yourself sooner? My daughter is all alone here. It is right that you should marry her." And the young man and the woman lived there as man and wife.

One time, his wife gave him a small parcel wrapped up in cocoon fiber. She said to him, "Don't unwrap it now. Just put it in the bottom of your string bag and carry it with you always. My father will speak to you later and then you will know what to do with it."

Another time, the cannibal said to the young man, "*Kauwa* [daughter's husband], let us go downstream." Eh, this is what my wife was talking about before, the man thought to himself. The cannibal took a ladder and inserted it down a deep sinkhole. The two descended. Under the ground there was a true place, a land, just like the surface world. The older man said, "You go this way, I'll go the other way," and he went upstream while the young man followed a path in the opposite direction. But after the young man had departed, the cannibal doubled back, reascended the ladder, and pulled it up after him. "You stay here and die," he called down to the young man, and he left.

The young man wandered around and discovered the bones of many other men whom the cannibal had trapped in the same way and then had returned to eat. The young man searched around and found a bundle of salt, and then some ginger and cucumber, and he readied these things. He then joined the bones of the dead men together carefully. When he was finished, he shouted out, "Men! men! men!"[5] The men awoke and cried, "Where are there men? Where are they coming from?" They saw where they were, and the younger brother revived them with the salt and ginger and they regained their senses. "Brother, that cannibal ate all of us! If he comes back here, we will eat him. But you must take cuttings of these flowers, this *geno'o* flower, this croton shrub, this black palm shoot, this *sesa'a* flower, tie them up in a bundle and put them near the opening of the hole. Then hide and wait until the cannibal returns."

Two days later, the cannibal and his wife returned. The younger brother hid near the base of the ladder. He removed the parcel his wife had given him. Unwrapping it, he found a *kaūgu* bird. This bird characteristically cries out whenever game, especially pythons and snakes, are nearby. He let the bird fly away and it cried "gua! gua! gua!" The cannibal heard it and said, "Eh, a python has been killed, I'm going to find it. Wife, there is a pig [i.e, a man] I left here—you go fetch it." The two separated in the land beneath the hole. After they left, the young man took the bundle of flower cuttings and ascended the ladder. He pulled it up after himself and destroyed it. "Eh, these men are eating me!" he heard the cannibal cry. They were also eating the cannibal's wife. The young man cried out, "I am going to marry your daughter," and he returned to the house. They lived there for a while and then they returned downstream, back the way the young man had come. As they traveled, they planted all the different flowers and crotons, at every house they came to. They arrived at the brother's house and saw that it had been abandoned. They built a new house and lived there. Thus, crotons and flowers came from upstream, so it is said. That is all.

In the narrative of a myth such as this, a sense of movement is appealed to, in at least two ways. First, of course, the plot of the myth centers on the outward movement of the protagonist from the human world to a place that lies beyond it, and then back again. But there is also the movement of the plot itself, as a series of key substitutions which force the plot in a specific direction. This latter movement delineates a more specifically discursive space, a region wherein the possibilities of the meaningful resolution of human actions are explored. Let us outline one such possible route for these substitutions.

The story, as do numerous other Foi myths (see Weiner 1988), starts off with the problematic situation of an elder brother with two wives and his younger brother who has none. Alerted by the cry of the *marua* bird, which in the context of the Usane Transformation (see previous chapter) always signals the transition from domestic horticulture to ceremonial hunting and exchange, the elder man and his elder wife depart to attend the Usane, in which the meat of game animals is given for that of domestic pigs (substitution *A*). While the pair are away, the younger brother uses and ultimately damages his elder brother's arrow while killing a pig, which we can interpret as the younger man's appropriation of the elder's sexuality, which for the Foi is intimately associated with a man's weapons (*B*). The young man tries to offer his elder brother pork (in recompense for the lost arrow), but this is rejected by the elder man (*C*). As a result, the younger brother himself departs, ostensibly to search for the lost arrow. He is offered meat along the way as a substitute for the arrow, which he refuses, a negative image of the elder brother's exchange which opens the story (*D*). Finally, he is forced to leave the area of human habitation entirely. It could be said that this radical separation of the brothers is the result of the improper flow of sexual identity between them earlier on.

The younger brother encounters a maiden who introduces him to her cannibal father (*E*). The cannibal, however, forbears from eating the man and instead offers his daughter to him as a wife. The cannibal's (positive) refusal to eat the man is equivalent to the elder brother's (negative) refusal to eat the pork which the young man offered him (*F*). The father-in-law, however, will eventually seek to eat his daughter's husband, an affinal version of the incestuous act by which the younger brother first obviated his elder brother's sexual/hunting prerogative. Another way of phrasing this imagery would be to say that in leaving the region of human habitation, the brother comes upon a place in which there is no relational space between human beings: hence, it is populated by cannibals, who instead of establishing the space between affines through affinal protocol, seek to consume them.

The myth achieves a temporary resolution when the maiden gives the younger brother the mysterious parcel, a hidden item in a parcel substituting for the lost arrow in the pig (*G*). Furthermore, because the cocoon fibers of the parcel are most commonly used to wrap pearl shells, the audience is led to believe at this point that if only the younger brother could return the imagined shell to his elder brother, the outstanding debt which has impelled the plot so far would be resolved and canceled out. But the myth provides its surprise—an essential component to many Foi myths—through this device, because the contents are precisely *not* revealed at this point, and the plot has to keep moving forward.

So the line of the story continues moving, beyond the space of this first closure. But this movement reverses all that went before. It reverses it by *undoing* it. The cannibal takes the young man down into a subterranean mirror world (underworld for surface world), and there he traps the man (inverse of *D*). The younger brother finds there the remains of men who have been eaten by the cannibal (perhaps, like the younger brother, they too were lured there by a disappearing arrow [inv. *C*]). Unlike the pig, the younger brother brings these men back to life with salt and ginger, which for the Foi are condiments that are "stinging, fighting," like arrows (inv. *B*). And he receives from them the first cuttings of decorative red and yellow flowers. This is an inverse of the first opening scene: the younger brother has received flowers (pearl shells in the context of pearl shell magic as we will see) for the gift of life itself, just as the elder brother received cooked pork for the fruits of hunting (death). But also at this point, the cry of the revealed *kaũgu* bird is like the cry of the *marua* bird which opened the tale (inv. *A*). The *marua* bird told men to leave their gardens and their reproductive life and go hunting animals; the *kaũgu* bird tells the hunter of men that a phallic game animal is at hand. Because there was a *G* point reached in the obviative resolution of the first part of the story, which related both *A* and *F* to the entire plot, this inversion in the second half also inverts that original *G* point (We can read this substitution as "alimentary gift of reproduction [pork] for geographic/uterine gift of reproduction [flowers]").

So the cannibal leaves off his consumption of men to find this sexual meat. And he himself gets eaten, because just as the younger brother initially did, he was unable to avoid an inauspicious cancellation of difference (inv. *F*). The younger brother and his wife return back to the man's house, planting the flowers as they go (inv. *E*; See Figure 5). Flowers and crotons originated by being brought from the "place source upstream" by a married couple, who plant them around every human house as they journey eastward back toward the land of human habitation. Like the Australian Aboriginal creator beings, they undertake a fertile journey which leaves an imprint upon the earth; like the Djanggawul brother, they insert the flowers into the ground. It's a peculiar form of a planting, a planting that moves, rather than one that is confined to the domestic space of the center of the human world, but it is precisely the point that the items planted are not quite domestic, but stand for the moving pearl shell. They surround each house, framing it, providing it with the space within which human sexuality, reproduction, and productive work emerge.

As is the case with both the Yolngu and the Cuna examples I began with, the spatial journey is an everted form of an internal, vaginal/uterine implanting, by which the productive powers of movement are channeled and made responsible for human reproduction. In the *ka sabora ira gari habora*, literally, the "maiden's tree-base spell," the Foi traditionally made a remarkably literal equation between this fertilizing, seeding, flowering journey and the act of human insemination itself. This sexual ritual (first described in Weiner 1984) was performed by a newly married couple if the woman was a maiden.

The two first collected the following yellow- and red-colored leaves

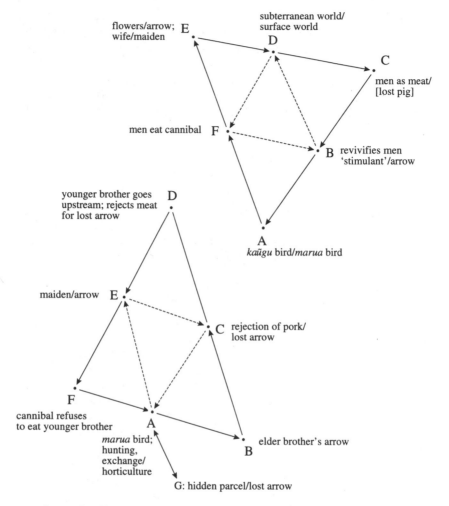

Figure 5.   Obviation and inversion in "The Origin of Flowers and Crotons."

from a garden that the man had previously planted for this very purpose: from the cordyline (Foi: kō varieties *dabura* (lit. 'red'), *ka'ase* (light yellow), *gogamu'u, foreyabe*; from the croton (*sihau*); from the plants known as *buba'o, hiname,* and *sawayo.*

They took these leaves with them into the bush, and located a *tu'u* tree, prominently identified as a resting place for ghosts by the Foi (it bears flowers which attract nectar-eating birds, many of which, like the birds of paradise, are thought to be the embodied spirits of the deceased). The man then took a length of reddish *dimu* bamboo and cut half of it transversely for half its length. In the resulting gouge-shaped exposed half, he placed small pieces of earth-oven leaves, the bark of the reddish *kegebo* vine, red ocher, red seeds of the *Bixa orellana*, scrapings from a pearl shell, dirt from the place in which a pig had been wallowing, and scrapings of white limestone. Small pieces of the leaves were placed on top of these items.

The man placed his erect penis on the exposed half of the bamboo cylinder, covering the leaves and other scrapings. In this manner he was said to deflower his bride. While he was copulating, he recited the following, which is the pearl shell spell that F. E. Williams also was told in 1938.

> the *tuma* marsupial portion, come to me
> the pig leg portion, come to me
> the *ba'abi* marsupial portion, come to me
> the rope of the *hē* cowrie, come to me
> the rope of the *wanema* cowrie, come to me
> the neck band of the pearl shell, come to me

The man's climax was supposed to coincide with the end of the spell. He would afterward carefully remove the bamboo in such a way as to ensure that the items remained in his wife's vagina. Later on, when the sexual fluids were leaving the woman's body along with the leaves, he collected this discharge and carefully wrapped it up into two small parcels of earth-oven leaves. Eventually the man and woman each planted one of the parcels in their respective fireplaces in their house. These would serve to "pull" pearl shells and other wealth items toward the man, while the woman would be assured of caring for many pigs. They also planted cuttings of the croton and cordyline they used near the *tu'u* tree where the procedure was carried out.[6]

These parcels of sexualized flowers are like the parcel with the *kaūgu* bird in it that the maiden gives the younger brother in the myth. They draw shells and animals to the house, just as the *kaūgu* bird draws people's attention to game, especially game in its most sexual form, the python. That is, the flowers are the route of the male python/phallus, always returning, always drawn to the place of human habitation, the domestic space of feminine reproductivity.

However, I am not merely pointing out an iconism between different kinds of spatial journeys or serial inscriptions. I am not just saying that the woman's internal uterine landscape "stands for" the whole of inhabited social space. Through the spell, and the myth which expands it, the man is able to articulate the female limit to male extensibility, as the Cuna shaman in fact articulates the uterine shape of Muu's mythical region. The phallus may inscribe itself on a landscape and make a whole named region, but the length it travels is only as far as a woman's body permits. It is the uterus which gives this phallus its shape, its status as human effigy, as fetus, as the boomerang is a vaginal space guarded by two phalluses, as the bamboo encircles the penis and makes a double enclosure out of the vaginal cavity, one for the internal phallus and one for the external phallus and its traces, which will draw pearl shells. The nodes or points that are created in a landscape and in a language are, in the societies I have talked about here, most vividly circumscribed by the bodily lineaments of sexual reproduction.

If the body provides the corporeal limits to inscripted space, then the myth itself creates an altogether different projection of the fertile space of the maiden's spell. The man performing the maiden's spell everts the sexual landscape of his wife's procreative tract onto the path of pearl shells themselves: the house will become like a uterus drawing to it inseminating shells. With his penis/arrow, the man injects the traces of these pearl shells (the flower cuttings) as a planting. Pearl shells—the medium of sexual/affinal exchange—are hence a result of a doubly fertile insemination.

In the myth, however, the younger brother loses his older brother's arrow—it is the inseminating weapon which the brother seeks to draw back, and to this end he refuses the fertilizing meat offered to him along the way. The cannibal draws human meat items to his house by way of his daughter (and her sexual organ by implication). In the myth, a thwarted act of cannibal consumption provides the path for an intersexualized reinscription of the brother's outward journey toward the source of shells and their flower icons themselves.

The spell, in its attempt to draw animals and shells into the space of copulation, seeks to make the regular rhythms and movements of sexual intercourse do the everyday "work" of the spatial journey described in the myth. A man's penis travels toward his wife's uterus, the real "place source upstream," the source of flowing blood; it is "eaten" by his wife's sexual organ and as a result it "dies." As a result of this act of anthropophagic swallowing, from the woman's uterus, traveling in the opposite direction, comes the neonate. The maiden's spell, in other words, is the route of the myth projected into the sexual space between and within men's and women's sexualized bodies.

We could be reminded of Ravel's *L'Enfant et les sortilèges*, where a recalcitrant boy is vexed by gigantic versions of household objects (see Klein 1929). We might say then that the whole Foi mythical complex was, like the Cuna curing ceremony and Ravel's opera, a play on the notion of scale, a realization that the space of the landscape is no bigger, from the point of view of meaning, than the space of the uterus, or that, in surrealist fashion, the Foi and Cuna uterus is itself a landscape structured by the inspissation of objects which form its interior spatiality.

III

It is no accident then that so many of the Foi myths I have described elsewhere detail a journey to a place beyond the realm of human habitation. This feature is related to one of the integral aspects of what Wagner has outlined in his theory of symbolic obviation: that human language and action involve the relation between the end point and the opening situation in the space of human habitation.

The Foi myth plays the linear mode of speech off against human historicity. It reveals that speech is not linear, that human action and movement are hence not linear. Because it inscribes a countermovement against the flow of human intention and anticipation, it obviates the linear equation between space, speech, and history. It draws attention to the real time of human subjectivity, wherein past and future are a consequence of intentional postures and retroactive memorations in the present, in the speaker's deictically constructed indexical field, rather than in the external cosmological time of unidirectional movement and flow.

Just so, place is not just about locales; locales achieve status only in their differentiation from each other, in the relationship between such locales as they are overarched by the temporality of human life, as they serve as *pointes de capiton* in the historical speech of humans. The myths themselves have no fixed "space," except perhaps in the sense of the fireside in the longhouse, where they were traditionally told. But they move between people, conveying the message of the limits to human movement and the limits of meaning itself in the Foi community, rather than a sheer geographic boundary.

But what is more, the Foi mythical view of place deprives the hermeneutical resolution of the myth of all vestiges of an origin story. The Foi myth is not about origins, which is another function of linearity. It only appears to project that after the fact. The origin emerges as an aftereffect, it has been deferred for the length of the myth. It is only after the younger brother and his wife arrive back home that the flowers acquire a fixed signification, that the space within the invisible parcel is revealed.[7]

The relation between the myth and its spell and the act of sexual intercourse they frame also images this concealment or containment of the nonlinear by the linear. The nonlinear back-and-forth movements of copulation are given a beginning and an end. Insofar as the myth speaks of an origin, it speaks of the origin of sexual intercourse, which while having no origin itself, is always seen as the most originary of human activities.

When we label the effect of these myths as "narrative," we automatically conceal the manner in which speech competes with and obviates experience, rather than gives it a cultural validation and conventional significance. But myth is not a narrative—it is neither the Kantian temporalization of space nor the Bergsonian spatialization of time. For the Foi, myth attests to the fundamental reversibility of all spacing and of the possibility of everting such intervals to make the spaces between them stand forth. The space between a man's and a woman's body is written over by the flower/pearl shell, the moving places that create their own world beyond the human one but also within it, within a woman's reproductive interior.

PART III

DETACHMENT AND CONTAINMENT

4

The Hunger People

A Hittite version of Aphrodite's birth attests that Cronus bit off the genitals of his father Uranus, swallowed some of the semen, and onto the surface of the ocean spit out the rest, which became the goddess. A Greek version subsequently averred that Aphrodite rose from the sea already pregnant with Uranus' severed genitals and that the shell merely bore her aloft and onto dry land. Is it a surprise to find that the Western embodiment of feminine sexuality has locked permanently within her body her father's male organ? Is this what the shape of Aphrodite's shell really outlines for us?

Jan van Baal describes a certain head-hunting raid undertaken by the Marind-anim in 1923. At the place Borem in the territory of the Kanum-anim people, eastern neighbors of the Marind, a party of armed Marind men laid an ambush for the Kanum-anim men who were known to be arriving at Borem for a feast. Whenever a small group appeared, the Marind invited them over to chew betel nut, after which they were slain and their heads taken.

This ambushing was not just a once-off trick. It has been reported by many ethnographers that the Marind would establish friendly relations with neighboring tribes who would thenceforth act as buffers between them and their main enemies in more distant regions. But as many other ethnographers also confirmed, their most populous neighbors, the Kanum-anim, who were frequently allies of the Marind and participated in their raids, were also themselves decimated by the Marind headhunters.

What then if the Marind merely lured their closest neighbors through acts of sociality into being sitting ducks for them? If so, would it amaze us that the Kanum should have fallen for the trick over and over again? Perhaps the acts of exchange, feasting, and making alliances call sociality forth irresistibly. But apparently such sociality was just a means to an end for the Marind, rather than an end in itself:

could it be that the Marind instigated acts of exchange and sociality only in order to set up the conditions under which they could continually cut off the head of such relationality?

I

The following is the principal myth of the Diwa-rek clan of the Marind-anim people of southern New Guinea (now Irian Jaya):

A number of dema [primordial creator-beings] came by canoe from the *mayo* [ceremony] in Yavar-makan . . . In front sat a dema-bird, *Yowi*, the white heron, and the canoe was loaded to capacity with victuals. The name of the canoe was *Diwa*. The dema went up the Torassi river and then, crossing inundated land, they made their way to the Wangu river . . . which they descended as far as Senayo. Here the dema made a big feast . . .

The main character is *Yugil*, who is also called *Diwa* and thus identified with the canoe. *Yugil's* genitals were of an extraordinary size; he had to carry his penis slung over his shoulder. *Yugil* had made the trip by land and on his arrival in the neighborhood of Senayo an old woman kindly ferried him across the Maro in her canoe. The old woman sat in front, her daughter in the middle and *Yugil* aft. During the trip, *Yugil* molested the girl with his long penis, but the mother took a piece of sago-leaf sheaf . . . and cut off the penis, which dropped overboard. Shrieking with pain *Yugil* continued on his journey to Senayo, where the *Diwa*-canoe arrived soon afterwards.

After the feast the dema proceeded again downstream, and *Yugil* went with them. *Zawi* had to get off because he had eaten too much sago and the canoe became overloaded. Not far below Senayo the canoe struck upon the cut-off penis of *Yugil*, which stuck to the bow and was thus carried down the river to the sea. After some time another dema was turned out because he wanted to eat himself. He is the ancestor of the *emér-anim*, the Hunger-people . . . a clan which is now extinct . . . *Emér-anem* is a term of abuse giving serious offense, used only in anger and then preferably in respect of one who was adopted as a child after having been captured on a headhunting raid . . .

Further downstream something more serious occurred; a sea-snake bearing the name of *Salendo* approached the canoe and stirred up a strong eddy. The canoe, which slowly followed Salendo down the river, had to be relieved of its load and successively a sago-pounder, an old woman (who changed into a tortoise), a couple of fishes . . . and a big load of sago were thrown out. The places where they were jettisoned abound in fish and in sago groves . . . (van Baal 1966:311–12)

The myth goes on to detail how other items and beings left the canoe and gave their characteristics to the places where they fetched up. Salendo reappears and capsizes the canoe, and other *demas* were stranded at various places. Salendo finally entered a swamp where he resides to the present. Meanwhile,

Yugil's penis was washed ashore at Kai-a-Kai, near Borem. Up to the present day a *ngor-uvik*-dema, a "dema of the top of a penis" has resided there in a swamp. *Yugil,* who is also called the *mit-uvik*-dema, "the dema of the penis-stumb [*sic*]," stayed with the other dema at Sirapu. He is the ancestor of the *Diwa-rek boan* [clan]. (1966:313)

Now it is very odd that the Marind-anim should apply to their captured war orphans the most derogatory epithet they know. It has been suggested (van Baal 1984) that because of their sexual practices—in particular, the high frequency of copulation that Marind women had to endure (about which we will hear more shortly), which produced a correspondingly high frequency of genito-urinary tract irritation and consequent sterility—the Marind-anim had a low birth rate. They supplemented the perceived insufficiency of their own endogenous reproductive efforts by bringing back these foreign children and raising them as Marind. The epithet emér-anem, however, suggests that such orphans are like those who wish to eat themselves. The severed head, the human caducity, obtained at the moment of death, is fertile: it is symbolized, as we shall find out, by the regenerable, plantable coconut for the Marind; while the young captive who will someday grow up and procreate him/herself is nothing but a deathly image of autoconsumption. It is the head with the whole live reproducible body and all its external relationships attached to it, hence complete and sterile. If it were the case that the Marind reproduced through acts of consumption, then we could understand why the emér-anim became extinct.

Yugil's penis is cut off when he attempts to sexually penetrate a young girl, and it is thrown overboard, along with the food items in the canoe. If throwing sago and fish overboard resulted in the land's becoming abundant with these items at those spots, what did throwing the penis overboard make appear in abundant quantity? Yugil's penis wound up at Borem, coincidentally, the place where the Marind set up their ambush of the Kanum-anim. Perhaps the penis made abundant not just *dema* of the severed organs themselves, but also the men who stage the raiding parties where Kanum-anim heads are severed, or perhaps it made abundant the Kanum-anim themselves, whose heads would henceforth be severed and harvested by the Marind.

We could then conclude that the penis is reproductive only when it becomes an illusory image of consumption, and not in its copulatory function. Is the Yugil myth saying in more general terms that the fertilization of the land with food items is a consequence of the abrogation of heterosexual intercourse? That production and consumption are consequent upon the *elimination* of sexuality? Is it too far-fetched to suggest that Marind men and women are not sexed beings at all, at least not as we understand sexuality? That the acts of cutting or castrating—of heads, of the sexual organ, of relationship itself—are the most productive acts they imagine? We would then have to compare the results of throwing overboard the whole person (the emér-anim *dema*), which leads to human extinction, the death of reproduction, with the jettisoning of the penis, which multiplies the heads of victims, the lost organ in its regenerable form, the head-coconut. And we would have to ask, how do acts of consumption operate to produce such metonymic contrasts with which Marind-anim personhood and gender are established?

In "The Signification of the Phallus," Lacan (1977a) talks of the phallus as the *ur*-symbol of human desire. Though the phallus is not merely the male penis, it always retains an iconic resemblance to the penis, the most everted, extroverted, and (apart from the hand and arm) extendable of human organs. Because of this iconicity, the phallus always retains an embodiment not privileged to other signifiers. Its ability to extend and retract readily allows it to become the detachable human organ par excellence. But it is not just this detachability that certifies its significational powers, but also its ability to make contact elsewhere—it is the logical copula as well (Lacan 1977a:287).

Yet the phallus is not just a mere part of the embodied person. Lacan explicitly rejects Melanie Klein's treatment of it as a "part object." It is rather "the signifier destined to designate as a whole the effects of the signified" (1977a:285), and with this phrasing, Lacan makes his own appeal to the regenerable caducity of signification itself.

As was the case with Freud, Lacan and Strathern seek to give an account of sexual difference that is not tied to sheer anatomical difference. Freud and Lacan both begin with the image of castration, that is, of a perceived lack. Both men and women wish to be the phallus, to embody the object of desire of the other. Metonymically, this organ always appears as the symbolic phallus—the drum, bull-roarer, string bag, pearl shell—the forms in which it presents itself to the displacing and euphemizing consciousness of the subject.

But human desire is always short-circuited or cut off in its confrontation with the other, leaving a gap or void. The phallus signifies this resulting void or disappearance or discontinuity. It is a *manque à être,* a "lack which is brought into being" (Wilden 1968:188; Lacan 1977a: 287; Muller and Richardson 1982:338), and thus stands for the whole of what would make a person and his/her drives complete. In Marilyn Strathern's terms, we might say that it stands for the drive as potential for relationship: that is, the person who is elicited by the (always socialized) desire of the other.

Because it always stands for what completes a person, the phallus as signifier stands for an absence. What is signified is hidden, repressed, or erased by the signifier; it "dies" in being covered over by the signifier; the object of desire disappears when the signifying phallus stands over it. What Ernest Jones (1950) called *aphanisis,* the disappearance or lack of sexual desire, is thus also an effect of the act of signification itself. And we might then surmise that some cultures might elaborate this function of the phallus, as a token of the death of relationality or sociality itself. We would then have to conclude that whenever the phallus comes into view in New Guinea—as pearl shell, as pregnant python, flute, drum, or bull-roarer—we should ask ourselves, what is being cut off from our gaze? What act of collapse or severing is the phallus covering over? And finally, what bounding container allows the phallus to appear as a whole thing, thus hiding the gap?

The appearance of the phallus presents us with a problem, then— we don't know what it is concealing. And the Marind-anim provide us with the most extreme version of this dilemma. At first, we are inclined to see the welter of phallic images, the repetitive invocation of the castrated male organ, the constant emphasis on ejaculation and its product as a sort of apotheosis of the sexual if not the erotic. It would be easy to read the myths and rituals in which these images stand forth most prominently as the manifestations of an ethos which glorifies the male version of the phallus and makes a social or relational image out of it. But our initial inspection of the Diwa myth and the others I will explore in this chapter should caution us. They seem to suggest that insofar as the Marind-anim can be said to be sexual at all, they are so in Gregory's (1982) terms: it is *consumption* that they find problematic, not the libido which for them is the energetic of consumption. For the Marind, as we shall see, relationship means being locked in a space within which nothing can emerge or move or be produced. What they must do is *sever the relationship itself*, to release the flow of nourishment, the flow of objects trapped within the relationship which serve as its body, to control the effects of consumption, and to make the death and the end of desire a precondition of it. If this is the case, then the Marind provide us with a critique of Lacan: they strive to produce breaks in the flow of life, to make what *we* call the phallus appear as a productive consequence of the gap or void produced by acts of cutting.

The head taken from the enemy by Marind-anim males (along with the victim's name, the true signifier) is about the closest we come to what we might describe as aphanisis as a social aesthetic. In its Marind form, what we call the phallus is what they employ as a signifier for the effect of obviation itself—that is, an image that signals its own exhaustion, the collapsing or cutting off of conventional relationality.

The problem of the ethnographer then becomes to announce the presence of the phallus without going overboard, to make the Marind phallus reveal itself in such a way that it is not merely the anticipated result of our own Western phallocentrism. For what appears to us as the detachable, inscribing male organ comes into view in its Marind form only when it is outlined by the female organ which stipulates both its efficacy and its limit. Insofar as it is a signifier at all, it is a signifier, as we shall see, of consumptive acts. And these consumptive acts are not the end and rationale of Marind sociality but merely images set up to facilitate the acts of cutting off that are the whole point of Marind mythos and social life. We must therefore approach Marind-anim myths as if their intent was to lure listeners with the promise of an origin story, but we must then realize that these myths are only using language to dismember sexuality.

II

The Marind-anim inhabited the southern Papuan coast of Irian Jaya (West New Guinea) between Kumbe and the present international border between Indonesia and Papua New Guinea. I speak here of their life as the Dutch colonials encountered it between the end of the nineteenth century until the 1930s when, devastated by introduced diseases, faced with a rapid decline in their birthrate, their head-hunting raids held in check by the European administration, and their ritual objects forcibly displayed to women and noninitiates, these

most flamboyant, aggressive, ritually extravagant, and sexually energetic people saw the collapse of their world.

Marind territory was located in the part of southern New Guinea
which was contiguous with the northern Australian savannah. The
productive and ceremonial life of the Marind-anim was dominated by
the marked alternation between the northwest wet season (roughly between April and September) and the southeast dry season (between
October and March). The latter was the season of head-hunting and
raiding, a time of plentiful food; the former was the season of sickness,
cold, and hunger. But the marking of this seasonal alternation was part
and parcel of a thoroughgoing dualism as manifested in their moiety
system. The moieties provided the framework within which marriage
and other sexual practices proceeded, and stipulated a complementarity to the ritual, mythological, and ceremonial tasks and functions
of each Marind-anim community.

The most comprehensive ethnography of the Marind is provided by
Jan van Baal in his thousand-page book entitled *Dema* (1966). The
analysis of Marind-anim cosmology and symbolism he provides summarizes the most useful contributions from all the Dutch and German
sources on the Marind-anim, most of them written in the early part of
this century.

Van Baal as well as others who have considered the Marind more
recently (Ernst 1979; Herdt 1984a; Knauft 1993) maintain that Marind-
anim life was dominated by the continual necessity to copulate and
inseminate. Much attention has been paid to the fact that the Marind
practiced what Herdt (1984a) calls ritualized homosexuality: older
men anally inseminated younger boys, for the purposes of "feeding"
them additional amounts of semen, a process that was thought to be
necessary to ensure their proper growth and attainment of male maturity. The heterosexual counterpart to this was enshrined in the practice of *otiv-bombari*, which literally meant "many/men's house rite"
(van Baal 1984:137): At regular occasions, a woman had to copulate
with her husband's lineage mates, the members of his men's house,
and sometimes other clan mates as well. This was done not only to
fertilize the woman, but in order to collect semen. Semen obtained in
this manner from a woman's vagina was considered a panacea—it was
a nourishing and curative substance that was mixed with food. It was
spread over tools, gardens, and garden vegetables, and applied as a
salve on human bodies as an enhancer of growth, efficacy, and health.
Their myths repeatedly illustrate the fertile properties of semen: humans, wallabies, yams, and bananas all appear spontaneously as a result of semen falling into various containers or cavities. Marind cere-

monial life elaborated upon the consequent necessity of continual copulation and supported it, and was also itself continual, one phase of the annual cycle moving without break into another.

In many societies of interior Papua New Guinea we find that the content of the husband-wife relationship rests on the restriction of sexual contact (see for example the Etoro [Kelly 1977]; Hua [Meigs 1984]; Daribi [Wagner 1967]) and its replacement by the flow of various foodstuffs. The food items themselves have male and female characteristics, so that a sexual exchange is effected or mediated through the imagery of consumptive acts rather than exclusively coital ones. What we find among the Marind-anim, however, is the literal unification of the consumptive and the sexual, for they use semen as food: they collect it, eat it, and consume it as if it were an all-purpose nutritive substance.

III

As I did in the case of the Yafar, I am going to consider several important Marind myths in relation to a total ritual cycle which they offered as an account or gloss on certain points of that cycle. Van Baal says that the Marind ritual year starts with the *mayo*, associated with the southeast monsoon, the dry season, the sun, the regenerable coconut, and other things pertaining to the benign forms of life energy. The *imo* is associated with the rainy northwest monsoon, with the aspect of life that takes the form of death: head-hunting, sorcery, the night, warfare, and hunger. To affirm the complete interdependence of these two principles, van Baal states that the *mayo* already includes the *imo* rituals which follow it. "Not one myth tells of the origin of the mayo. The mayo is simply there, as the origin of all things, the imo ritual included" (1984:146). And the myth of *mayo* can be seen in the same way. It is identified by van Baal as the most important myth of the Marind-anim. The image of a man locked in permanent copulation supervenes all other Marind notions of intersexual mediation. And van Baal repeatedly finds other imagery in the ritual cycle that refers back to it. In fact, there is no point along this ceremonial cycle which does not bear upon the story of Uaba and Ualiwamb (also spelled Ualiuamb). The problem, then, is not to identify analogic relations of equivalence within this world of imperishable flow but to locate the effective images of motivation and punctuation within this continual sexual energetic. The myths emerge as one of the Marind's important forms of discursive ligature; they make concrete these images of severing, and mark out the beginnings, ends, and origins within a lifeworld which is cyclical and continuous.

UABA AND UALIWAMB (abridged)

It was the time for the *mayo* initiation ceremonies in Yavar-makan. *Uaba* was among the initiates. He had brought an *iwag*, a woman of his age-grade, to participate in the *otiv-bombari*, the rite of sexual promiscuity. Her name was *Ualiwamb*. But she managed to escape and the *otiv-bombari* could not be held. She ran away to Mopa near Gelib, in Eromka country, the part of the southern coast that is farthest west. There she made sago.

Uaba followed her and found her at Mopa. He watched as *Ualiwamb* came home after her day's work, carrying a load of sago. She went into her hut. *Uaba* hid and waited until it grew dark. He then stealthily entered the hut.

The next morning *Uaba* was found moaning and groaning in copulation with *Ualiwamb*, unable to extricate himself. A *dema*, *Rugarug-evai*, hurried to Kondo and told the people what had happened to *Uaba*. Some of them left immediately to fetch him. *Uaba* and *Ualiwamb* were laid on a stretcher and covered with mats, and taken back to Kondo, preceded by *Rugarug-evai*, who laughed at and mocked *Uaba*. When they arrived at Kondo the couple were carried into a hut and laid on a bench. A young woman from his totem group (of the category men call *nakari*) covered *Uaba* with a sleeping mat and gave him a piece of wood for a neck rest. Crotons were planted outside the hut (as is the case with any *dema*-house) and *Uaba* remained there until this day.[1]

Uaba first killed *Rugarug-evai*. Then *Aramemb* came from Yavar-makan. He had been looking for *Uaba* as far as Imo. When he heard of his whereabouts, he returned and came to Kondo. He went straight to *Uaba*'s hut where he was still locked in copulation. *Aramemb* seized *Uaba*, shook him, and turned him over to disengage him. Suddenly, smoke developed and flames flared up. The friction of their parting had produced fire. Simultaneously, *Ualiwamb* gave birth to a cassowary and a stork. The cassowary and the stork owe their black feathers to the fire. Moreover, the stork has burned its legs, and the cassowary the lobes on its neck. These are still red.

The fire, fanned on by the east monsoon, spread all along the coast, leaving a broad beach. All animals fled into the water, but the lobster burned itself and turned red, and up to the present day lobsters, when roasted, will give off a hissing sound like water being thrown onto a fire.

In different places, the fire spread inland, burning long, woodless valleys into the earth, which became the present-day river beds. Other natural features are still related to the primeval fire. The *dema* of Kondo were so impressed by the event that since then they did not come to celebrate the *mayo*. They had something more impressive, fire, which they now knew how to make. Moreover, they had the fire *dema*. And this is how the *rapa*-cult originated from the *mayo*. (van Baal 1966:243–44)

Like the Foi Usane Transformation, this myth begins with a general substitution of *mayo* ceremonial for nonceremonial time, a time when the ritual intensification of heterosexual intercourse in the form of *otiv-bombari* takes place (A). But Ualiwamb flees from this ceremony; she disengages herself from continuous copulation and runs away toward the west (B). Uaba pursues her and after dark enters her hut. He then finds himself trapped in copulation with her (C). This is the literalization of A. To be obliged to copulate repeatedly is to be trapped by the female sexual organ, to be swallowed by it.

The two are carried back to the east, covered with a mat. Van Baal identifies the sequence as symbolic of the movement of the sun: when the sun sinks in the west at the end of the day, the Marind-anim say it is copulating with the earth. At night, it travels underground so that it may reemerge in the morning in the east. He suggests that the reason why the two are covered with a mat in the myth is to symbolize that theirs is a hidden, underground journey.

So Uaba and Ualiwamb are carried back to the place of the *mayo* ceremony (D), the pair is placed in a hut, and crotons are planted outside it, "and Uaba remained there until this day," so the myth says. Uaba, unlike the sun, is rendered immobile—his whole body, and not just his sexual organ, is in a state of stasis (a nonrelational image of sexuality, hence obviating the implied temporal movement of A). The first half of the myth thus tells us that the Marind do not see finding opportunities for attachment or copulation as problematic; what is difficult is to *disengage,* to create the *absence* of copulation, to make the activity discontinuous, to introduce aphanisis.

Aramemb comes to the place of the *mayo* looking for Uaba. When he finds him, he shakes the man and manages to separate him from the woman (E). While in B the woman was able to disengage herself, in this episode Uaba has to rely on another man to help him do the same. Further, I suggest that what the myth does is not to account merely for the separation of Uaba and Ualiwamb but to show how this separation creates a space into which the phallus is inserted, in the form of the stork/cassowary/coconut which is the initiate. The parting of the couple is accompanied by fire and sparks, and the fire itself spreads from east to west (*F*). The woman gives birth to the stork and cassowary (*G*), that is, the male Marind-anim initiates (*G* → *A*: initiates for the *mayo* ceremony, i.e., the retroactive motivation of *A* and *D* by *F*). The external triangle *BDF* plots the movements: east to west, back east underground, followed by the westward spread of fire (sun), creating the north-south division of inland and coastal ecosystems, and this sequence obviates *A*: inland/coastal spatial division for temporal ceremonial division and east/west diurnal division, which is both spatial and temporal. But this motivating seasonal pulsation is itself the background against which the reversible time of facilitating human procreation unfolds (*A* → *C* → *E*: intensification of heterosexual intercourse → man locked in copulation → disengagement, a three-point scheme of conception, making *G*, the birth of the stork/initiate, a product of such disengagement, rather than of the permanent copulation of *A* and *D*). As is the case with Foi Usane Transformation, a permanent separation (ritual-ecological) is made responsible for the reproduction of children-initiates.

Rugarug-evai laughs at Uaba, because it really is a joke to see a man and a woman locked in copulation. But he loses his life as a result of his not taking Uaba's predicament seriously, and you might say that we Melanesianists have been afraid to laugh at the joke ever since. But it is a joke, one of cosmic proportions.

Now, *rapa* was a cult of the Kondo people, and the rites of the *rapa* were performed in a *dema*-house of Kondo. Paul Wirz, the German anthropologist on whose ethnography van Baal based most of his analysis, surreptitiously visited the *dema*-house in Kondo in the early part of this century. He found everything painted red inside, but what he noticed immediately were two big mummy-sized packages, also painted red. One of them was full of red-painted human bones. There were also many implements for fire making, all painted red. Wirz then plunged into wild speculation, van Baal says, and concluded that the *rapa* was a cult of human sacrifice.

Wirz gave the following version of what he thought was the order of events in the *rapa* rite. First a large pig is prepared for cooking and roasted whole on the fire. When the pig is thoroughly cooked, an incision is made in its abdomen, releasing the hot vapors and fat which issue forth in a gush of flame, visible to the women standing off at a distance. "That is the fire-*dema*," the women then say to each other.

After this, a married woman, an *iwag*, must submit to *otiv-bombari*, the ceremony of multiple copulation. Toward the end of this session, fire is drilled, and the woman is thrown into the resulting flames alive. The roasted pig is also thrown onto the fire, and it and the woman's body are eaten. The bones of the *iwag* are subsequently collected and painted red.

Van Baal dismisses this account as preposterous for a number of reasons, not all of which are relevant here. Most likely, he concludes, it is an imaginary version told to initiates to frighten them, when all that is happening is the quite ordinary consumption of a roast pig. But after all, Ualiwamb, alias Kanis-iwag, belongs to the same phratry, Nazr, as does the pig.

Well, van Baal does his best to take the joke seriously. Uaba and Ualiwamb get locked in copulation, and when they are finally prised apart, fire shoots out of Ualiwamb's genital. This produces the ecological division between treeless beach and forested inland. After that, men left the *mayo* cult behind, and took up *rapa*, the cult of fire, because "now they had something more impressive." More impressive than what? The *mayo*? Or are they saying that it is preferable to the massive amounts of copulation they have to engage in during the *mayo*? In the *rapa*, the act of penetration of a woman was seen as tantamount to the incisions made in a pig for the purposes of consumption. It was Roy Wagner (1978:201f.) who suggested that the thought of killing and eating pigs and other game animals most likely aroused far more passion and desire in a Daribi man than the thought of having sexual intercourse with a woman. Instead of producing the stork/initiate, Marind-anim men make the creation of fire result in edible pork. Is it so preposterous to conclude that Marind men should have wished that sexual intercourse was as easy as fire drilling—and as rewarding, since after all it results in edible meat?

IV

We saw in the Uaba myth that the initiate is the product of what could be labeled the Marind *Urspaltung*, the act of productive disjunction that is the death of copulatory relationship. In the next myth, the product of this disengagement takes a different form—it appears more visibly as the embodiment of killing and head-hunting as the productive and reproductive nexus of Marind life.

SOSOM (abridged)

Sosom came from Waruti, west of the lower stretches of the Kumbe River. He was a giant *miakim* who resided in the subterranean waters of Mabudauan, from where he comes every east monsoon to the eastern part of Marind-anim territory, fertilizing man and soil.

Sosom became trapped in copulation with an *iwag* during an *otiv-bombari* rite. The *iwag*'s mother took a piece of sago-leaf and cut off his penis. The severed part remained stuck in the girl's vulva. Finally a stork managed to extract it with its beak. Sosom, however, went to Kanum-anim territory across the border where he still resides as a *dema*. (van Baal 1966:267–68)

SOSOM'S SON (abridged)

Sosom came from the far east, from the Fly River, in a beautiful *dema*-canoe, the *gaream*-canoe. He arrived at Pater (east of Kondo), where the people only had the *uga*-canoe, and where they bartered their canoes with Sosom. Continuing on his journey by *uga*-canoe, the sea became turbulent, so he disembarked off Yobar and continued on foot, his footsteps raising the waves of the sea. His *nakari* [young women of one's totem group] named Nagi and Runggu accompanied him . . .

He went westward as far as Komolom, but the people there killed him. They cut off his head, but the head ran off and went eastward under the ground. Sosom himself became a *hais*, a spirit of the dead. He returned by land to the east. He went to the Kumbe River, to Moha near Wayau and subsequently to Burb near Saror. Here, unnoticed, Sosom entered into the vagina of an *iwag* (in effect, a married woman) called Wanumb. She became pregnant and gave birth to a son, Sosom.

He was a very noisy boy, always singing to himself *mu-u, mu-u*: a nuisance to the other people when they had their *wati* [kava]. Grown up, Sosom seduced the girls and beat the smaller boys of the village after having first decorated himself. At last the older people lost their patience and cut off Sosom's penis and chased him from the village. The penis fell into the river and became a water-snake.

Singing *mu-u, mu-u-u*, Sosom went from Burb to the coast. He slept in Song-ad-warin, which means "there he sounded the bamboo pipe." Then he went to Tamu, a swamp in back of Wendu, where he masturbated. This stirred the water of the swamp and the women, thinking that the ripple was caused by fish, took their nets and tried to catch fish. Thus they caught Sosom who went on singing *mu-u-u*. Wishing to soothe him, the women sang *waiko* [a ceremonial dance] but Sosom kept singing. Then the women tried *yarut* (the song for the dead) but Sosom never stopped. The women brought him to Imbarim, a dry place close by, where the men were gathered. The men sent the women away and sang *manggu* [the introductory song of the *sosom* ritual]. Sosom became very restless and his growling grew louder. Then the men sang *bandra*, the main song of the *sosom*-rites and now Sosom's growling rose to a roaring so tremendous that the few women who had been lingering around ran off as fast as they could. Then at that place Sosom taught the men the *sosom*-rites and after that he returned eastward to Mayo and Yavar-makan. Here he met with women celebrating the *sosom*-rites. For two days they had been whirling the bull-roarers but Sosom went up to them and said, "Women, from now on you may only follow the *mayo-kai* [the *mayo*-road, or the *mayo*-rites]; men only may go with me." Therefore, Yavar-makan is the place of *Sosom*, and Mayo that of the *mayo*-rites. Thereupon Sosom went to Sota where he has remained until this day. (van Baal 1966:271–72)

Sosom is also the Marind-anim word for the bull-roarer. The bull-roarer is, as van Baal described it, "a flat, lancet-shaped slab of wood" with a hole at one end through which a cord is tied. "When whirling the instrument at the end of the cord, the operator gives the bull-roarer a spinning movement of its own . . . thus causing it to produce a surprisingly loud noise . . ." (1963:201). Among the Marind-anim, the cult of Sosom and the bull-roarer involved the anal insemination of boys by older men (see van Baal 1966:472–94).

In the first myth fragment, Sosom is in certain respects the metonymic version of Uaba. Like Uaba, Sosom is also trapped in copulation, but here a woman (in fact, the mother of the female in whom he is trapped) frees him only by severing his organ. A woman detaches Sosom's penis, whereas Aramemb, a man, leaves Uaba's penis intact but causes him to be replaced by the stork, the human phallus.

The second myth can be said to include the first fragment as the hidden expansion of its opening *A* point. Journeying from east to west, Sosom encounters the people of Komolom, who kill him and cut off his head (*A:* head for Sosom; head for penis). This has the effect of turning Sosom into a *hais*, a spirit of the dead, and it is in this form that he impregnates a woman (*B:* [headless] spirit for penis/Sosom). Sosom's son is born and he is called Sosom too. The son continually produces noise; he is, in effect, a bull-roarer/penis: Sosom has reconstituted himself as a miniature phallus, a live bull-roarer (*C:* bull-roarer for head; son's voice for father's voice).

Sosom seduces young girls and acts aggressively toward other boys

(*D:* unruly bull-roarer/penis, obviating *A,* as the small Sosom is both voice and phallus at once, the returned head turned into a penis). The people in response cut off his penis (*E:* man without a penis for *B:* woman without a penis). The detached organ turns into a water snake (*F:* snake for penis; the snake is nothing but a detached penis while Sosom's son is a metaphorical penis, a whole body as phallus). The internal triangle *CAE* plots the successive detachments of son, head, and penis, all equivalent and interchangeable castrations, and all of which reproduce the entire Sosom; as was the case with Yafar caducity, in this Marind myth, each detachment results in the same product.

The inversion of the myth begins when the women, thinking there are fish in the water, actually are seeking Sosom's detached member (inv. *D:* women seek Sosom's penis). They succeed in catching Sosom, who, instead of copulating with them as before, emits sound (rather than semen), and forces the women to dance to soothe him, which has the opposite effect of increasing the volume of Sosom's roar (inv. *C:* deafening roar for childlike buzzing, the effect of a maturing Sosom). The sound becomes so loud that it eventually drives the women away—the more the women try to anticipate the desire of Sosom, the more firmly do they ensure aphanisis. Desire is *anathema* to sexual reproduction in these myths! (Inv. *B:* driving away of women for impregnation of woman.) Finally, Sosom sets the precedent for the *sosom* rituals, which involve the whirling of the bull-roarer (inv. *A:* bull-roarer for severed head).

Sosom's penis becomes totally detached as a result of his being trapped in heterosexual copulation. The detached penis, the bull-roarer, henceforth serves to separate women from men; it drives women away when it is sounded. As Wagner puts it, "it celebrates the abrogation of normal (i.e. heterosexual) intercourse through the severing of the organ" (1972:21). The consequence of the disengagement of Uaba and Ualiwamb was the permanent separation of inland and coastal zones, also a female/male distinction, but here it is the detachment of men and women and the attachment of men through inseminatory ritual that are produced as a seasonal, productive spatial division.

V

What we see in the Uaba and Sosom myths is a glimpse of the real Marind male interest in the world: they are always ready to abandon the *mayo,* to leave it all to women, to get through it in a hurry and on to their real passion: head-hunting, sorcery, *rapa*, and *sosom*, the supreme acts of ligature in the Marind world of consumptive disjunction. In the last myth I consider here, this is caricatured in a pronounced form, and the phallus, as a signifier of the primal cancellation of Marind life, achieves perhaps its final form.

YAWI AND ARAMEMB (abridged)

A *Mayo* ceremony had been celebrated at Yavar-makan. *Uaba* was among the initiates. The ceremonies having been brought to a close, the *mayo* boys went westward with their mother, a python of the variety called *bir*. Her real name is kept a secret, but she is known as *Nangewra, Wangor, Wangus,* and *Kadubar*. She carries the boys in a *kabu*, the cradle used for new-born babies.

The python stops in a number of places. On the fifth day she stops near the Maro River, where she stays for a few days. One of the little boys climbed out of the cradle and changed into an *Inocarpus edulis*, a fruit-bearing tree frequently found near the beach.[2] The python crossed the Maro and slithered through the area between Maro and Kumbe, to arrive at a place called Koandi.

In Koandi the python became pregnant. She bore a son, *Yawi*, who was found by two females from his totem group from Moha, which used to be a village near the mouth of the Kumbe River. They took the child with them to the village, but the python tracked them down by their smell. She encircled the hut and shattered it, without doing much harm to those inside. An old woman chased the python away, throwing glowing charcoal at her, whereupon the python fled and hid in a swamp in Kanum-anim territory, where she has remained ever since.

The python proceeded to swallow a number of women who were fishing in the swamp. The last to be swallowed was a pregnant woman, who was too big to be swallowed and stuck in the python's throat. Later, the men killed the python and slit her open. All the women emerged alive, except the pregnant one, but her unborn baby was still living, and it is from him that the *Bugau-rek*, a *Geb-ze* subclan of Tomerau, are descended.

In the meantime, *Yawi* grew up into a very handsome boy. *Aramemb* heard about him and wanted to steal him. He went to Imo. At Imo, *Aramemb* was informed that the boy was in Moha. When he arrived there, the village was deserted; the men were out hunting and the women were preparing sago for a feast. *Aramemb* used his time to prepare a collection of ornaments. He had brought rattan from the interior and nautilis-shells from Komolom. Up to that time, body-decoration had been unknown among the Marind.

While the people were out at their tasks, a boy was sent back to the village to fetch fire. Astounded at the beautiful decorations which *Aramemb* had exhibited on wooden puppets, the boy forgot everything. The same thing happened to each boy who was sent to fetch fire by the puzzled village people. Gradually, they all return home to crowd admiringly around the decorations. The excitement gives *Aramemb* the opportunity to seize *Yawi* and bring him to Imo.

When he is grown up, *Yawi* commits adultery with his foster-mother. *Aramemb* finds out and decides to kill *Yawi*. To that end he goes to the east to call in five Kanum-anim men, reputed to be sorcerers. The five men, *Mangasesse, Mangaueru, Ueru, Doyam,* and *Enod-anem,* belonged to the *Sapi-ze* subclan of the pig clan. They are the mythical *kambara-anim,* and they kill *Yawi* with their magic (*kambara*). *Ueru* was the one who led the killing.

Soon it is over, and when *Aramemb* hears that the boy is dead he hurries off to the bush to collect medicine. He feels sorry that the boy is dead and wants to restore him to life, but it is too late. When *Aramemb* returns with his medicine, he finds that the boy has been buried already. Thereupon, *Aramemb* takes the bowl of medicine and pours it over a snake. The snake becomes quiet, turns cold, and sheds its skin. Ever since, snakes have not died. When they are sick, they just shed their skins and live on. If *Aramemb* had been on time to give the medicine to *Yawi*, not only would *Yawi* have survived, but man would have become immortal, shedding their skins when they are ill. From *Yawi*'s head, severed from his body before it was buried, sprouted the first coconut. (van Baal 1966:247–50)

This tale is cognate with the Foi myth "The Origin of Usane" (Weiner 1988:224) and with the Yolngu Wawilak myth from northeast Arnhem Land, Australia. Like those myths, it concerns itself with the paradox of the double container: a uterus within a uterus, an image of double birth—and, potentially, double loss. In this case, the image of the double container is also a version of permanent copulation rendered in terms of containment. For a fetus to be trapped in its mother is for that woman to be trapped within the phallic organ itself. The python is a hollow penis, the penis which enters the vagina but gives birth by itself, that is, the penis which is itself fertilized rather than being the fertilizing organ.[3] The image of the snake phallus represents the answer to the problem of permanent copulation, to *otiv-bombari* itself.

The snake mother swallows a pregnant woman. The woman dies after being swallowed by the snake, but the unborn child lives to be "born" when the snake is cut open. In other words, the penis swallows the uterus and becomes a uterus itself; hence, it gives birth to the intact child. This child is the ancestor of the Bugau-rek line.

But what happens to Yawi? He was born in a normal way from the snake; that is, he is not protected by the double container, which makes an eversion out of containment itself. He thus becomes vulnerable to *kambara* sorcery. Let me now detour momentarily to discuss the nature of *kambara*.

The *kambara* men are said to approach a victim and hit him over the head from behind, rendering him unconscious. Then, without visibly damaging the skin, they cut the victim's flesh and viscera, tearing strips of tissue from the interior of his body. When they are finished, the victim is brought back to consciousness. He begins to feel symptoms that night, and is dead the next morning.[4]

Of interest to us is the implement by which this magical death is accomplished. It is called a *tang,* which is another word for the bull-roarer or Sosom's penis. And Sosom himself is also the *dema* of *kambara* sorcery (van Baal 1966:486). The *tang* is also said to be a snake. The apprentice sorcerers learn to fling the arrow-shaped *tang* while seeming to make it disappear. It lodges in the victim's body, an alternative way of "striking" the victim unconscious. Van Baal says: "It flies off and when it has got near to the victim, it changes into a snake and bites him" (1966:896).

The *mangor* is another such implement, considerably more dangerous than the *tang.* According to van Baal, "It is made of a dwarf-coconut and has the form of a pig's head with a gaping mouth" (1966:897). There is a hole at the other end through which a cord can be threaded. The sorcerer can therefore retrieve the *mangor* after he has flung it at his victim. It is like a bull-roarer then, which also is tied to a string, but it is also a coconut head at the same time, a detached head.

So, to return to Yawi. He is attacked by a sorcerer's snake/pig's head/bull-roarer/phallus, the *tang* or *mangor.* He is born of a snake and is killed by being penetrated by the sorcerer's lethal "biting snake"—he is swallowed by a very big snake and is reborn, but is bitten by the little *kambara* snake and dies. His dead body gives birth to the first coconut, the detached (pig's) head, which is the phallus itself, insofar as it too stands for death. Men's penes cannot produce life by themselves, but only when they are swallowed. Castration, the severing and bringing back of the heads of other men, is the only way to obviate that—they cut their losses, as it were.

VI

I want to consider now in obviative terms the entire Marind ritual cycle as van Baal (1984) summarizes it. Let us identify as point *A* the image of Uaba and Ualiwamb, locked in permanent copulation, the effigies of which herald the beginning of the ritual season and announce that the practice of repetitive copulation for the purposes of collecting semen and vaginal juices—*otiv-bombari* (lit. rite many / men's house)—will begin in earnest. The young male initiates enter the *timan*, the enclosure in which are placed the effigies.

This phase of the cycle ends with the destruction by burning of the effigy of Ualiwamb, who is also the Old Mayo Woman or Mayo Mother. In the next phase (*B*), Ualiwamb in this guise takes on a sinister, threatening form; she becomes the Excrement Woman. The initiates are mistreated and have their faces smeared with excrement mixed with semen. They are made to believe that they will be beheaded. In contrast to the opening sequence, the Old Woman remains in the enclosure and

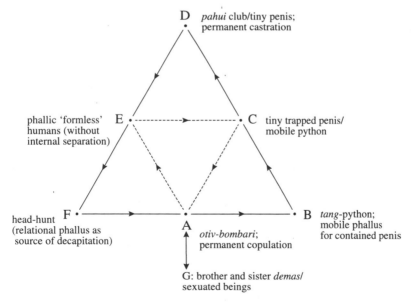

Figure 6.   Obviation of ritual cycle of the Marind-anim.

does not leave to fetch the young boys; they, in turn, wait outside the *timan*, rather than in it. In other words, everything is done to emphasize the boys' separation from and their negative attitudes toward a maternal figure, a definite heightening and intensification of castration anxiety, a dramatization of the primal splitting and aphanisis.

In the myth cycle, it is at this point that Ualiwamb, the Old Mayo Woman as van Baal (1984:149) identifies her, turns into the snake who gave birth to Yawi. The woman who originally trapped Uaba's penis has turned into a mobile penis, the *tang*, which swallows women but is also capable of giving birth.

The next phase of the ritual cycle (C) is the *bangu*. The dominant image is again Uaba and Ualiwamb locked in copulation. Only now the proportions are altered. The initiates screw arrowheads into holes in the ceremonial shields that surround the pit. As van Baal observes, this is an image of copulation itself. But if it is, it is a surreal image even in Marind-anim terms; it is as if a very tiny penis is being locked in copulation with an enormous vagina. The snake has "swallowed" the men, the consequence of their being trapped in copulation.

Van Baal recognizes a crucial turning point now, and I will identify it as point *D* in this obviation sequence, the point at which the sequence of images has acquired enough momentum to carry itself through to its end point. Two beautifully decorated men, impersonating Uaba and Ualiwamb, have been dancing all night in the pit. The initiates, painted dead black and wearing masks representing the spirits of the dead, surround the pit. As night is about to end, a man surreptitiously climbs a coconut palm. He begins to throw down coconuts. There is an uproar from the participants. The two impersonators climb out of the pit and the initiates throw their shields into the vacant hole. Uaba and Ualiwamb are about to be carried back to the east, the journey that represents the sun's underground journey during the night (reversing the direction of the snake, the Mayo Mother).

But the *D* point has already been reached before this occurs. It was reached the moment the arrowheads were screwed into the shields, for from that point on, the shields are called *pahui*, the word for the ceremonial club taken on head-hunting raids. The *pahui* consists of a very long wooden shaft which at one end is inserted into a donut-shaped stone disc. A frail, carved bamboo blade is attached to the shaft above the cincture of the stone disc. This blade is apparently designed to snap off after the club is used to strike a victim. In other words, the blade is broken off in the act of "copulation," revealing the rim of the circular stone head which becomes the effective and visible limit of the phallic weapon. What is left behind is a plain disc-headed club.

(And nothing is said of the fate of the detached blade. Is it merely left behind by the head-taker, as the Keraki headhunters do [Williams 1936], as a token of what has been detached?) To the Marind, it represents a very long penis copulating with a very small vagina, which reverses the proportions represented by shields themselves. In turning to head-hunting, the men reverse the proportions of the sexual act itself: in head-hunting, unlike copulation ($D \rightarrow A$), they are efficacious. They themselves bring back the fruits of this copulation, the heads, a totally externalized version of what women create in gestating the phallus-fetus.

Point E follows the *bangu*, the "life-giving" ceremony of the *aili*. The imagery at this point centers on two lengths of bamboo tubes, called *imo*, which is the secret word for canoe. Phratry by phratry, all of the women dance with the bamboo tubes between their legs, moved jerkily back and forth by the leaders of each group. They dance until they fall down with exhaustion. When all the women have had their turn, the men do the same thing. The bamboos are burned at the end, and when they burst in the fire it signals that sickness, pollution, and danger have been banished to the west.

A major hunt follows several days later, after which there is a night of heterosexual promiscuity. Van Baal mentions that often before this night a sham fight occurs between men and women, and that among the eastern Marind on this occasion the men throw excrement at the women. The sickness, as represented by the excrement, is thrown back, literally, onto the woman.

What seems to be unfolding in the sequence is the elaboration of an image of permanent copulation against a background of intersexual separation and hostility. However, it does so not in copulatory terms strictly speaking, but by drawing attention to the opposed associations of the mouth and anus. At every point in the ritual cycle, initiates are fed sperm and vaginal secretions with their food; hence, the numerous acts of *otiv-bombari* that must be performed during these ceremonies (notice that they are not being "inseminated" directly by men as part of this ritual cycle). It is the mouth that is the real site of "permanent copulation," the consumptive focus for the Marind: the mouth is like the vagina. Defecation, elimination, on the other hand, becomes the site of separation, pollution, and castration. Does it not appear that for the Marind, permanent copulation is their image of aphanisis, the death of relationship, of desire, of sexuality? That it is only through consumption, and not through sexuality, that they can reproduce at all? That the Marind, both men and women, have to exhaust themselves in coitus in order to make the appropriating of semen a matter of consumption?

The actual head hunt occurs at the point we would label *F*. In *C*, the initiates were as tiny arrows in relation to the Imo Mother; in *F*, the long shafts of their war clubs pierce a tiny female organ.

The final feast we can label as *G*, the "not-not" of *A*. The most important feature of the final feast is that the participants impersonate the *dema*, the totemic deities themselves, analogous to the way in which many Australian Aboriginal ceremonies attempt to recreate the dreaming creators. Each male *dema* is accompanied by his *dema* sister counterpart. This couple are neither locked in permanent copulation, nor covered with the phallic excrement of their full and antipathetic *separation*. Rather, it seems as if the sister is the female shadow of the *dema*. The man and his *dema* sister counterpoint are not sexed beings at all. In fact, women are lured into having sex with their men when all men want is to accumulate semen for their own consumption.

I wish first to focus on the androgynous image of reproduction that is being precipitated in the internal, facilitating sequence which is punctuated by *G*. The *imo* canoe in the *aili* ceremony figures in the myth of origin of the two Marind-anim moieties (van Baal 1966:85–86). The *dema*, after celebrating a feast at Sangasé, traveled by this canoe underground toward Kumbe. Near Kondo, they encountered the first humans floating in the water, where they had the appearance of lumps of loam (semen?). The stork *dema* removed them from the water. Aramemb, whom we encountered in the story of Uaba and Ualiwamb, made a fire and gave them their human shape.

This process is given further detail in another version of this myth (van Baal 1966:209–10). The loam creatures are in fact fishlike in appearance. They were the *anda*-fish, "in reality human beings whose arms, legs, fingers and toes were still one with their bodies, and who had neither mouths nor ears" (1966:210), which we can see as a projection of total closure and permanent attachment onto the image of the Marind body itself. The *dema* ordered the stork to place these creatures on dry land.

> Then the dema made a big fire on which he threw a number of bamboo-stems. First a small bamboo cracked . . . whereupon two holes burst in the head of each of the beings and became ears. A second . . . bamboo exploded, and caused two other slits to appear in each head, and these were the eyes. A third explosion gave them a nose, and a still louder one . . . resulted in another crack, the mouth. Now the dema cut them their arms, legs, fingers and toes with a bamboo knife . . . (1966:210)

This is an eversion of the Uaba and Ualiwamb story, for the stork causes the separation, rather than being the product of it himself, and fire gives the loam creatures a human shape rather than being the product of sexual disengagement (hence, in this ritual sequence $A \leftrightarrow G$). The human form is as much a product of the imposition of *internal* separations as the *external* disengagement of Uaba and Ualiwamb is responsible for productive relationality. In the *aili* ceremony, both these versions of separation, the one internal and the other external and intersexual, are equated, for both men and women are locked in their copulatory dance of exhaustion with the bamboo tubes, the canoe which brings the *dema* into contact with the human race, and which causes the fire and explosion that give the human body its internal divisions.

It is clear that the cycle itself takes shape as a result of the alternation of facilitating images of death, closure, and total attachment (*ACE*) versus motivating ones of life, immortality, and detachment (*BDF*). The total ritual sequence plots the substitution of copulation by head taking, from penis to pregnant snake (*tang*), to the war club which *stands not for the penis but for the act of copulation itself*. Being a total relational organ, it allows for the detachment and death of relationality. We can also say that acts of *otiv-bombari* and the collection and ingestion of semen figure prominently in the internal sequence $ACE \rightarrow (G)$, which images the essentially asexual end product of permanent consumptive copulation— that is, totemic reproduction. Head-hunting, on the other hand, results in the recapture of the real reproductive moment of Marind life: the return of the names to Marind territory, the retention of the *logos* of the myth's reproductive format. We thus encounter the masculine viewpoint that, although confronting us in its most flamboyant and intense form among the Marind-anim, is general to Melanesia, as Marilyn Strathern (1988) has suggested: the extension of the body through detachment of its organs—even though this detachment occurs through an act of aggression or violence—is a life-giving, socially positive, and constructive image. The contrastive images of total attachment, of stasis, of the fetus within the womb, of fish creatures with no gaps or orifices, of being locked in copulation are merely the temporary facilitations through which these disjunctive acts are set up.

VII

How then do *we* learn to see the Marind as sexed beings? In the second segment of *The Four Fundamental Questions of Psycho-*

analysis (*Seminar Book XI*), Lacan, in discussing desire in relation to the human gaze, directs his attention to a painting by Hans Holbein entitled *The Ambassadors* (see Illustration 2). Completed in 1533, it depicts two young French diplomats, one on either side of a low table on which shelves stand. Displayed on the table and shelves are various objects. On the top shelf is a celestial globe, astronomical instruments, a book, a sundial. Below it on the table's surface are a globe of the earth, a set-square, two compasses, a lute, two books. The objects, as Jurgis Baltrusaïtis points out, all have to do with the quadrivium of the liberal arts of the Enlightenment: arithmetic, geometry, astronomy, and music. In the upper-left-hand corner of the painting, behind the ambassador on the left, is a silver crucifix, partially covered by the curtain backdrop.

Above the floor between the two men, at an acute angle pointing to the right, rises a strange object. Baltrusaïtis (1977:91) remarks that it looks like a cuttlefish bone, and perhaps Lacan was reminded that the cuttlefish was sacred to Aphrodite, the Western goddess of desire. Its fuzzy edges make it appear as if it is flying; yet again it has a vaguely phallic outline. But in fact it is an anamorphic representation of a human skull, whose normal proportions are revealed if one stands very close to the painting and looks down upon the object along its length. In order to make the skull visible, one has to assume an oblique perspective, one's gaze has to strike off the surface of the image at a very acute angle (as a myth has to strike off the surface of language at a tangent in order to impinge on it). The effect is startling, because, as the viewer moves closer to the surface of the painting, just as the two human figures and the objects between them disappear from the field of vision, from the line of sight, the skull reveals itself (just as language reveals itself at the very moment when it is collapsed in a myth). The appearance of skull is made to efface the entire edifice of Enlightenment Man, his political power, his artifacts and science, his laborious accession to perspective. "All this shows that at the very heart of the period in which the subject emerged and geometrical optics was an object of research, Holbein makes visible for us here something that is simply the subject as annihilated . . ." (Lacan 1977b:88–89). Even then, Lacan saw fit to mention Salvador Dali as another painter whose visual traps provided the same surprise of cancellation for the Western viewer—and we will find one of Dali's traps useful later on.

The skull is the "other" form of the phallus; it stands before (in the foreground) all the other objects which define the space between the two men of Holbein's painting. (Holbein in 1525 also made a drawing of an earlier version of this image, which showed a well-dressed man and woman holding between them a shield with a skull as its coat-of-arms. Between the skull's teeth, by the way, is a serpent or adder.)

I now want to direct the reader's gaze to a strikingly homologous *tableau* that van Baal unearthed from his patient sifting through the early archives, photographs and records from this part of New Guinea. The photograph I refer to (see Illustration 3) is examined at length by van Baal. It was originally taken by an assistant resident named L. M. F. Plate in 1913. Van Baal's comments are worth recounting at length:

> Plate—or his deputy—went to Sangasé and other villages in the western section of the coast because the villagers had been on a headhunt. He reported that all the houses of Sangasé were searched and that 8 "fresh" heads were seized. Apparently it was not only heads which were confiscated. What happened is evident from the photograph. His police-sergeant or whoever was in command contrived a unique still-life with all the heads, the mandible, the arrows, the spears and the paraphernalia symmetrically arranged round and on a small table covered with a cute rug. We owe him a debt of gratitude for his morbid fancy. (1966:737).

Although this is the closest we have come to finding an outsider (although apparently another Papuan) who gets the joke of Marind relationality, van Baal again treats it seriously. "Everything connected with headhunting is there," van Baal continues (but we already know that that can only be meant in the strictest sense of what Heidegger called *das Zeug*, "equipment," [Heidegger 1962:97f.] for everything the Marind-anim do is connected with head-hunting). But, as in the Holbein painting, the catalogue of objects framed by the two anthropomorphic death's head drums on either side is critical.

In the center there is a phallic pole belonging to a head-hunt house, the *kui-aha*; on the right and left two *kui-ahat*, forked poles used to hang heads on (labeled with white letters *a* and *b* on the photo); the left-hand one is identifiable by the inverted V markings which are made in parallel along its length; three big oars (left, right, and center) with painted blades, and finally, labeled *c* in the photo, a *pahui*. The *pahui* looks like a long thin spear. Van Baal says:

> It is not easily recognizable as such because the *pahui* made a quarter turn and stands showing the fretwork blade sideways. It was not until I had the picture enlarged that I discerned the object and established its identity. (1966:737–38)

If the *pahui* had been cinctured by its stone band, there would have been no doubt as to its identity. But the absence of the stone disc, which the Marind-anim have already likened to the female genital, points to what is missing in the photograph, which is any reference to the feminine shape, function, and origin of these artifacts.

Apparently, these stone discs were both rare and valuable and were safely kept in between the times they had to be fastened to their shafts and taken on raids. Van Baal comments on the reports made by Kooijman (1952) and Grottanelli (1951) concerning the same clubs used by the neighboring southern Boadzi. On the clubs he collected, the stone disc fits loosely around the shaft and slides up and down in the process of being swung and wielded (Illustration 4). A length of plaited fiber is used to retain the disc and keep it from moving too far in either direction. Kooijman notes that the mechanical moment of the club is thereby enhanced: "In battle the warrior brandishes the club over his head, making the stone slip backwards; when he delivers a blow, the disc shoots forward, greatly adding to the impact" (1952:97). We seem to be confronted with another version of the movable, detachable female genital which slides up and down along the shaft of the trapped, immobile male genital, and which we already encountered in the Foi myth "The First Married Couple" (see above, Chapter 2).

Administrator Plate and we ethnographers of the Marind who have glanced uncritically at that photograph for the last thirty years have continued to make of those skulls and objects the artifacts of Marind social integration. But they do not have this function at all. Aramemb uses wealth objects only to divert people's attention away from his real interest: the stealing of children. Does this not strike us as the most comic indigenous reply to our current Melanesian models of circulation and reciprocity? In the Yawi myth, wealth objects are of no other use to the Marind, for the real work of the brief moments of transaction in their life is accomplished through other objects—arrows, stone club heads, bamboo fretwork blades, and invisible sorcerer's projectiles. What these weapons do—we call them weapons and in so doing conceal the fact that they function to objectify parts of persons every bit as effectively as do pearl shells—is to establish the opposite of what we labor to reveal by our attention to ceremonial exchange: the cutting off of such ceremony from all its relational functions.

VIII

In Plato's *Symposium*, Aristophanes relates the story of how the two sexes originated. At first, the human race consisted of "circle-men": each had four arms, four legs, and two faces set on opposite sides of a single head, with four ears. These beings couldn't walk, they could only somersault around. Their genitals were on opposite sides of the circle of their bodies, so they could reproduce only like grasshoppers, by leaving their seed on the ground. There were three kinds of these circle beings, one composed of two male halves, one composed of two female halves, and the third, the androgyne, composed of one male and one female half.

Zeus decided to do something about these creatures and ordered Apollo to split each one down the middle and sew each half up, which created a navel for each. Their genitals, however, were still around the back. These sundered half beings then spent all their time searching for their missing half, and when they found each other, they would clasp each other and not let go. When alone, they would not eat or do any of the work that people needed to survive, and so they began to starve, for they would not eat except in the presence of their other half. Zeus then ordered that their genitals be moved to the front of their bodies, so that when they embraced, at least the half beings of the original androgyne would reproduce.

Our view of sexual intercourse, as Ricoeur almost lyrically asserts, is that it is a striving for oneness, an attempt to fuse two bodies into one, and of course this is the literal and practical result of such intercourse, in the form of a fetus developing within its mother's womb. But one would have to reverse this myth entirely to make it speak to the Marind-anim: for them, as we saw, reproduction happens only in the splitting apart. Fusion is a cosmic bad joke, and men attempt as much as possible to mate like grasshoppers, spreading their seed on the ground.

> The Marind were well aware of the symbolic meaning of Diwa's penis and castration and cannot have had the slightest difficulty with such misleading details of the story as Diwa's continuing his way "shrieking for pain." They will have interpreted it as his song of triumph. (van Baal 1984:160)

Van Baal's analytic conclusion is that for the Marind, continuous warfare equaled continuous copulation. If we are to take this literally, then Marind copulation has nothing to do with fusion, nothing to do with sexuality, and everything to do with identifying the cuts and breaks in the flow of life substance that makes reproduction possible. Death, not coitus, results in children, since it is the permanently detached penis, the *pahui* stone club, which kills/copulates and reproduces. Head-hunting is an act of copulation which results in the initiate-phallus in external form, rather than the internal phallus—the fetus.

Evidence of the depth of van Baal's understanding of Marind-anim usages is provided on page 187 of *Dema*. There he explains that *dema* refers not to the ancestral creator beings as such but rather to "the supernatural in its mythical form . . . These manifestations of the supernatural are the object of a cult." That is exactly how we must approach Marind sexuality, through its epiphanic manifestations that become the objects of productive and consumptive efforts: coconut–bull-roarer–*tang*–penis–head.

5

The Lost Drum

I know what I eat
I do not know what I do
—Salvador Dali

Let us picture the time of the evening meal at the Foi long-house. Women prepare the main part of this meal—that is, the staple, roasted sago—in their own houses next to the men's communal long-house. The sago is cooked in sectioned internodes of bamboo, which turn black from the fire. When there are no children around, a woman may walk underneath her husband's sleeping area in the longhouse (the structure is raised four feet off the ground) and push the tubes through a hole or gap in the flooring. At other times, one also sees children both male and female leaving their mother's houses with bamboo tubes of sago and cooked food, running up the steps of the men's longhouse and going inside to lay the tubes by the fireplaces of their fathers and elder brothers and then sitting down to eat with them.

Now let us imagine the night of the Usane habora ceremony, when the *samoga*, the nighttime beating of the drums, takes place. The men have decorated themselves with *kara'o* tree oil, giving their skins a reddish, oily, glistening appearance. They hold the *sa'o*, the Foi drum, either the fish-tailed (*fare*) or the round-ended (*gauwage*) variety. The men beat the drum, drawing forth its hollow, plangent voice; unlike the *sorohabora* dancing when men sing songs composed by women, during the *samoga* dancing, only the drums speak. The women hold torches to illuminate the men's skins and their decorations. And they hand bamboo tubes of water to the men who have succeeded in arousing their desire, so that these men may quench themselves during their exertions.

When the evening meal is over, when there are no ceremonies being performed, at that time of night in the longhouse when most of the children have gone to sleep, we shift to another scene. Men are sitting near their fireplaces, or perhaps gathered around the sleeping area of another man. They converse, sometimes argue, or tell myths to each other. And weaving in and out of their conversation, from out of the dark, from the sides, percolating into the smoky interior of the house, slipping in through the gaps and interstices of men's conversation come the

101

voices of women, disputing, correcting, affirming, emphasizing, distracting. No barter of silent bamboo tubes here. Above men's heads, in the rafters alongside the shields and bows of remembered battles, are stored their ceremonial drums, almost invisible in the dark, camouflaged by the soot they have accumulated from the men's fires, like great bamboo tubes slowly cooking over the years in the rafters. Silent these drums usually are, or do they echo ever so faintly the voices of the men over whom they are suspended?

I

After having learned of the dilemma of Sosom and his son, we might now consider that the "speech" of the bull-roarer—and other New Guinea sound-producing instruments such as the drum and flute—is its rendition of its own myth. These instruments speak to people with the voices of the ancestors, or the culture heroes. These voices must, like all voices, compete or converse with, or respond or talk to, those of their human players and listeners. We would also not know in the first instance whether it was incumbent upon humans to interpret or control the voices of the instruments, or whether it was the power of the instruments to dub over or drown out the voices of those who give them the power of speech. And as was the case with Sosom's son, to make too much noise, to have too much voice, to penetrate too hard with the substance of sound, might in the end result in enforced silence or castration of the signifying, inscriptive organ.

In her analysis of the mythology of the Gimi people of the Eastern Highlands of Papua New Guinea, Gillian Gillison claims:

> Gimi women possess myths of their own that, looked at in combination with men's myths, seem to be part of a conversation with men, as if the myths themselves were engaged in discourse. (1993:xv)

The Gimi enjoin strict residential separation between the sexes: men and women live in separate houses, as is the case with the Foi. Since all young children initially reside with their mothers in their mothers' houses, they grow up first hearing women's myths, called *nenekaina*. Later in life, male children leave their mother's houses and go to live in the men's house. There, they will hear *bidokaina*, or myths of the men's home. Gillison states that these stories may be thought of

> not simply as the male equivalent of the *nenekaina* but also as a response or appropriation of the *nene*, incorporating, elaborating,

translating into the terms of a male ethic stories men heard in infancy. Whatever the direction—or mutuality—of influence, the tales told "in secret" inside men's and women's separate houses seem to speak to one another across the night. (1993:8).

Gimi boys apparently fetch myths from their mothers to their fathers. And these myths are . . . consumed in some way by Gimi men. The most important item contained or wrapped up in these myths is the bamboo flute, the sacred aerophone which is the focal object of the secret male cult among the Gimi. The Gimi boys thus, like their Foi counterparts, carry bamboo tubes from their mothers to their fathers— only in the Gimi case, they are virtual flutes, whose shape is given by the mythic discourse which contains it. But these myths feed the real flutes, lend to men the discursive resources they require to legitimate their own soundings of the flute.

According to Gimi women's myth, the First Man had a very long penis which he carried coiled within a string bag. The string bag hung from his neck so that it "protruded in a lump over his belly" (1993:7). Such a man might very well be said to be pregnant with his own penis, or carrying it around with him like an infant in a string bag, or a fetus in utero—or all three. The myth of this man—and Gillison refers to him as *the nene* man, as if *the nene* man was paradigmatic or metonymic of the whole corpus of *nenekaina*, or women's myths—is as follows:

While the *nene* man lay fast asleep inside his house, his penis awoke "out of hunger" and went out alone to search for the vagina. The penis was blind and followed his nose into the woman's house. But she was fast asleep and her vagina closed. "The man slept. The woman slept. The penis came alone." He searched in vain for the opening and finally "ate a part of the hole to open it. Then he entered and ejaculated." The woman awoke with a start and took the penis in her hand. She walked to the man's house and, while he still lay sleeping, cut his penis to the length of a section and a half of sugarcane, throwing the huge severed portion into a river. The blood of the maimed giant was the blood of the first menses. (1993: 10–11)

Gillison pairs this myth with the male myth of the origin of the flute:

the first couple was composed of a woman and a boy who were sister and brother. One night, the cries of the woman's flute awoke the "small boy" asleep in the men's house and he crawled to her house, hiding himself in the tall grass outside her door. In the morning, after his sister had gone to her garden, the boy crept into her house and stole her flute from the head of her bed or, as told in other versions, he took it from the grass where she had left it. When he put the instrument to his mouth to play, he found that she had closed the blowing hole with a plug of her pubic hair. The boy's lips touched the plug and his sister's hair began to grow around his mouth, which is why men nowadays have beards. By stealing the flute, the boy not only acquired a beard; he also caused his sister to menstruate for the first time. But when she saw that her flute was gone and heard it "crying" inside the men's house, she was not angry . . . and did not try to take it back. "She forgot everything that happened and died," their myth says. (1993:10)

Now if these myths are speaking to each other, in what way do they converse? They both account for the origin of menstruation (which patently cannot be a literal origin, since there are at least two divergent accounts of it). But Gillison goes on to say the following:

The myths . . . are alike in one feature: each deletes or deactivates the Moon or primordial father. In women's myth, the Moon, or first *nene* man, lies fast asleep while his penis "does the walking" to woman's house. But in the flute myth he is entirely absent. (1993:11)

And she concludes:

Analyzed together, men's and women's myths reciprocally imply that, in the very first instance, before time began . . . only the other sex "had the penis," only the other was grown-up and possessed sexual appetite. (1993:12)

Let me first question the extent to which the issue of Gimi sexual identity is already established in these myths. Consider first the flute myth: a woman plugs the hole of the flute with her pubic hair (and could this hole not then be a vagina which is penis-shaped, or a vagina which is a mouth hole?). Her immature brother tries to blow the flute, but acquires a beard instead when the pubic hair attaches to his face—so that his mouth has replaced the sister's vagina, by virtue of its contact with a (vagina-shaped) penis. Here, the vagina plugs an empty penis, rather than the other way around which presumably is the conventional image of heterosexual penetration, as intimated by Gillison (for example, 1993:204–5). The vagina, in other words, "eats" the penis. So if there is a "penis" in this myth, its functions have been taken over by the vagina.

Now the *nene* myth: here the penis is undisguised because it is still attached to the man. Let us keep in mind that the penis is never disguised in its undetached form in these New Guinea myths, whereas it is always disguised in its detached form. Or perhaps we should say that in its detached form, as whole, nonpartial object, it acquires its relational complement and thus takes a different form.

We don't know whether the penis is also the *nene* man's child and umbilical cord at the same time, in light of the manner in which he carries it around in his string bag, or even whether it is some extruded form of his alimentary tract. At any rate, the penis/(child)/intestine has to "eat" the vagina, rather than merely fill its already empty hole.

Neither do we learn what happens to the huge severed remnant of the *nene* man's penis. Unlike the Marind-anim remnants of Sosom and Diwa, it disappears from Gimi discourse. The penis disappears or dies after having intercourse. But the blood remains. The blood is the first menstruation blood, which the Gimi say is "'the same as a firstborn child'" (Gillison 1993:11). The penis dies, but it remains as blood, the relational *phallus*, the form in which the penis is made to connect or have an effect on others. The cause is replaced or substituted by its effect.

The *nene* man loses his penis but yet lives on. He lives insofar as the detachable, signifying organ acts on others. He lives *through* and *in the form of* its elicitory powers. But the first woman, in losing the flute, dies—that is, disappears—as a result. Is it too far-fetched to suggest that what these myths are depicting is not the absent father but two alternative *relations* to what constitutes the name or power of the Father in Gimi, that is to say, the embodied phallic signifier?

But how are the real flutes transferred from person to person? When a woman is to marry, her father makes a new set of flutes and plugs their openings with chunks of cooked meat. He then hides the flutes inside his daughter's string bag, and unknowingly she carries them to her husband. The husband knows what he will find in the string bag. He removes the flutes, the silent gift of his wife's father, removes the meat plugs, and places them in his bride's mouth.

What she carried inside the flute (and the flute is her father's child which she carries in her string bag/womb), that is, its flesh, she now consumes. What her husband does by feeding her is to make her pregnant again, especially as her mouth has already been tattooed with a pubic "beard." I find it not unreasonable to conclude that insofar as the Gimi are talking about sex and sexuality, and the closure and self-closure that sexuality inevitably involves in New Guinea, then, as do the Marind-anim, they do so largely in consumptive terms.

As both Gillison (1980) and Strathern (1988) maintain, in these myths and in all of Gimi social imagery, we are unable to attribute specific organs, or their functions, or specific consumptive or sexual acts to one sex or another. Both men and women have penes and vaginas; both men and women emit sound and substance and receive or consume such emissions; both men and women are consumers as well as consumed. There is no sexual difference in any form in which we are familiar with it. In fact for the Gimi, "maleness and femaleness seem defined to the extent in which persons appear as detachable parts of others or as encompassing them" (Strathern 1988:107).

The flute and the penis are the same organ, but they are shown in their different, perhaps opposed, relational capacities. They are not merely the oral and the genital, or unmarked and marked, form of the penis. They embody the contrast between relational and nonrelational outcomes of the same acts of consumptive dissemination. What we must determine is the differential relation to such acts that allows maleness and femaleness to appear, at least temporarily. In Strathern's words, "In order for the distinctive gender of [genitals], like the particular and distinctive gender of the participants, to be made apparent, bounding mechanisms are necessary" (1988:121).

By itself, the phallus cannot secure sexual identity. Being relationally constituted, it has the capacity for unlimited expansion in scale. It can be the organ, the part organ, or the whole person. What we saw in the Foi flower myth was the way in which the uterus emerges as the shape and space of male inscription.

But if we then wish to appeal to men's and women's mythical points of view, what form will such viewpoints take? Will *having a viewpoint* then also display features of encompassment and detachment? Will the alimentary, consumptive image of New Guinea sexuation not inflect the shape of myths themselves and their relation to each other?

Just as these images have to provide the framing boundaries for each other within the embodied, specular field, so do the discourses to which they are attached and which they draw into their orbit: that is, associated myths and other glosses. The myths make visible the *social implications* of each other's imagery by limiting the range of obviative expansion in other myths with which they share part sequences.

One of the singular features of language which I have been focusing on in this book is its self-referential properties. Language always has a tendency to fold back onto itself, and in so folding it adheres and conforms to the shape of the body whose posture-in-the-world it outlines. Language is an extrusion of our various perceptual modalities; it itself remains faithful to its bodily origin and embodied intentions.

So we should not be surprised when Wagner speaks of the holography of meaning, nor when Lacan speaks of the anamorphic properties and effects of certain forms of figurative speech (Lacan 1992:139–54). We saw in Chapters 2 and 3 above that the retroactive properties of myth's obviational structure implied that in some sense an external sequence within the myth was framing an internal reflexive movement or sequence in the opposite direction, which emerged as a counter-invented image of life made possible by the obviating episode itself.

I have taken a cue from Freud and Klein and maintained that internal relations model external ones, and in fact are a function of them. The same thing is true in myth, within discourse itself. In myth especially, we see language taking advantage of its own form, playing a seeming linearity of narrative off against its self-referential, self-folding effects. We might expect that if different myths are related to each other thematically, that is, in terms of the images they produce, then they might relate not so much in terms of their semantic or narrative structure as in how they fold around each other; how they provide a framing, external form for each other, how myths can be as inside and outside to each other.

II

In the Foi myths I consider in this chapter, the establishment of a male voice is very much in evidence as a foil for all of those influences which serve to make the effectiveness of such a voice contingent and restricted. The danger that Foi men face is that the extensibility of their male power brings with it the possibility of loss, of castration. An object which serves as "metonymic" extension of the real phallus winds up being a "metaphorical" phallus which becomes humanized to a certain extent and travels on its own. And what it marks out is the route that the signifier plays in tracing the shape of Foi social discourse itself, the way that speech embodies desire by creating its intersubjective space. The phallus announces itself, as a drum which speaks, and in speaking it hangs over the heads of men and women, effaces the subjectivity of those between whose relationships it obtrudes itself. Strathern, in what could be a Lacanian paraphrase of Gillison's remarks about the Gimi flute, says similarly:

The indivisible flute is symbol of a thing that "cannot be shared," but "is wholly possessed by one sex or the other"; it is "transmissible but indivisible." (1988:113 [all quotes taken from Gillison 1983:49])

In Chapter 8 of *The Heart of the Pearl Shell,* I analyzed the myth "The Fish Spear" followed by "The Milk Bamboo." In "The Fish Spear," a man takes his elder brother's fish spear in his absence and this is later discovered by the elder man. Since the elder man had also left his wives behind with the younger brother, the appropriating of the phallic weapon is tantamount to the younger brother's supplanting the elder's sexuality. "The Milk Bamboo" I called a female complement to this story because there a man and his sister's son become linked to the same breast, which plays the same role as the fish spear: in the act of establishing itself as a mediating, nonpartial object, it actually creates the gap in which male contingency can emerge.

The myth I am going to discuss here, "The Lost Drum," seems to combine "The Milk Bamboo" and F. E. Williams' original story "The Lost Drum and the Snake-Man" (1977). What I want to do here is isolate and examine the mediative obviation that makes two myths into a single myth or vice versa.

THE MILK BAMBOO

Once there was a longhouse where only women lived. One time, the woman who slept in one corner disappeared. The next day, the woman with whom she shared a fireplace also disappeared. The next day the woman who slept across the house from her also disappeared. This kept happening down the line of fireplaces until there was but one woman left in the opposite corner on the east [downstream] end. "What shall I do?" she thought. She killed her pig, and not eating any of it herself, she put it in her bilum and went to look for her sisters. She searched for them but could not find them. But there on the other side of the latrine fence, she saw that the ground was muddy and churned up from many footprints—as if the women had climbed over, jumped to the other side, and left that way. She too went in that direction.

Along the way she came upon a cave where the women had slept. She kept travelling until she came to a wide river. How shall I get across? she thought. Sitting there, she heard the sound of a paddle being struck against a canoe and looking, she saw a worthless *uga'ana* approaching. She called out, "*Uga'ana!* Come and get me." But he replied, "No, your sisters also asked me the same thing and mixed pig excrement with the sago bundles they gave me. So I won't take you." And he continued on downstream. She sat there helplessly. But then she heard the sound of splashing and saw the *uga'ana* returning. He backed the canoe toward the harbor and told her to get in. Taking her to the other side, he told her to get out, but she said, "All my sisters wanted good men, but I myself am a rubbish woman so you and I will be all right together; I won't leave the canoe." Then the *uga'ana* said to her, "All your sisters used to give me pig shit with the sago bundles: Look at the base of that *damu* cordyline there!" She looked and saw that the ground was dark and muddy with discarded sago and excrement. The two paddled downstream. They shared a pig kidney and a roll of sago. As they paddled they passed a large bamboo grove, *hagenamo* trees, *arase* edible leaf, amaranthus, bamboo shoots, sugarcane, wingbean and yam. The *uga'ana* said, "These are my sister's son's." They disembarked, and the *uga'ana* tied up his shabby, broken-down canoe. The house was atop a small ridge, and it was well-made and surrounded by beautiful flowers and shrubs. Then the *uga'ana* said to the woman, "Cook sago, I will fetch water," and he left. While she was cooking sago the woman heard someone coming up the steps and she looked up to see a handsome young man. He said to her, "Wife, give me sago." But she replied, "No, the *uga'ana* will beat me, I won't give you sago." He answered, "But it is I who brought you here from upstream. This is your house now; those pigs underneath the house and the garden and vegetables you saw are yours." Then she exclaimed, "All my sisters abandoned these good things when they left you!" and the two of them lived there as man and wife.

The woman bore a female child. At the time the child started walking, they heard the cry of a *marua* bird. The husband said, "Wife, what is that bird singing about?" and she replied, "No, 'garden food will ripen,' it is singing." But he said, "No, it is not saying that. 'Your sisters' line will have an Usane—go hunting' it is saying. You stay here and make our decorations. I am going to find game" and he left. The day before the Usane was due to be held, the man returned with two string bags of game. Then they decorated and saw that each one was beautiful. The man took his *fare* drum and his Usane ceremonial skirt and it swayed gently back and forth very beautifully. They both smiled with pleasure. They then embarked and paddled downstream. They arrived at the longhouse of the Usane and saw that one of the two dance lines still did not have a leader. But the man himself took the place and, together with the other dance-line leader, they were satisfactory. The man looked perfect and the two together led the dance very well. Their two wives went first, and everyone thought that no others could have led the dancing so well. They danced and then they exchanged their game for pork.

There was another woman who kept following the man around, and when the handsome man noticed her, she averted her eyes flirtatiously. The exchange was finished, and the men all decorated again for the nighttime dancing. While they were getting ready, the woman explained to her sisters, "The worthless man to whom you gave pig excrement is this handsome man here." They all cried, "Aooh! You're lying!" "No" she replied, "It is he." "Oh, we did that to that handsome man!" they lamented. "Sister, look at us now!" and the woman noticed that her sisters' children were emaciated and had swollen, malnourished bellies, and that her sisters too were poor looking, and their husbands were bad men. "Ai!" the woman thought, "It is these bad men who are having this Usane."

Then the men returned ready to begin the nighttime dancing. The two dance leaders arrived, and the man went over to his wife and gave her two thin bamboo tubes. "Put these in your bilum and hide them under your cloak. Do not let anyone else see them. If one of your sisters' children cries out for water, do not give them this. When it is almost light, you will hear me tell you to give them to me." Then the men danced. The other woman who had been staring at the handsome man, she had a child who started crying. The woman tried to give the child things to settle it, but nothing worked. The child said, "I want my mother's sister's little bamboos." But the woman said, "But I'm not carrying anything in my string bag." "No," the child insisted, "They are there." So the woman took one of the bamboos and gave it to the child saying, "Drink just a little, or else your mother's sister's husband will get angry." But the boy drank all the water. The woman took back the empty bamboo and squeezed her own breast milk into it, refilling it. Then, as it started to get light, she heard her husband say the thing he told her would be the signal for her to give him the bamboos: "River stone moss water, I want to drink, want to drink; *urabi* moss water water, I want to drink, want to drink; water found at the base of the trees, I want to drink, want to drink; *hekana* aquatic grass water, I want to drink, want to drink," he sang as he approached. The woman removed the bamboos and gave them to him. He drank the one with the good water in it, but when he drank the second bamboo, he knew there was something wrong and he broke it over his wife's head. Then the dancers left the longhouse and prepared to leave. Below at the harbor, the man and his wife loaded their pork into the canoe. As they did so, he said to her, "I want to sleep; put the child here with me in the back and go get the pork." As she was almost finished and had come back from putting the last ribcage in the canoe, she saw that her husband and child were gone. "Where have you two gone?" she called out. Aiyo! There under the water were her husband and child sleeping, he with his *fare* drum as a head pillow. She dived in to try to retrieve them, but she only managed to grab handfuls of leaves and grass. Five times she tried unsuccessfully. Then she took a piece of sago bark and went up to the longhouse and struck her sister's child. She then struck all of her sisters, and they ran away along with all their husbands. She looked and there behind a section of *kewabo* vine she saw that all the men and women and children had turned into marsupials and were lined up. She turned around and went back down to the water. Again she tried to retrieve her husband and child but failed. Walking back and forth along the bank she turned into an *abeyaru* aquatic rodent, dived into the water, and lived there. That is all. (Weiner 1988:199–202)

In my original obviative analysis of this myth (1988:202–4), I drew attention to the identification between a man and his mother's brother (substitution *B*) and how it is canceled by a parallel identification between a man and his own child (substitution *E*). It could be said that just as the female breast provides the metaphorical link between a man and his sister's child, so does it always provide the same identification between a man and his child, which identification is masked by the normative constraints of patrilineal ideology which effaces the breast (the penis, in this reasoning, becomes the patrilineal form of the breast). The myth, in other words, reminds us that there is as much matrilateral continuity between a man and his offspring as there is between a man and his sisters' children.

We can thus say that in substitution *B*, the woman protagonist has married male matrilateral succession. What she reveals in the obviating point *E*, then, is the breast and its milk, the organ and product which mediate such succession. Alternatively, the obviating hinge could be phrased as "child's voice for man's drum's voice": the phallic drum is effaced by the child's cry for the breast, and it will be my duty to remind readers that in much of interior Papua New Guinea, we are likely to find the domain of the Imaginary phrased in acoustic terms as frequently as visual ones.

In many regions of southern New Guinea, breast milk is seen as the female analogue of male semen (Wagner 1967), an equation that is explicitly recognized in such areas as Anga (Mimica 1981; Herdt 1984a) and Bosavi (Sørum 1984) where the nutritive qualities of semen are elaborated. But it is also clear that in the case of the Foi, who do not elaborate oral insemination as an alternative form of substance transmission, milk and semen are complement rather than equivalent substances, and their mediating roles (from a feminine perspective) are localized at opposed points of the body's *topos,* the mouth and the vagina, respectively. Nor do the Foi even transitively equate the two by way of a dual identification of semen and breast milk with meat, as do the Daribi. Hence, the product of the breast, milk, is opposed in these series of myths not to its complement male substance, semen, but to the embodiment of male signification itself.

The obviating hinge of "The Milk Bamboo" is used in the next myth to achieve a similar effect, but in the following case it is more explicitly played off against the contingency of patrilateral continuity, mediated by the phallic drum.

THE LOST DRUM

There once lived two brothers. The elder brother had two wives while the younger brother was unmarried. One day, a *marua* bird sang out from the nearby tree. The elder brother asked, "My two wives, what is that bird saying?" They answered, "It is telling us that garden food is about to ripen: bamboo shoots, *hagenamo* leaves, *kõya* shoots will ripen, and children will grow." But the man replied, "No, it is saying that our mother's brothers are going to have an Usane pig feast. It is telling us to go hunting." The man then said to his younger brother, "I do not wish to go hunting. Take my younger wife, your sister-in-law, with you and go yourself." The younger man did so.

He filled two string bags with marsupial meat and returned to the house. He then took his brother's fishtailed drum and put a new snake skin on it. He also broke off cordyline sprigs for decoration and unwrapped his ceremonial string skirt.[1] Then, preparing these things he told his sister-in-law to carry the bags of meat. "I will now go and join the dancing," he said to her. "Our mother's brothers and cross-cousins are waiting. Take the meat and distribute it to them so that I may join the dance line."

Arriving at the longhouse, he found that the men were searching for another fine-looking young man to lead the dance line. When the men saw him arrive, they decided that he was to lead. And so they danced the *samoga,* and when they finished they received gifts of pork from their maternal relatives. The young man gave portions of pork to his sister-in-law, and she in turn shared it with her sister who had also come to the Usane. It was almost time for the nighttime dancing, the *usanega* [*samoga*] which is done to the accompaniment of drumming. Before taking his place, the young man gave two small bamboos of water to his brother's wife. He then said to her, "At some point in the dancing, you will hear my drum speak—at this time, give me the bamboo tubes of water." She then busied herself with cutting and sharing the pork they received. Meanwhile, the young man took his brother's drum and the men began their dancing. His sister-in-law wrapped the two bamboo tubes in bark cloth and sat watching him. But as the women watched the men dancing, her sister's small boy said to his mother, "Mother I want to drink breast milk." The woman tried to give him her breast but the child refused, saying, "No, I want the other milk." The woman tried filling a bamboo tube with water but this too the child refused. The child began to cry and the woman fretted, not knowing what he wanted. Finally, the child became such a nuisance that the woman's sister, the young man's sister-in-law, gave the child one of the bamboo tubes she was saving for her brother-in-law. The child drank the entire tube of water, and the woman took the tube back and filled it up with her own breast milk. Meanwhile, the men were still dancing. When her brother-in-law approached, she heard the drum sing out, "*Submerged tree, water, water, I want to drink; submerged stone, water, water, I want to drink.*" The woman thought, this is the signal he was telling me about. The young man approached and took the bamboo tube she offered. But when he drank the contents, he struck his sister-in-law over the head with the tube saying, "You have done a bad thing. You did not follow my instructions." After this, the young man felt very fatigued and so he took his drum and bade the men continue dancing without him.

As he left, he noticed another man following him. "The sound of your drum is very sweet," this man said to him. The young man flourished the drum proudly and then went off to sleep. He found an empty fireplace and put the drum under his head as a pillow. But when dawn arrived he awoke and found that the drum was gone. Someone had taken it. He searched all around for it, but no one could tell him who had taken it. Finally, he came upon some men who told him that a large dark-skinned man had been seen carrying the drum downstream [i.e., eastward]. "My brother will hit me when he learns that I have lost his drum," he exclaimed in consternation. Then, giving the pork to his sister-in-law he told her, "Take this and give it to my brother. Because you acted wrongly, my brother's drum has been stolen." And the woman left. When she told her husband what had happened, he became angry and struck her several times, saying, "Return and tell my brother to bring back my drum." She told her brother-in-law what her husband had said, and the young man went off alone to search for the missing drum.

The young man followed the footprints of all the men that had left the longhouse, after the Usane feast was over. He first arrived at another large longhouse and, inquiring as to his drum, the men told him that they knew nothing of it. But one man told him that he saw someone take his drum toward the east, downstream. He continued on, stopping at all the longhouses along the way. At each place, the men could tell him nothing of his drum, except that they thought they had seen someone carrying it toward the east. Still, the younger brother traveled on.

Now he had to start cutting his own trail as he traveled, for he was leaving the area of human habitation and there were no paths through the bush. He finally arrived at a longhouse deep in the bush and again he asked about the drum. There they also told him that they had not seen his drum. Then the men said to him, "We have not seen your drum. This is the last house of men. There are no others living further downstream. Return to your home." But the young man did not heed them and pressed on through the trackless forest.

He kept walking and finally came upon a small path. Following it, he found that it led to a great garden. There was much food growing around it. He followed its edge and found where the path continued on past the garden. He kept walking and then he heard the sound of his brother's drum off in the distance. He followed the path over a small hill and there on the other side he saw a longhouse. On the verandah of the longhouse he saw the drum hanging from the rafter. He approached the house, but looking closer, he saw that a huge python was circled on the verandah floor, and with his head he was striking the drum, thus producing the sound. The young man approached the python and spoke to him, saying "Brother, I have come searching for that drum." The python said nothing but moved aside and took the drum down from the rafter and gave it to the young man. There were no men in that longhouse. The young man took the drum and left the longhouse, but as soon as he left the steps and touched the ground, he himself turned into a python. He stepped up again onto the verandah and this time he turned back into a man again. He went back and forth between the ground and longhouse with the same results: when he touched the ground he became a python and when he returned to the longhouse he turned into a man again. Finally, in sorrow, he said to his brother's wife who by that time had followed him to the python's village: "Here is my brother's drum that he wanted. I am unable to return with it, but tell him that he should cut a large garden with it, that he should marry a young maiden with it, that he should kill many pigs and hold his own pig feast with it. I am unable to live with him and help with his work, but the drum can take my place." And there he remained in the house of the python.

The woman returned and gave her husband the drum, repeating the last words her brother-in-law had instructed her to say. The elder man, in his sorrow and anger, broke the drum in many pieces. The woman herself turned into a *kabayame* snake. That is all.

The story begins with the substitution of a man's human interpretation (that is, his "voice") of the *marua* bird's call for that of his wife. What this male-for-female substitution also signals is the replacement of female gardening and child raising by male hunting and ceremonialism (and ceremonial matriconnection, since the Usane is an affair of male maternal relatives). As I mentioned in Chapters 2 and 3 this is what I have called the Usane Transformation (1988:175), a common device in Foi myth to shift the action from the domestic sphere of sexualized production to the ceremonial sphere of consumptive sexual display and decoration.

The Usane Transformation invariably begins an obviation sequence, being located either at the beginning of the myth (often signaling an anticipated collapse or resiting of sexual differentiation in the myth's resolution as we saw in the flower origin myth of Chapter 3) or as the point of attachment of an inverted internal myth, as is the case here. In other words, as does the *mayo* with respect to Marind-anim life, the Usane Transformation always stands as the most encompassing contrast in Foi life, since all other substitutions keep referring back to it, and all mythic themes take place within its frame or shell.

The next substitution, *B*, is younger brother for elder brother in regard to the transfer of the younger wife to the younger brother's keeping. The essential sexual nature of this transfer is underlined by the elder brother's giving of his phallic drum to the younger brother as well. In the next substitution, *C*, the drum itself acts as the younger brother's voice and asks the woman for a drink. But since it is the elder brother's drum, we can see this as continuing the hegemonic extension of the elder brother's subjectivity. In substitution *A* he spoke for his wife, and in *C* he now speaks for his brother via the drum.

Substitution *D* marks the turning point of the myth, the obviating point which defines the limit of the elder brother's sexual/vocal extension. But it is the younger brother who bears the consequences of such limitations, for it is he who is infantilized by the drinking of breast milk (the woman has shifted the signifying power of the drum onto her breast), subverting the implied leviratic transfer initiated by his elder brother.The drum's cry for water is made equivalent to an infant's cry for the breast. The substitution can also be rendered as domestic, female breast milk for the male "bush water" imagery evoked by the drum in a specifically ceremonial poetic fashion, hence canceling the initial terms of the opening Usane Transformation.[2] By responding incorrectly to the drum's call, the woman cancels the effects of A where the man's voice (interpretation) took precedence over the woman's. Finally, the phallic, protuberant breast intrudes into the men's ceremony by resiting maternal connection between the two brothers, rather than between exchangers (performers and audience) in the Usane.

The next substitution, E, is drum for younger brother. Because of the way in which the assessment of male public stature focuses on the manipulation of such metonymic extensions as the drum, the drum can become an object of either male or female desire. In this case, a strange man follows the younger brother after the dancing, just as unmarried women will follow unmarried men after a ceremony among the Foi. But here he admires not the younger brother himself but the voice of his drum, which after all is now his identity and the elder brother's as well. The strange man takes the drum, and in so doing cancels the relationship between the younger brother and the elder brother completely. In the previous substitution, D, it was only the leviratic mediation that was *aufgehoben*, canceled. But as Lacan says, "the phallus is the signifier of this *Aufhebung* itself, which it inaugurates (initiates) by its disappearance" (1977a:288). That is, the intrusion of the breast between the two brothers anticipates the disappearance of the mediating phallic drum— and I use *anticipate* in its special Freudian/Heideggerian sense: to actively set the conditions for something to appear (we can thus read it as the futurial form of retroactive motivation). The drum then is made significant, is made to signify, by its removal. It is only because Foi male identity is made to repose in such artifacts that, as a signifier, the drum can elide this sibling differentiation.

Hence, the next substitution, F, is the drum itself, the actual tympanum, for the drum's male human voice. The younger brother discovers that the sound of the drum he has been following is the sound of a snake beating on the drum. But since those who listen to the story know that the tympanum is a snakeskin, then a snake beating a drum is a snake beating on a snakeskin, or the drum beating on itself. In other words, the snake beating the drum is a self-sounding tympanum, a spontaneous (human) drum, as opposed to the human beaten drum we encountered in substitution C. What this effects is a collapse of the mediations that governed the younger brother/elder brother relationship, which collapse was anticipated by the intrusion of the younger wife's breast. Hence, the myth closes with substitution G, snake for younger brother, which is the consequence of the younger brother's original identification with his brother's drum. As a drum, he is "human" in relation to snakes, i.e., he is a man in their longhouse, because a drum is a human metonym made from a snake, a snake converted into human use. But when he leaves this framing house of snakes and attempts to rejoin human society, he turns into a snake, because his human social identity has been appropriated by the sound of the drum, that is, the snakeskin. He is a man with a snakeskin, or in a snakeskin, that is, a snake. This is the *Aufhebung* of D in that it cancels the assertion of domesticity effected by the woman's breast milk (since the snake man lives in a longhouse beyond the limits of human habitation, that is, in the bush). This substitution is also the "not-not" of A. The cancellation of D does not result in a return to the original starting point A, but in its second-order sublation: the man as snake, in a longhouse beyond human space, is neither domesticity nor hunting, neither matrilaterality nor patrilateral siblingship. What it is is pure unmediated phallus, a sounding without continuity or social extensibility.

What could also be explored here is the extent to which an implied equivalence between infant and phallus helps to achieve the firm anchoring of the G point: that is, the man is made into a phallus in D by acting like an infant, who is the phallus of the mother. Support for this interpretation could perhaps be found in the explicit snake = infant imagery of a related Foi story entitled "The Origin of Usane" (Weiner 1988:224–30), where a man kills the infant snake children of his sister and subsequently the sister's python husband. On a portion of the dead python's internal organs, two maggots appear and later turn into the sister's human children. The man gives them two ceremonial drums which the two boys beat at the first Usane ceremony. Here too the drums replace the python, and paternal continuity is seen to be encompassed by matrilateral connection.

III

"The Milk Bamboo" was told to me by women, and "The Lost Drum" was told to me by men. Their relationship to each other is one of containment, a containment made possible by the holography of mythic language itself, by the manner in which it creates a space of meaning by folding signification back upon itself. In this respect the relationship of the two myths is iconic of the feminine act of containment or encompassment itself.

What would "The Lost Drum" look like without "The Milk Bamboo," however? Williams obtained the following version of such a myth in 1938. In it, we see that without the framing story of "The Milk Bamboo" to expand upon the obviating point at which the elder brother relinquishes control over his second wife, the striking of the younger brother and the subsequent departure with the elder's brother wife are framed in a different, more sexually explicit way.

THE LOST DRUM AND THE SNAKE-MAN

Wanagani lives with his younger brother, Sisimano [a small snake species]. A visitor comes to tell them of an *usanehabu* dance at another village. Wanagani does not care to go, but sends his wife together with his younger brother. They carry two bags full of smoked meat, and Wanagani allows them to take his drum, telling them to look after it.

At the end of the dance, which goes on till dawn, Sisimano lies down for a sleep before returning home, placing the drum under his head for a pillow. He awakes to find it gone. After searching everywhere without success he and his sister-in-law return to tell Wanagani that his drum is lost. At first he thinks they are joking; but, finally convinced, he hits them both on the head with a stick.

Sisimano and the woman go off weeping. They travel from place to place enquiring for the drum. They can hear nothing of it until they come to a certain village where the people tell them that there was a strange drum left tied to the front wall of the men's-house; it was making a noise by itself; but now it has gone again. Encouraged by this news Sisimano and his sister-in-law go further till at last they come to a very attractive village, and there, tied to the front wall of the men's-house, is the lost drum.

Sisimano climbs up the steps to take it; but, looking in at the door before doing so, he sees that the men's-house is inhabited only by snakes. He beats a quick retreat; but as soon as he sets foot on the ground he finds he is a snake himself. He darts back on to the verandah and becomes a man again; then on to the ground, and becomes once more a snake. Thus he tries again and again, until he finally gives up in despair. He hands the drum down to his sister-in-law, saying, "You take it to my brother. I must stay here and be a snake."

The woman goes back to her husband and gives him his drum.

At first she is afraid to tell him what has happened to his brother; she prevaricates, saying he is on the track behind and will shortly arrive. But at last she breaks the news, Wanagani, overwhelmed by sorrow, smashes the drum to pieces, while his wife turns into a snake and slips off into the bush. (F. E. Williams, 1977:305)

Without the breast milk and matrilateral succession theme to counterpose and enrich the *D* point of leviratic replacement, this myth is something like a joke that has lost its punch line: it has to carry itself through on drum imagery alone. The first substitution we can label younger brother for elder brother, as escort for both the wife and the drum to the Usane. In this regard, it is the drum which legitimizes the unusual escort arrangement, acting as a token of the elder brother's sexual propriety.

But in the next substitution, *B*, the younger brother loses the drum, and hence the above-mentioned rationale for the younger brother-elder brother's wife relation is removed. The younger brother is in a precarious position because he can no longer mediate his relationship with his sister-in-law via his elder brother's phallus. Hence in *C*, the elder brother strikes the younger brother and the wife with a stick, inverting the image set up in *A*: there we anticipated a human beating a "stick" (that is, a drum), and now we find a man using a stick to beat humans. The brother and sister-in-law are joined through aggression rather than the drum, which is the object of striking.

In substitution *D*, the younger brother and elder brother's wife depart once more, against the wishes of the elder brother, although they do so in his interest (to recover the drum). But this cancels *A* by removing the mediating rationale of their original partnership because this time they leave without the drum.

Since the couple has joined without the mediation of the signifying drum, the drum itself is "detached" and can signify only itself; hence in the next substitution, *E*, the drum takes on a life of its own and, making a sound without being beaten, travels from place to place ahead of the pursuing couple. Note that this is a figure-ground reversal of *B*, where the couple traveled without the drum.

The younger brother reaches the house of snakes as in the other version, and in taking back the drum becomes a snake himself (*F*). This is the same substitution we find in "The Lost Drum." But in Williams' version, because of the association already established in substitution *C* between stick, drum, and elder brother's sexuality, this point acquires a more emphatic sexual imagery. It is the drum as penis rather than as phallus per se—that is, without benefit of the expansion provided in

"The Milk Bamboo" of drum as voice, and voice as mediator between water and milk (which in substitution C obviated F in this manner). And by the same token, this version does not begin with the cry of the *marua* bird and the Usane Transformation, because it is not the male voice which is at issue but the male "signifier." The sexual equivalent of a self-sounding drum is a self-operating penis, that is, a snake. It is the animate transformation of the elder brother's "stick." This substitution also stands in obviating relation to the opening point A, since the younger brother has now become a game animal associated with the hunting imperative preparatory to the Usane.

The last transformation, G, is snake for wife. The woman becomes a female self-operating penis, a snake-mate. She is neither the affinal escort of the younger brother, nor a co-refugee, as in D, but a self-contained member without relationship to the younger brother. In other words, the woman *becomes* a phallus because of the way she was attached to the brother (through the sexual imagery of aggression). But the brother becomes a phallus as a consequence of what he originally *had* (as a bodily sexual adjunct) but subsequently *lost*—that is, the drum. Lacan's distinction between being the phallus and having the phallus, intended as an analogue of the distinction between metaphor and metonymy, is also a restatement of the Foi contrast between female self-sufficiency and male contingency (see Weiner 1988; Wagner 1978).

"The Milk Bamboo" provides a female "shell" over the "male" myth of "The Lost Drum." It turns Williams' rump account of male contingency into a story about how the effective limits or social efficacy of such contingency are provided by women's domestic capacity; hence, the consanguineal elision of "The Milk Bamboo" tale is used to "make appear" the leviratic succession problem in "The Lost Drum" ($D \rightarrow A$; $G \rightarrow D$).

IV

In *The Heart of the Pearl Shell*, I presented the myth "The Milk Bamboo" followed by "Fonomo and Kunuware," to demonstrate the manner in which women act to confirm and maintain the contingency of men. Having interposed between these two myths the story of "The Lost Drum," I wish to briefly return to "Fonomo and Kunuware," because now the drum symbolism in the latter myth has been made to stand forth in a somewhat different manner. In "Fonomo and Kunuware," it is a woman who gives a man a drum, and the drum speaks with a woman's voice, rather than an elder brother's.

First, a summary of the myth. A young unmarried man encounters a woman fishing from his father's stream. They engage in fisticuffs and the woman comes out the victor, leaving the young man unconscious. He awakes to find her nose plug, the Foi *saboro*, between his toes, and he realizes that he has been "marked" by this woman and that she is his wife. He sets out in search of her.

He comes upon longhouse after longhouse inhabited only by maidens, where, as in *Cinderella*, he tries to fit the *saboro* in the nose of each woman he finds, each time finding that it does not fit. When they discover the man, the maidens aggressively pursue him in Sadie Hawkins fashion. Each time he escapes. Finally, leaving the region of human habitation entirely, he comes upon a lone house. There he meets the original woman. Again, they have an aggressive, competitive encounter where the woman demonstrates her superior strength and also her formidable hunting prowess. They live there as man and wife.

By way of the Usane Transformation, an Usane ceremony is announced. The man goes hunting and obtains meat, while his wife stays home and makes decorations for him. Before he goes, the woman gives him a drum saying to him, "During the *samoga* dance, when dawn is about to break, this drum will speak to you. You will know what it is saying. At that time you must return home. But if you wait until it has become light, well then, you'll see what will happen." He went to the Usane, and was chosen to lead the dancing. Close to dawn, the men there heard the drum cry out, "Fonomo, go!" Amazed, they urged Fonomo not to listen, and he remained and finished the dancing. The next morning he returned to his house, only to find that the dwelling had disappeared down an enormous sinkhole that had opened up in the ground.

He made a container for himself out of *kabosa* (*Ficus* species) bark, sealed himself in it, and threw himself down the hole. He found himself in a beautiful land and walked until he came upon a dwelling. There he found his wife, who told him, "Did I not say what would happen?" Fonomo then discovered that his wife was living there with her husband, Kunuware. The two men when they encountered one another simultaneously fired arrows at each other, and both perished. Each man turned into a different species of *hinanu* (*Zinjerberaceae* species). The woman wailed a death lament for both of them. Thus, *hinanu* grows crooked and bent when it bears fruit.

There is a play on size here, reminiscent of the play on scale we found in the Marind-anim ritual sequence. The young man has only a "small" *saboro* with which to mark women, piercing their noses transversely instead of their vaginas vertically. The woman in turn gives him a long drum; her marking phallus is more prominent and more male than the young man's. The nose plug sits atop the mouth: it doesn't speak, because it functions to cancel the human voice. By contrast, the drum which is held across the man's groin does speak, for it signals the intrusion of the male principle in discourse. It could thus be said that the woman regains her voice by discarding the *saboro*, and she herself marks her husband with a speaking version of the *saboro*, the drum.

Here we have both Gimi images—that of the mouth marked by the phallus, and the detached phallus as sound-producing hollow tube—combined in one myth. Can we say that Foi men's and women's relation to the part phallus are speaking to each other within a single myth? That the myth itself is mirroring the androgynous compositional qualities of the very items it seeks to account for? And that any appropriation or swallowing of this myth would be an appropriation of the androgynous aspects of the phallus, that is, both its male and female properties simultaneously?

The man seeks a wife and the women seek a husband, but none are successful, because the marking artifact has to mediate their desire. What then does the drum mediate?

Let us return to the Usane Transformation, which, as I have indicated, always signals the juncture between progressive and retrogressive movement when it appears in Foi myth. The sequence outlined from that point on in "Fonomo and Kunuware" is an inside-out version of the milk bamboo/drum theme: In "Fonomo," a woman gives her husband a drum rather than a man giving a drum to his brother; the drum therefore speaks with her voice rather than a man's voice as in the drum stories. And in both stories, the voice of the drum is disobeyed. But whereas in the drum myths, it is the loss of the drum which is a consequence of this, in "Fonomo and Kunuware" *the man loses his wife, a whole woman rather than the drum.* In not obeying its voice, he loses the source of the voice which the drum mediates. Only a man can lose the phallus; a woman, on the other hand, is herself a self-procreating phallus and cannot, like a male, lose the phallus and therefore cannot be marked or represented by it.

As a direct consequence of this, the boy Fonomo must masquerade as a drum in search of his wife (rather than accompanying his wife in search of the drum, as in the previous stories). And what he finds when he gets to her is that all along she had another man, Kunuware. Fonomo and Kunuware become "joined" in reciprocal aggression, through the agency of the drum/*saboro*/woman.

Now we know why the Foi child carries the bamboo tubes from his mother to his father: the child may be the signifier of the father but is the embodiment of the mother. A woman's bamboo tube is filled with food, and it is this transactional moment which is secured through childbirth. A man's tube, however—his drum—is hollow, from which a voice is brought forth: the voice that instaurates the concealing detachments of social life.

6

The Stolen String Bag

So far, I have referred to three kinds of containment. One is bodily, another is scopic or visual, and the third is linguistic or verbal. Now I will attempt to establish the terms by which these containing functions can be compared with each other. And I will also argue that all three are implicated with each other at all times—that is, that we cannot make an argument for the ontological primacy of the bodily over the visual, or of either over the verbal.

In his first seminar of 1953–54, given on the topic of Freud's papers on technique, Lacan (1991a) employs an optical metaphor to explain his notion of the Imaginary. Take a concave spherical mirror, he says. In front of its reflecting surface place a box open at one end, with the open end facing the mirror. The box is placed on a stand so that it is in the center of the half-spherical mirror. On top of the box place an empty vase and inside the box, hidden from the sight of the observer, an inverted bouquet of flowers (see Figure 7).

If one stands above and behind the vase, but always within the orbit of the half sphere's projections, and looks toward the mirror, one will see an imaginary bouquet appearing in the vase.

In its early months, the human subject is just a disarticulate bundle of things—objects, drives, desires. It's not aware of itself as an integrated entity. It first gets a sense of this totality by recognizing its own shape externally, in the visual confirmation of another's unity. "The box represents your own body, the bouquet, instincts and desires, the objects of desire which rove about. And the cauldron [i.e., the mirror], what's that? That could well be the cortex" (Lacan 1991a:80).

We introject the objects, desires, and drives that constitute our experience of the world into the *image* of the body—the vase—that we perceive externally, whose source is *external* to our perceptual apparatus, and which becomes then the bounding container of such objects and drives. Introjection can be seen here in visual terms—and we should remind ourselves of what Gillian Gillison reports for the Gimi: they

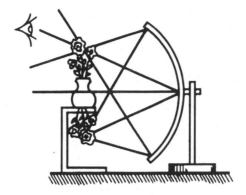

Figure 7. The inverted bouquet. From *The
Seminar of Jacques Lacan, Book I: Freud's Papers
on Technique, 1953–1954*, edited by J. A. Miller,
translated by John Forrester. 1991 (New York:
Norton).

consider seeing as tantamount to possessing. What we see, what we
locate within our scopic field, becomes part of us.

If the processes of conception, gestation, and parturition are seen as
literal manifestations of such processes of introjection and ejection, they
are literal in the sense that they are subject to confirmation by visual
cues. The "ego" is the name we give to this collection of drives and
objects so bounded by the body's image. That is, they are framed and
bounded by our body image and contribute to its internal solidity and
continuity.

What if these objects were already embodied themselves, however?
What if they were already relationally constituted, or constitutive of a
relationship? By what assumed process of introjection did such objects
come to have an inside and an outside? And since they have an inside
and an outside already, in introjecting them we would be everting
them: the outside of the embodied object would become the hidden inside, and what was internal to the object might, through the resulting
cancellation of its external boundary, become revealed.

What if we were to see the bodies of language that we call myths as
the body of such objects? In what sense does such language enframe
and give an external shape to the flowers (both Lacan's bouquet and the
Foi flowers we've already encountered), the child in the womb, our desires which we locate within our selves? Our linguistic apperception
provides the refractory device by which the introjection is accomplished—and we should see language itself as an organ of perception,

ranged alongside and in conjunction with eye, cortex, and body. We thus never introject the naked object. That object has already been fixed by the linguistic signs that have identified it, named it, and traced its history.

I raise these questions because so often the language we use to describe such bounding functions of language makes use of images of woven containers, of threads and warps and woofs creating the outline of a container, yet one that we can see through to its contents in the center, by virtue of the spaces created by the interlocking fibers.

What I want to raise is the question of how we can compare verbal and graphic images—in terms of the *effects* of these images, rather than their formal properties—for it is in terms of the effects of such images that we perceive meaning and recognize its presence. And does not the image, itself lying beyond language, precisely make equivalent what appear to be nonequivalent modes of representation? Is it not also the case that we present our analyses of both verbal and visual images in terms of the same narrative form, and we adduce their commensurability as a result of their ability to be transposed into such a form? What Lacan's theory of the Symbolic and the Imaginary offers us, however, is not a reductive theory—a theory which reduces the verbal and the visual to the textual—but a dialectic, whereby the visual and the verbal fields are made to be iconic of each other, by virtue of the verbal and visual functions of ego formation. In such a case, a different sort of flowers is introjected into the container of our analysis—the "flowers of the mouth," as Mallarmé termed them, the metaphors of our narrative threads, that are as essential to painting and to myth as brush, canvas, and voice, and without which we cannot identify the narrowing down of interpretive space that makes the juxtaposition and comparability of these images possible.

Let us consider, for example, Freud's (1914) famous interpretation of Leonardo da Vinci's painting *The Madonna and St. Anne.* Freud found in the folds of the Madonna's skirt, the outline of a vulture (See Illustration 5). The vulture figured prominently in one of da Vinci's childhood "memories" which endured for him throughout adulthood. The memory took the form of a verbal account in da Vinci's journals—da Vinci wrote that he remembered himself as a baby in the cradle, watching as a vulture descended upon him, opened his mouth, and struck him across the lips with its tail.

Freud called this memory a screen memory (see also 1899:301–22): it acted as a displacement or substitute for a more critical or dramatic memory which for one reason or another was repressed from consciousness. But it is on the idea of a screen, and what lies behind a screen, that I focus. Jane Van Buren, writing of Freud's account of da Vinci's memory, says the following:

> Freud . . . found an example of his notion of a screen memory, which according to his theory is a synchronic structure *woven* out of the condensations and displacements of inner life. The screen memory brings together layers of reality with dream, history with fantasy, desire with limitation, and the diachronic with the synchronic. In this way, we can view the painting and Freud's interpretation of it as mythic structures of the incarnation of madonna and child. (1989:129–30; emphasis added)

What I would like to focus on is this third perceptual container, the function of speech in the constitution of our visual images. For the Foi and others like them the flowers are never seen outside of their container—they travel with it. For the Foi, to whom appeals to an organ such as the mind would be quite misleading, their mirroring "cauldron" is not the cortex itself, as in Lacan's analogy, but an origin myth of flowers, a net bag of signifiers which plants the flowers. Speech is their organ of social perception, and a myth as a speech form is a locus or node of such perception, rather than a representation of it. It contains the flowers, and the various organs into which we see the flowers literally introjected—the bamboo tube or uterus or larvae nest parcel—are iconic of this more encompassing bounding function of verbalized perception.

The two Foi myths I discuss now focus on the string bag, the woven artifact that has become as prominent an icon of Papua New Guinea culture as the pearl shell and kula valuable. The myths focus on each of the two main functions of the string bag in New Guinea life: as a container of infants, an external womb, and as a container for food, an external stomach.

Foi men under certain circumstances also display their pearl shells in small versions of these bags, as most New Guinea men also hid their cult stones in others. And in such cases, what is the bag an external version of? Is this what Marilyn Strathern might have been alluding to in the title of her article "Culture in a Net Bag" (1980)? This phrase effectively captured the critique of a whole way of doing anthropology in Melanesia, an anthropology that kept its attention fixed on objects and neglected to characterize the framing conditions under which such objects can appear at all. It is to this issue that Strathern turns in *The Gender of the Gift*.

What most Melanesianists have conventionally thought important is

what these string bags hold, the pearl shells, food, and children; they
have ignored, however, the phenomenon of being held or hidden by the
bags themselves. But around the same time as Marilyn Strathern was
identifying the social conditions of Melanesian form in the course of her
debate with Annette Weiner, another alternative glossing of this image
received far less attention, the publication of Hylkema's ethnography of
the Nalum entitled *Mannen in het draagnet* (Men in the net bag) (1974).

"Men in the net bag" is how I want to continue talking about object
relations, the way that men seek a bounding frame around themselves
and these objects so as to anticipate and prevent their alienation. It
could be said that once we have decided to focus on objects, then alienation (and reappropriation) are the only interesting things that happen
to them (see Lacan 1977b:203–15). But to consider a relational image
like men in the net bag is to presuppose the possibility of something
other than alienation: the unmediated extension of men through objects
which because of their metonymic constitution can never be merely
partial. It reminds us that what is at issue is not the relationship between person and object so much as the limits to extensibility itself that
the objects afford, and what that extended space consists of. "Men in
the net bag" focuses our attention on the human body that is always
providing such enframing limits, and urges us to consider that signification always runs up against the contours of embodied consciousness,
what I am calling desire. We look inside a net bag full of material "culture" and see a constellation of signs; we look inside a net bag with a
male baby in it and see the image of embodied life in interior Papua
New Guinea.

The word *imago* technically refers to "the final and 'perfect' stage or
form of an insect after its metamorphosis" (*SOED* p. 1023). Freud used
the word to refer to "a mental object, an unconscious prototype based
on the infant's earliest experiences" (Bowie 1991:31; Freud 1912:100).
The Foi, however, are not inclined to see the relationship between these
two meanings as anything but literal. In several Foi myths, both male
and female characters receive gifts of parcels made of the leathery cocoon of the *Opodipthera joiceyi* moth. Inside these parcels the character
finds two tiny pigs no bigger than insects, or two similarly sized dogs.

Foi men normally use this moth nest as wrapping for large pearl
shells when in storage, and perhaps men invoke the incubatory powers
of such nesting material as well as the explicit resemblances between
the imago of the moth and its embodied image, the nested pearl shell
(also, as we discovered in the myth "The Place of the Pearl Shells"
[Weiner 1988], equated with the bush fowl egg within its mounded nest

of twigs). According to Marilyn Strathern, for the Melpa of Mt. Hagen, the pearl shell mounted on a board is like an infant curled in its mother's womb. We see that the fetus is appresented against the limits of its incubating container: an insect's cocoon, a uterus, a net bag, the house and its tools, the nimbus of moving pearl shells that enframes human nurturance and protection. What is shed or discarded in insect reproduction becomes the outline or container of human reproduction.

The image of the Gimi flute, itself a hollow tube, hidden in its string bag (which is a womb), is a figure-ground reversal of the following Foi myth, in which a child turns into an insect and hides in a bamboo tube of water which is swallowed and hence taken into a woman's interior.

THE STOLEN STRING BAG

A boy and his grandmother once lived. The boy would habitually climb a large *tegare* tree and from it shoot birds. He would bring them back to his house and they would *mumu* [cook in an earth oven] them and eat together. The grandmother gave him a large *magini* string bag [the large, long kind used for carrying children and food]. This he would hang on a branch near the ground and climb the tree to shoot birds. One time, as he was in the tree branches, a *ka buru* arrived. She took his string bag and left. He watched as she disappeared toward the downstream direction. Where has she taken my string bag? he wondered. He climbed down the tree, but when he reached the surface he turned into a *kãga* marsupial [a species of ground-dwelling marsupial]. He ascended the tree again and turned into a boy once more. Again he tried to reach the ground but turned into a *kãga* marsupial when he touched the ground. He ascended the tree and stayed there as a boy. He called out to his grandmother, "*aya!* come!" She arrived and he showed her how he turned into a marsupial when he reached the ground and how he turned back into a boy when he reached the top. She told him to ascend the tree once again. He said to her, "*aya*, it is hard for me to stay here. Take me back to the house. Later you can fetch my bow and arrows and the birds I killed." The grandmother cried as she did this. She put the marsupial boy into an empty fireplace and covered him over with earth. She brought his things back and *mumu*ed the birds. She cried as she cared for the marsupial boy in her house.

One time a drizzly rain came. She heard a soft rustling outside the house and looked to see two small boys, flitting swiftly toward her. They asked her, "Old woman, how are you?" She replied, "no, my two children. My grandson has turned into a *kãga* and is here in the house. I am forlorn." The two boys said to her, "old woman, there is a *me'o* banana on the verandah of the house there. Would you give it to us?" She gave them the bananas and some sago also. She picked a large taro and gave it to them. The two divided the food and toward the downstream direction they departed. In the middle of the bush they built a house and gathered firewood. They divided the bananas between them and the elder boy said to the younger, "Stay here and eat these bananas and sago and taro. Stay here yourself and eat these things." Then he left alone, going downstream. He came upon a large path and arrived at a longhouse. There were bamboo tubes of water lining the sleeping areas inside the house. He looked inside all of them and found one with dirt and debris floating in it. He turned into a tiny fruit fly and went inside the water bamboo. Presently, he heard the sound of loud voices laughing as many women returned to the house. It was a village of maidens only. They each took their bamboos and drank water. The woman whose fireplace was at the corner took her bamboo with the fruit fly in it and drank, thinking that the fly was only a bit of leaf debris. The women continued to live there. Presently the woman who had swallowed the fly became pregnant [the narrator used the Foi colloquialism, *agikobo aso ho'obo'o*, "a stolen marsupial," to refer to her condition]. Her sisters said to her, "What has happened to you?" She replied, "Sisters, have you seen me go somewhere else? Now, we are together all of the time. I have made sago, fetched firewood, gone to the gardens with all of you all the time. I have seen no man." They lived there, and the woman became very pregnant. The other women built a birth house for her. She went inside and soon she took the child "in her hip" [i.e., she was ready to give birth]. She bore a male baby. All the women were very happy. The other women gave her choice pieces of meat while she nursed her child and did all the work for her. The boy grew up. When he was walking around the house yard, one day he said to his mother, "make me a small bow." She gave it to him and he shot grasshoppers with it. Another time the women wanted to go to the gardens. The boy said to his mother, "Mother, I want to eat sweet potato." She gave it to him but he said, "No, I do not wish to eat this, I want to eat sugarcane." She gave him sugarcane and he said, "No, not this; I want to eat pig heart." This too she gave. "No, I want to eat cassowary heart." This too she gave him, and all other kinds of food, but he refused them all. The boy became angry and started striking his mother and biting the hands of the other women

in rage. Finally, in exasperation, the woman said, "Son I do not
know what you want." The boy said, "No, my *aya's magini bilum*
[string or net bag] which is underneath her cloak there, take it and
give it to me." The woman's mother, who had the *bilum* under her
cloak, said, "Daughter, I am not carrying a *bilum*." But the boy said,
"No, you are carrying it; give it to me." The boy's mother said,
"Son, I am tired of this." The boy kept crying, and finally the old
woman took the *bilum* and gave it to him. She said to him, "Little
boy, don't let it get wet, take care of it." He took the *bilum* and saw
that it was the one he wanted. Then he said to his mother, "Mother,
put a strip of cassowary meat inside and some sago, two yams also,
put them inside." This she did. Another time, they went to the
garden to pull weeds, and the boy shot grasshoppers. While he did
so, he climbed over the garden fence. He kept pretending to shoot
grasshoppers and meanwhile hid underneath a large pile of garden
debris, and taking the *bilum* he ran away back upstream. He came
up to his brother's house and saw that he had but two bananas left.
He took the cassowary meat and other food from the *bilum* and
shared it with his brother. The next morning they went to the
grandmother's house. She was crying still when they arrived. The
boys arrived and the elder brother took the marsupial boy's bow
and tightened its string. He removed his arrows which were stored
in the rafters. He said to the woman, "Old woman, you must call
out. Take your sago-pounding stick and call out." The two boys
decorated themselves beautifully. Then the two boys cried out,
"men! men! men!" and the woman cried out. The elder boy hung
the *magini bilum* from the fireplace. The marsupial took the *bilum*,
and turned back into a boy. He put his decorations on and took his
weapons and assumed a martial pose, thinking that they were
crying the warning of an attack. He ran from one end of the house
to another and then saw the two boys sitting on the verandah. He
thought he was still a *kāga* marsupial but he saw that he had turned
back into a boy. He kissed the two boys and rubbed noses with
them and so did the old woman. She wanted to give the two boys a
reward for what they had done. But they said, "No, just give us two
small cowrie shells each." She did so and she and her grandson sat
there. From the upstream direction they heard a chirping sound
and they jumped up and looked around the side of the house. There
where the floor beams protruded from the end of the house sat two
tarebo birds [New Guinea bare-eyed crow]. They had put the white
cowries over their eyes and became *tarebo* birds. "What have you

two boys done?" the grandmother cried. The two birds jumped up and down and then left. The grandmother and her grandson continued to live there. That's all.

This story begins with the problematic situation of a young orphaned boy in the care of an elderly grandmother. The grandmother is not physically reproductive but is in a maternal relation to the boy. Hence, she compensates by giving the boy her external uterus, the string bag, which is a token of the string bag that a woman carries a child in, and also resembles the pouch in which a marsupial carries its young (*A*: string bag for mother). One day, the boy climbs a tree (like a marsupial) but leaves his "pouch" on the ground, and another woman of dubious reproductive potential, the *ka buru*, comes along and steals it. As long as the boy remains in the tree, like a marsupial, he is able to retain human form, for his position compensates for the strange fact that as a human boy he was a marsupial in relation to the old woman's pouch. Another way of putting this is from the opposite perspective: the string bag, the external womb, compensates the grandmother for not having a functioning *internal* uterus but has the effect of turning the boy into a marsupial. When he descends, as he must eventually since he is not a real marsupial, he turns into a marsupial, for his *human* pouch, the artifact that affirmed his humanness, is now gone (*B*: marsupial for child). The old woman now has a mere animal to care for. But at that moment, two boys, who are really transformed versions of other tree dwellers, birds, come to her aid and elicit further maternal behavior by asking for food (*C*: bird-brothers for marsupial child). One of the bird-brothers leaves his brother behind in a safe place and, going in search of the missing string bag, comes upon the longhouse of the unmarried young women. It is revealed that it is one of these women who stole the string bag. Despite the insufficiency of these women's maternal capabilities, the bird-boy gains the confidence of the young woman only through the same kind of appeal to her "motherhood" that initially impelled him to take pity on the old woman. So he turns into an insect and in this form is swallowed by the woman and becomes her fetus (*D*: insect-fetus/boy). This image is a figure-ground reversal of the opening substitution: the young woman's internal "immaculate" pregnancy matches the old woman's external pregnancy by way of the string bag.

The bird-boy becomes the woman's child, and his presence makes the women jealous of one another, for what he elicits from them is their desire for a man. This desire on the part of the young women is opposite to that of the old woman's desire for her boy. That is, motherhood is elicited by the desire of the other (in this case, the boy).[1]

The boy asks his new "mother" for a string bag and will accept only the one which she stole. Taking it is tantamount to accepting her motherhood (*E:* "Amazon" mother for old [grand]mother). The string bag is strictly speaking a *total relational organ* (cf. Lacan 1991b:95); it relates a person to another and at the same time provides the shape—the embodied image—of that relationship. As soon as he receives it, he runs away, rejoins his brother, and returns the pouch back to the old woman (*F:* string bag for "Amazon" mother). His human pouch restored, the old woman's son is now free to resume his human form (*G:* boy for string bag), and this allows the brothers to turn back into birds.

The partiality and incompleteness of all the characters are outlined most vividly in this myth—and this is what makes the string bag both an item of relationship and an image of it at one and the same time. Neither the old woman nor the "Amazons" are true mothers, for one needs an external pouch and the other needs an insect: that is, the myth counterinvents a world of female contingency which is revealed by the absence of men. We are forced to conclude that the much-commented-upon self-sufficiency of New Guinea women is elicited only in the presence of men—a feminine perspective on the more common ethnographic observation that men are contingent only because women are around.

The boys are not real boys either, for one needs a pouch and the other two have to appeal deceptively to the maternal desires of women to maintain their human form. We can see a parallel between the man who loses control of the mediating drum and the boy in the "The Stolen String Bag" who loses the mediating human pouch. What maintains their human form in each case is their bodies' sexual extension through a partial object, a phallus or its everse, the framing external uterus (note that the old woman's male-like status, her *contingency*, that is, her nonreproductive state, makes problematic the possession and transfer of her string bag, contingency being the sine qua non for the partiality of metonymic objects). When this extension is lost they become nonhuman caricatures of those part objects, in other words, part humans.

For Lacan, the eye, the subject, moves around, but the container, the body image stays fixed. For the Foi, the container moves around—it can be stolen, reappropriated—and whoever owns it controls the fate and shape of those who desire it: boy, marsupial, bird, insect.

Freud (1925:237) originally phrased the imagery of introjection and projection, however, in consumptive terms. Of what gives pleasure, we say that we should like to take this thing inside us, that is, consume it, and of what we dislike, we say that we should like to spit it out, eject it.

Now the other thing that a string bag is used for in New Guinea is to carry food. Although the food most commonly carried, especially in the large *magini* bags referred to in the story, is garden food, what excites the imagination of the Foi is the thought of such bags crammed with cooked pork, the bounty claimed after having brought pearl shells to a pig feast. Here, rather than a uterus, the string bag might be thought of as an external stomach, the organ which in so many ways is contrapuntal to the uterus, particularly in their diametric relationship to their respective accessing orifices (cf. Tuzin 1978).

So the image of an animal's body parts in a string bag would have to stand in an inverse relation to that of the child in the bag. The following myth provides some of the anchoring points that make such a relationship plausible among the Foi. This myth has been found widely in interior Papua New Guinea, and there exist published versions for the Kewa, Daribi, and Enga (LeRoy 1985:207–9; Wagner 1978; Meggitt 1976).

THE BOY AND THE FLYING FOXES

A small boy once lived with his grandmother in a place where there were no other people. One time they went to set crayfish traps in the river and the boy saw pig viscera floating in the water. Someone is eating pork and throwing the viscera in the water, he thought. He gathered them up and he and his grandmother cooked and ate them. They found floating viscera another time and again ate them. This continued for some time. The boy was curious as to who was doing this, so one day he and his grandmother paddled their canoe upstream. They came upon a canoe harbor and the boy alone disembarked. He hid and waited. Presently, a large, light-skinned man came carrying viscera. He threw it into the river saying, "Whoever lives downstream, whatever women and children live there, so that they can eat this, let the water carry it downstream." Oh, so this is how these viscera arrived, the boy thought. He took the viscera again and he and his grandmother ate once more. The next time, he and his grandmother again paddled upstream and the old woman left him there. He went ashore and came to where the light-skinned man had prepared his earth oven. He hid and waited. The light-skinned man arrived carrying leaves to line the oven. He left and returned with greens to eat, and then again left to fetch bamboo tubes of sago. There was a large red pig there. He butchered the pig and removed the viscera and proceeded to throw them in the water once more intoning, "Whatever men and women live downstream, let them eat this." He waited until everything was cooked. He removed the meat from the oven and cut it up. Then he removed his head and put the food directly into his throat. At this time, the boy came out from his hiding place and filled up his string bag with pork. The headless man could not see, he was feeling around for the pork with his hands. The boy took the pork back to where his grandmother was waiting. They returned home and ate the pork. They did this time after time, stealing pork from the light-skinned man when his head was off. The man discovered that someone was taking his pork. One time when he had removed his head, he reached out suddenly and grabbed the boy's wrist while he was taking pork. He put his head back on and said, "So it is you who have been stealing my pork." He then took cassowary thigh bone spikes and stapled the boy's legs and hands together and then put the boy in a string bag. He covered that string bag with nine more bags. Then he took the imprisoned boy to a mountain where a river cut through and made a waterfall. There was a long *gawayu* palm growing near the edge of the waterfall and far beneath it were large stones. From the palm fronds the man hung the boy in the string bags and departed. The outer bag broke away and dropped off, and then the ninth, and then the eighth . . . and soon there were only two other bags besides the one he was in. He saw that he would soon be dashed on the rocks below. At this time he heard the cries of many hornbills approaching. He called out to them, "Hornbills, come and save me!" but they replied, "No, you only mean to eat us," and they turned around and flew away. He saw *gega'o* birds coming and the same thing happened. All the other kinds of birds came by and refused to take him, saying that the boy only intended to eat them. The boy despaired of being rescued, when he heard the high-pitched cry "*gai, gai, gai!*" and looked and saw flying foxes coming. "Come and save me!" he called out, but they replied, "No, our intestines, our skulls, our legs, these you want to eat," and they flew off toward the west. They had all but disappeared when they suddenly returned and lifted the remaining string bags and carried the boy off. They carried him back to the grandmother's house and left him on the roof. The grandmother heard the noise and went outside and saw the string bags, and when she took them down she discovered her grandson in them. He explained to her what had happened. He was nearly dead from hunger and had forgotten how to eat. The grandmother took a cassowary bone spike and pried his mouth open and filled it with food. The boy revived. He asked the flying foxes, "What kinds of things do you eat?" and they replied, "Cordyline leaves, *kosa'a* tree leaves, ripe bananas, *hāya* fruit [*Ficus copiosa*] . . ." and they went on to list all the leaves and fruit they ate.

The boy became a young man and built a longhouse with women's houses along the sides. He cared for many pigs. He planted *hāya* trees, *kosa'a* trees, and all the kinds of fruit and leaves that flying foxes ate. When he finished, he readied much firewood. He then told his grandmother to make a skein of *hagenamo* (*Gnetum gnemon*) rope. She made a large skein of it and the young man took it and hung it from the rafter of the house. Then he announced his Dawa pig feast. He watched carefully as each man arrived and noted that the light-skinned man who had imprisoned him also arrived. He distributed his pork and gave tobacco and food for all the visitors. He made two latrines. One he constructed in the normal manner but the other he made especially for the light-skinned man with soft wood that broke easily. Underneath the latrine he dug a large hole and he planted sharpened sticks in the bottom of it. He then covered the pit over and made it look like a normal latrine. The men ate pork, danced, and began to leave. The light-skinned man visited the latrine the young man had prepared for him. When he climbed onto the post to squat, the soft wood broke and he fell into the pit, impaling himself, and so he died. The other men asked, what is the meaning of this, and the young man explained what the light-skinned man had done and how he had finally paid him back. The flying foxes also came but they didn't come to eat pork. They young man thought, what shall I give them to repay them? He offered them the pearl shells and cowrie shells he had received from his pig feast, but they replied, we never eat these things. Now at this time, flying foxes had no internal viscera, they were just empty inside. But they now ate the *hagenamo* rope that the grandmother had prepared and they finally had intestines. Then they ate the cordyline and *kosa'a* leaves and all the other things the young man had planted especially for them. They didn't eat pork. Then they flew away and all the men who had come to eat pork also departed. The young man and his grandmother lived there. That is all.

The obviating sequence of this myth is closely parallel to that which Roy Wagner (1978:133) provides for the nearly identical Daribi story entitled "The Headless Man." As is the case with the Daribi story, this tale focuses on the effect of different parts of the pig on human com-

munication, weaving this theme around that of alimentary insufficiency—the idea being that when digestion is incomplete or insufficient, so is exchange! The tale begins with a boy and his grandmother
who inexplicably find pig viscera floating in the river near their home
(*A:* viscera for normal communication; viscera for normal pork presta-
tion). They travel upstream and the boy discovers the source of this
meat: a man who eats without a mouth (that is, by removing his head)
is in the habit of eating pork and discarding the viscera for those who
live downstream of him (*B:* headless man for viscera). The boy thereupon steals the more desirable pork (*C:* stolen pork for viscera) and
returns to do so several times until the headless man manages to trap
him, whereupon he imprisons the boy in a mass of string bags and sus-
pends him from a tree to face certain death (*D:* man's string bag for
pork; man's string bag for boy's string bag). In *A,* the viscera floated
down the water, while in *D,* the mass of viscera-like string bags remain
motionless over the moving water. The string bags which are like viscera drop into the water one by one, and the boy is about to become a
floating gift of viscera himself.

After appealing unsuccessfully to various avian creatures for help,
the boy is at last rescued by flying foxes, "whose intestines are just like
goai," say the Foi. *Goai* is the string made from the underbark of the
Gnetum gnemon tree (Foi: *hagenamo*) from which string bags are woven.
Only at this stage, the flying foxes are empty inside, having no intestines. Hence, *E:* flying fox for headless man, or viscera-less creature for
headless man, *E* → *B.*

Now grown into an adult, the young man holds a pig kill to trap the
headless man; he lures the headless man to death by playing on *his*
desire for exchange and sociability. He kills the man through his pos-
terior orifice (*F,* hence *F* → *C:* lethal defecation for lethal consumption,
obviating *C* by making pork as lethal to the headless man as it was for
the boy). The flying foxes return and refuse all gifts, including pork,
"which they never eat," and instead swallow the *goai* which gives them
internal viscera (*G:* viscera for string bag). This substitution is the inverse of *D* ("boy 'swallowed' by string bag" for external string bag) and
hence the "not-not" of *A* (string bag for viscera).

Because of the developing string bag–viscera theme, the obviation
sequence of the Foi story has to begin with the appearance of the viscera
in the river, rather than the discovery of the headless man, as does the
Daribi story, in which the same theme is absent.

The two Foi myths do not touch; they separate the functions of the
string bag as stomach and as womb. Would it then strike us as ironic to
see this demonstration that Foi myth worked as a result of the *repression*

or foreclosure of synonymy as well as the revelation of such tropic expansion? We might also remind ourselves that in the Foi marriage payment sequence which I described in *The Heart of the Pearl Shell*, the named payments of the *arera bari* (cowrie given in exchange for women's string bags, sago washing baskets, and other domestic items, usually of apparel) and the *ka aso* (the cooked meat portion given by the groom's to the bride's relatives) also "do not touch"—the domestic and sexual/consumptive images of the marriage transaction are kept distinct.

Let me then contrast this situation, this encapsulation of imagery, with something that first appears to be very nearly its opposite in Western terms.

Salvador Dali painted his second version of *The Madonna of Port Lligat* in 1950 (see Illustration 6). The painting draws one's attention immediately to the series of spaces nesting within each other in the center of the painting. The child Jesus has suspended within the enframed empty space of his body the heel of the Eucharist bread; the same bread held within a basket floats just to his left, almost pointed to by the child's left hand, as if drawing attention to the basket which holds the body of Christ as his body itself holds the bread which is its external, divisible, and consumable form. But this containing of the bread within the body and vice versa is itself nested within the empty space of the Madonna herself, in the guise of Gala, Dali's wife (who was the subject of many of Dali's paintings). We are not looking at visceral spaces within the body created by the pushing of tissues against each other, or by the growing fetus within its mother's virgin womb creating its physical space and dimensionality as it causes that womb to expand; here, space is a void that is not filled but only superimposed by form. What we are allowed to see once more is the double container, the eucharistic body of Christ within the child, and child within the Madonna. The superimposition of these spaces upon each other makes food, stomach, and womb collapse into each other, for the Eucharist bread comes out at once from both the body of Christ and the womb of the Madonna—and we get a confirmation of what we learned was the case in Marind-anim: that consumption cancels sexuality rather than merely disguises it.

It is this superimposition which I feel is brought out in the Foi myth of the flying foxes. For it is not just an internal organ that the young boy gives the flying foxes, but an organ which is itself the body, that is, the framing womb, of the human form, and which as a string bag (also as container of food) is the external body of women. Only it appears differently, depending upon whether it is inside or outside the body. Inside, it is the uterus; outside it is the string bag (the little boy in the

Illustration 1.   Wiru man: "Home of Value." Drawn by Kaiyape Wilson. Courtesy of
Jeffrey Clark.

Illustration 2. *The Ambassadors,* by Hans Holbein. Photo courtesy of National Gallery, London.

Illustration 3.   A Marind head-hunting display. Photo courtesy of Photodepartment Koninklijk Instituut voor de Tropen, The Netherlands. All rights: Koninklijk Instituut voor de Tropen.

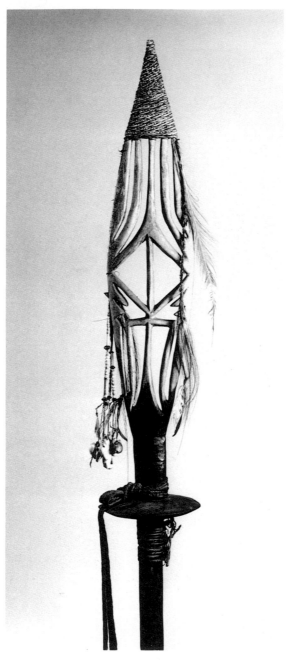

Illustration 4.   Hayam club of the Marind-anim. Photo
courtesy of the Rijksmuseum voor Volkenkunde, The Netherlands. Copyright © Rijksmuseum voor Volkenkunde.

142

Illustration 5.   *The Madonna and St. Anne,* by Leonardo da Vinci. © The Louvre, Paris.

Illustration 6. *The Madonna of Port Lligat,* by Salvador Dali. The second verson, 1950, Minami, Tokyo. Copyright © 1995 Demart Pro Arte / Artist Rights Society (ARS), New York and © photo Descharnes & Descharnes.

Illustration 7. A New Guinea drum-man, courtesy of The Field Museum Chicago (negative number A102554, catalogue number 142777).

Illustration 8. Bull-roarer from the Papuan Gulf (photo by author; specimen courtesy of the South Australian Museum).

Illustration 9.   Foi woman's string bag (*gō magini*), with pandanus leaf child's mat inside (photo by author).

string bag myth affirmed his old grandmother's maternity by carrying her uterus around with him). Inside, the Christ is the infant; outside, he is a piece of Eucharist bread in the breadbasket. Inside, the Foi boy is a boy or *imago,* insect; outside, he is a marsupial, a meat item. Swallowing is revealed and affirmed as the essential fertilizing act in both images (the little boy tricks the young woman into an immaculate conception by assuming the form of a homuncular insect and being swallowed, just as the consumption of Christ's flesh through the Eucharist is the mortal version of the Madonna's own internal conception). The young woman in the string bag myth swallows the insect in the bamboo tube, thinking it is just a bit of leaf debris; leaves or insects, both make their nests, as we saw was the case in the Foi maiden's tree-base spell (Chap. 3, above). "Covered by flies, I went on painting [my Christ] better than ever," Dali recounts.

What is miraculous for Western Catholicism is what is self-evident for the Foi, for under the terms of Foi procreative theory, conception for *all* women is autogenesis. Foi men do not *fertilize* women, they merely provide a shell or bowl within which female blood can coagulate to form the body of the fetus, to which the shell will eventually contribute the bone and other hard white parts. The flying fox, with its detachable string bag stomach/womb, is a "female" animal for the Foi, just as the vulture is the female animal in the Egyptian mythology which da Vinci and Freud were absorbed by. The vulture enveloped da Vinci's desire with its female phallicism, just as the flying foxes did for the boy. And perhaps this enveloping function of birds is also manifested in both the Foi and the Western "birds of enunciation": the *marua* bird which wraps female domesticity with male hunting, and the dove of annunciation, which made of a mortal woman a vessel for the son of God.

As if to underline the central image of growth within the framing confines of form, the form-enhancing properties of shell ontogenesis, the painting displays shell and egg images at top and bottom. Above the head of the Madonna, an egg hangs by a thread from the half seashell. This image was used by Piero della Francesca in his fifteenth-century painting *Madonna and Child, 1470–75,* which Dali saw shortly before painting *The Madonna of Port Lligat.* Below the Madonna's feet, in the central section of the sideboy at the bottom of the painting, is a fragmented, schematized version of a nested egg, or an egg within an external shell, a key perhaps to the double containment of Madonna and child. A slightly opened bivalve shell hangs suspended below it. In the distance beyond the Madonna stretches an expanse of the Bay of Port Lligat, and arranged in a circle with their backs more or less toward the center are five feminine angels, the nearest of which, like the Madonna herself, also bears the face of Gala Dali. The angels on the left-hand side have their backs toward the viewer and they look like cuttlefish. We see the immaculately pregnant Madonna framed by the shells of Aphrodite who was also immaculately pregnant with her father's genitals when she arose from the sea.

But what is that little rhinoceros doing there in the left-hand compartment of the sideboy? Dali wrote, "All curved surfaces of the human body have the same geometric point in common: the one found in this cone with the rounded tip curved towards heaven or towards the earth, and with the angelic inspiration of destruction in absolute perfection— the rhinoceros horn!" (1990:47). As if Holbein had painted a Have-a-Nice-Day face on his death's head! As if some waggish Dutch colonial had put a lit cigarette between the rictus jaws of a Marind-anim victim's skull!

Dali wrote in his diary that he once thought of painting Christ's body as composed totally of a mosaic of rhinoceros horns. If so, it would look very much like the Foi heart of the pearl shell which was given its contours by the pearl shell fragments flying around it, circling and orbiting it, outlining it like iron particles in a magnetic field, as the flowers that Foi men plant around their houses give it its shape, make of the house a uterine place of fertilization; flowers which in the origin myth were given by men who had been resurrected from the dead by the gift of flesh and food by the protagonist.

What the Foi do through their marriage spell is to make a mirror with which the flowers can be projected into the woman's internal vase, to see the flowers of the uterus as a function of the "flowers of the mouth."

There is one more image that belongs to this series of Madonnas. The poster for the film *The Silence of the Lambs* depicts a woman's face. Superimposed over her mouth, the organ of speech, is the death's-head moth, the moth which, upon emerging from its woven cocoon bag, first displays the skull of mortality on its back, the version of the skull whose anamorphosis is its reproductive genesis. On closer inspection, the segments of the skull are seen to be composed of the contorted, semaphoric figures of three nude, dead women.

The male serial killer who is the subject of the film's story wishes to wear the skins of women so that he can be reborn as one himself. He is an everted form of the Gimi woman who is born with her dead father's penis inside her womb. For the killer is a phallus himself who seeks to make his own penis disappear by encasing himself in a woman's skin. Both reproduce through an act of killing, for as Gillison reports, the husband must "kill" the father of the bride before he can impregnate her himself.

What would the Marind-anim make of this serial killer? Would they see the guise that Yawi takes in the Western world? Would they be amazed that one of their most passionate images of rebirth is one of our most grisly depictions of horror? Would they be revolted that we saw this in erotic rather than reproductive terms? And would they conclude that we were to be pitied because we saw only the death in this image and refused the rebirth to men?

7

The Origin of Petroleum
at Lake Kutubu

We play a recording role by assuming the function, fundamental in any symbolic exchange, of gathering what *do kamo*, man in his authenticity, calls *la parole qui dure* [the lasting Word].

—Jacques Lacan

In 1989 I was in southeast Irian Jaya briefly, and while in Merauke, the regency capital, I visited several craft shops that sold artifacts—mostly Asmat-style carvings of the male body in its sexual potency, many depicting anal homosexual intercourse, some even suggesting self-intercourse in that manner, as in two men depicted head to toe or back to back. Even to my inexpert eye, it was clear that these artifacts were produced solely for tourist consumption, and after having visited Irianese villages I was doubtful that there was any form of Asmat religion within which the artifacts played a role. As crude as some of the carving was, the wood was nevertheless of a rich black color, with a satisfying smoothness and sheen, quite ebony-like in its look. I asked the shopkeeper about the kind of wood used by the local carvers and the process by which it was prepared, and he replied that the Asmat artists used old crankcase oil to achieve that beautiful shiny luster. What poetry in those new artifacts! How effectively has the procreative, generative substance of Western society coated the bodies and tools of pagan peoples, erasing the old blood, sweat, and semen that they hitherto embodied, leaving the oily trace of the West's most artificial organic substance, the most fragile blood of our machines.

That greasy patina of subterranean (hidden) regenerate organic matter, that black fecal fertile fuel, so perfect a mix of organic decay and machine vitality, how well it mixes in the political economy of fluids of other societies. Our anthropological view of such societies, particularly those in Melanesia, is that they are oriented around a concern with the production and control of various fertile body substances such as blood, semen, and breast milk, and if we were entitled to speak of a Gresham's law of corporeal liquids, we might think that petroleum would blanket and drive out all those other more organically nervous and contingent body fluids. But whereas the Asmat body and their embodied religious art may well have been covered over by the unctuous missionaries and leaky machines of the Christian economy, the Foi people, located in Pimaga Subdistrict, Southern Highlands Province, in neighboring Papua New Guinea, have proved to be a bit more immiscible—at least so far. They have met oil with oil, as I shall explain shortly.

When we talk about Papua New Guinean societies we characterize them in just these terms of variably dissolvable, adherent, generative fluids, and we let these mixing metaphors stand duty for our hidden (subterranean) interpretive flow of words. We gauge the rightness of our translation, its ultimate *therapeutic value,* by the degree to which our terms encapsulate the essence of these flows. Because these words embody our own most cherished commitments to rationality, order, and intellectual stimulation, we see the substances themselves as a suffusion of the savage mind,[1] instead of an internalized social movement. And if the substances are variably sticky and soluble, do we pay any attention to whether the words themselves have variable qualities of adhesion, smoothness, miscibility? Referring to André Green's book *L'Affect,* Gilles Deleuze and Félix Guattari recount the author's characterization of a successful session of psychoanalysis. It is typified neither by what Green calls "Type I," where the patient's discourse is "viscous, weighty," sodden, bogged down by interminable detail, punctuated by leaden silences, where no break in the ooze allows entry; nor by "Type II," where, conversely, a hysterical torrent of words and images gushes forth, in a liquid rushing stream, where nothing can be made to "stick to" the unconscious.

> Only the third type remains, whose characteristics define a *good* analysis. The patient "speaks in order to constitute the process of a chain of signifiers. The meaning is not attached to the signified to which each of the enunciated signifiers refers, but is constituted by process, suture, the concatenation of bound elements . . . Every interpretation furnished by [the patient] can offer itself as an already-signified awaiting its meaning. For this reason interpretation is always retrospective, as the perceived meaning . . . (Deleuze and Guattari 1983:66)

Whether we phrase it in this way or not, as anthropologists listening to myth we are in the same position as the analyst before the reclining patient. We are faced not with a laborious search for one hidden, true meaning of a particular instance of symbolism, but with a sorting out of the burgeoning possibilities of alternative interpretations that the enchained, embedded symbolism of a myth creates. The charter theory of myth seems to be a variety of "Type I" analysis; in its tendency to reify a myth into a text, to turn it into a recipe for social protocol or principle, to see it in some sense as an enabling *rule* for social interaction, it slows down, makes more viscous and inert the fluid properties of mythic projection. Nor should we go completely in the opposite direction, that of structural analysis, in which a torrent of unchained signifiers gushes forth from every myth, where an image's negation means the same thing as its affirmation. Both of these approaches stress the codified properties of myth as (recorded) text over its dynamic and contextual properties as interpretive response, and choose to ignore the fact that as interpretation, myths emerge out of people's interest in the world. As Wagner suggests in *Lethal Speech*, "Myths are constructed (told, retold, analyzed) by people who are in certain situations, interested in certain situations, reflective about things and situations" (1978:257). In other words, myth does its best work when, recursively, it acts to retrospectively examine and rephrase the situation and terms of its own creation.

Fluid facts, the social facts about body fluids, and the mythical fluidity of factual embodiment come together in the New Guinea world felicitously in their own origin myths. As Strathern, Wagner, myself, and others[2] have elaborated, the essence of many interior New Guinea social systems is the way certain objects and substances both embody and represent central aspects of vital human corporeality. Among the Foi, for example, bridewealth consisting of shell ornaments, live pigs, and the cooked flesh of game animals is given by male relatives of a prospective groom to male relatives of the bride. This attests to the interchangeability of human and animal corporeality, and the raising, nurturing and transaction in such animals, primarily domestic pigs, are intimately associated with the making and nurturing of humans.

In practical terms, however, men first acquire and raise pigs and hunt game, and then obtain shells by trading animal flesh for them. Human marriage and reproduction are thus contingent on the acquisition and nurture of animal reproductivity. These animals and wealth objects are constantly transferred from one person to another, and a lien on such tokens is a lien on a comprehensive range of bodily human productive and reproductive values. One's body, thus, is always extended, apportioned, and displaced in partible form to others, by virtue of its commensurability with wealth items, and others acquire an influence over one's corporeal and reproductive destiny as a result of the protocols surrounding the management of meat and other wealth objects. The model of control and dispersal of such objects, in simple terms, is of sexual reproduction expanded into a model for communal formation and inscription.

It is important for us to understand that the actors in this kind of society completely personify this process, since it is the controlling model for their most centrally important socially reproductive practices. But the local myths that detail the origin of these items exert a relativizing effect on such personification: they make of a self-evident moral situation a "natural" and cosmologically meaningful one as well.

In *The Heart of the Pearl Shell*, I examined a myth concerning the most important Foi wealth item, the crescent pearl shell, introduced to them in large numbers since the 1930s. Although the Foi know that pearl shells originate in coastal areas of Papua New Guinea and are traded to peoples of the interior like themselves, the myth which I titled "The Place of the Pearl Shells" posits an originally local, hidden source of these shells and identifies them as the eggs of a bush fowl who turns into a man. A normal man accidentally discovers the bush fowl man and his large stock of eggs/pearl shells and is promised a continuous supply of them providing he keeps secret their existence. When the man nevertheless publicly reveals the name of the bush fowl man, a landslide carries the shells down into the river and they are carried all the way to the sea, their present-day location. The myth, in other words, distills the essence of one of the problems with this kind of world where social efficacy is mediated by external valuables: insofar as these shells have a source, the source itself is nowhere, for it is coextensive with the total range of social obligations that are mediated by shells and which make their social flow possible and efficacious. The system works only if men do not secretly hoard their shells; if they did, no one would know their source at all.

The myth is not intended as a "correction" of real life, nor as some competing version of it, to be mediated or canceled by the discovery of inversion or opposition. One might be tempted to say that since myth telling is not as important as exchanging real wealth items for real brides, then the illocutionary effects of myth are of an inferior kind to those of the protocols of bridewealth negotiation and transfer. But the myth reveals—and in revealing, overturns—the background against which the related bridewealth and other exchange practices emerge: that is, a set of tacit comparisons between birds, which give birth to their own pearl shells, and humans, which never "hatch" theirs but instead pass them around and in so doing make human reproduction possible (see Wagner 1978; Weiner 1988).

But this story about human reproduction and its objectified tokens also mirrors a story about the very relation of the myth to the phenomenon it comments upon, and it projects the same dilemma onto this mirror image, a dilemma that Jacques Derrida (1981) sums up in the notion of the word as *pharmakon:* both poison and cure, both bush fowl and egg, at one and the same time. We pass around our words and myths and let them get as dirty as dirty can be, as dirty as money, dirty with all the accumulated greasy residue of interpretation and transmission error, secure in the knowledge that the real world is safely nested and as naked and as pure as an egg. In fact, if we return to our Foi image of the bush fowl man, we seem to find exactly the mechanism by which our valuable words are magically created: in the case of the Melanesian bush fowl, its eggs are encased within a huge mound of dead twigs and other plant debris from the forest floor, whose decomposition releases the heat by which the eggs are incubated, just as our words get nourished by the decomposition of dead, accumulated metaphor. The Foi myth, however, because it supervenes a world of human productive values, tells us what we need to know about this process: that it is the passing around of the word/egg/shell/coin that is its reproductive moment (for Foi men), that is, its *use,* and not only its brooding detached encapsulation (its differential Saussurian *value*), which is simultaneously the result and the precondition of its circulation.

The pearl shell, its myth, and our gloss on both close off—at least temporarily—the possibility of further miscibility, of further Type II enchaining. The whole point of the myth is that it allows a final answer (again only temporarily), a negotiating closure of some problem posed by the open-endedness and contingency of everyday life and the conventions by which people make their way through it. The temporary closure achieved in the analysis of the pearl shell myth focuses on the implications of Foi men's sustained comparison between human and ovarian reproduction and the role that the double image of egg/pearl shell plays in effecting this comparison.

But there always exists the possibility of reopening this temporary closure; there are many other Foi myths which achieve many other effects, other temporary answers, and only if we were interested solely in typologizing this kind of discourse would we think there was a fixed recipe for achieving the displacements the Foi make in this way. You might say that the interpretation we put on a myth only defers the problem; all that results is another image which we then have to examine anew, which is why I appeal to the temporariness of the whole process. The pearl shell myth argues for a certain reading of Foi exchange. But the pearl shell itself is only one, albeit the most common, item of Foi social mediation. In fact, it achieved preeminence only since the middle of this century, following the introduction to the Highlands of large quantities of shells by Australian colonial administrators.[3] It is itself still a new currency and like all new currencies it is still "bad" in

Gresham's sense, still rather too volatile and disreputable for Foi liking. The Foi experienced a great inflation of their bridewealth payments and devaluation of their other shell items as a result of this mass influx of high quality pearl shell. The pearl shell myth naturalizes this historical origin of the shell by positing a local origin for it that has no time referent at all, by transforming an effect of external foreign culture into an autochthonous moral and cosmological structure. It is tempting to see this process as a variety of *bricolage,* of the appropriation of an exogenous item of significance and its embodiment within a local moral landscape. But although it is true that "the elements which the 'bricoleur' collects and uses are 'pre-constrained' . . . by the fact that they are drawn from the language where they already possess a sense which sets a limit on their freedom of manoeuvre" (Lévi-Strauss 1966:19), what is more noteworthy is precisely the way the mythical naturalization of the pearl shell obliterates its contingent and completely detached origin and turns it into the embodied, localized metonymic bodily extension it is for the Foi.

What then *is* the original, indigenous Foi wealth item, and what shape does its mythological self-objectification take? The Foi are known throughout the Southern Highlands and Western Highlands Provinces as the manufacturers of what Highlanders call in New Guinea Pidgin *wel gris,* "oil grease," and what the Foi call *kara'o.* It is the sap of the *Campnosperma brevipetiolata* tree and it is an inert, yellow-orange colored oil highly sought throughout interior New Guinea as a body decoration. The Foi export this oil, which they carry in ten-foot-long bamboo tubes, to their immediate Wola-, Anganen-, and Kewa-speaking neighbors to the north, who then pass it on to more distant Central Highlanders. In return, the Foi receive shoats, pearl shells, and Papua New Guinea currency (as well as stone axe blades and cult objects in the pre-European days). The Foi were fond of telling me that "in the beginning, there was only *kara'o,*" and that when they learned how to tap the oil and collect it, they traded it for the pigs and pearl shells they now own and which form the basis of their internal economy.

During his stay with the Wola people, Paul Sillitoe visited Lake Kutubu and collected the following version of the myth of origin of *kara'o:*

> Long ago a woman called Verome was wandering along the Mubi Valley to the longhouse community at Hegeso. One night she slept near a *kara'o* tree and took it into her head to cut a hole in its trunk. She was menstruating at the time and some of her menstrual blood fell into the hole she had excavated. When this happened the tree started to "menstruate" too and oil gushed from the hole. It

produced an incredible amount of oil and in one day she filled two long bamboo tubes, one of which today takes a man with a number of trees several months to fill. She gave the oil to some men and they were delighted with it and used it to anoint their bodies and give them a beautiful glistening appearance. Soon they asked Verome how she had obtained the oil and when she told them, they decided that tapping the oil from the tree was not women's work and forbade her to continue. They searched for kara'o trees and started cutting holes in them but they produced no oil. They were furious and started to curse and threaten Verome, and as a result their trees started to yield oil. Today men still have to curse her in a spell as they cut holes in new trees or else they will not produce oil. (1979:293)

In order to approach the imagery of this myth, it is first necessary to summarize the Foi theory of sexual reproduction. Female menstrual blood, the product of the uterus, is the essential regenerative bodily substance in Foi theory. A woman releases this blood for the purposes of reproduction every time she has her monthly period. If it is not held back within the uterus, it flows out of her body and must be disposed of cautiously, as it and any other vaginal fluids (as well as, to a somewhat smaller degree, issues from her other body orifices) are extremely debilitating to adult men.

A man attempts to retain his wife's menstrual blood in her uterus by copulating with her, thereby providing semen which forms a bowl-shaped receptacle. This prevents the blood from leaving the uterus and provides a container within which the blood can begin to coagulate and form the fetus. Up to thirty copulations may be necessary to achieve this result, since the amount of semen a man produces during any one ejaculation is small. Foi men are ambivalent about sexual intercourse, and they unjokingly refer to the task of impregnation as "hard work": their sexual desire is always tempered by the knowledge that the more they copulate, the more they are impairing their health by contact with women's vaginal secretions.

The most compelling image of kara'o for those Foi with whom I lived likens it to menstrual blood, produced from a uterus-like cavity in the interior of the Campnosperma tree. In the myth, men confront not only the spontaneity of women's menstrual capacity but exaggerate its productivity; the tree, after being quickened by the woman's blood, produces copious amounts of kara'o (as women are thought to produce much blood in contrast to the minute amounts of semen that men provide). So much oil is produced, in fact, that it can cover the bodies of all the men, and in this "territorialization" of (human) blood into (vegetative, and hence propagative) tree oil the original internal flow of the woman becomes transformed into an external socializing (decorating) substance. As long as the woman Verome alone mediated this production, as Foi women mediate all vegetative production, yields remained high. But when men attempted to expropriate this talent, they were confronted by their own lack of spontaneous reproductivity: the tree ceased to produce oil. Men cannot initiate "menstruation," they can only attempt to exert post factum control over it. Men have to treat the tree as a woman, cursing and intimidating it, in order to have it produce.

Both Sillitoe and myself heard some version of the magic spell referred to in the last line of the myth, which men recite when they are making the delicate incisions on the tree that will initiate oil flow. Sillitoe mentions one line of a spell:

Verome your skin I am cutting.

One line of the spell I heard, and which I discussed in *The Heart of the Pearl Shell*, mentions a maiden named Wagiyomo rather than Verome:

I am not about to cut this *kara'o* tree
But Wagiyomo's chest I am cutting.

In its explicit focus around the dialectic of objectification and aggressivity, the *kara'o* myth seems to call to mind Jacques Lacan's (1977a) description of the *mirror stage*. Lacan first points out the prolonged period of motor uncoordination and helplessness of the newborn.[4] The newborn lacks a "coenaesthetic" sense, a sense of the integration of the multiplicity of its body's sensations. Freud himself described the ego as essentially an effect of sensations experienced at the body's surface: "[The ego] may thus be regarded as a mental projection of the surface of the body, besides representing the superficies of the mental apparatus" (1923:26n).

When the child reaches the age when it can recognize itself in the mirror, an important possibility is opened up. The child sees its body as a whole, apprehends the totality (more or less) of its body, but without yet having control over it; it recognizes only an alienated, ideal unity of its diverse motor "superficies."[5]

The child, confronted with the discord between the spatialized external unitary image and the subjective experience of kinaesthetic atomism, experiences an "aggressive disintegration of his own body" (Benvenuto and Kennedy 1986:57). The internal lack of integration is projected and literalized outward as a detotalization and lack of fit amongst body parts. "These are the images of castration, mutilation, dismemberment, dislocation, evisceration, devouring, bursting open of the body . . ." (Lacan 1977a:12).

Now, there is no reason why we should not take this myth of the origin of Western fragmentation in exactly the same way as we did the Foi pearl shell origin story, that is, as an allegory, albeit unintended, of the way we try to make our narrative flow reveal the shape of the object being described (since every narrative also contains within it a comment upon its mode of symbolic figuration). The aggressivity of Foi men's response to Verome's tree, cursing and cutting it, could well be interpreted as an illustration of this primordial recognition of narcissistic fragmentation, this traumatic loss of men's external surface control. Lacan identifies this loss as a lack or deficit, a lack of completeness. In this gap, language finds its space, as a totalizing regime of signification. So although Lacan presents the mirror stage as an allegory of the body, what we most practically feel as a loss is the lack of embodiment of our words and interpretational strategies, a locutionary fragmentation which manifests itself as an abstracting aggression against the body of the word. But for a people like the Foi, for whom the body is always the site of articulation, the flow of words is not the alienating mechanism it is for us, and fragmentation may be as strange a notion to Foi views on embodiment as metonymy is to ours. In fact, the Foi never doubt the metonymic nature of speech. For them, the name of a thing is a part of it, and goes proxy for it, like wealth items—these too are part of the same domain of embodied markers and substitute for people and their diverse bodily capacities in the same way. Each word or wealth item retains an iconic sense of the whole of which it is part. Under such conditions, the Foi would hardly see the attainment of totality as an issue at all.

Foi men, therefore, are inclined to manipulate the bodies of words and signifying objects, and the discursive forms which shape them, as a way of controlling the processes of embodiment over which they lack direct power. Foi men perceive that they lack a spontaneous power of internal embodiment—that is, they do not embody within themselves, as do women. Their social agency is always projected outward onto other surfaces, other bodies. Men's physical endowment allows them only limited success in corporeal regeneration. Although a man's semen does contribute something to the formation of the fetus (it forms the "hard, white parts" of the body, the bone, teeth, and nails), the largest portion of physical reproduction is provided by a woman's menstrual blood, out of which all other body parts cohere.

Men assert control over women's physical capacity to reproduce by way of wealth items in the context of the bridewealth system. Through an appeal to an ideology that stipulates that children should belong to the clan of their fathers, they compensate a bride's male kinsmen for the loss of their woman's reproductive potential by transferring to them a quantity of these wealth items.

In other words, Foi men confront their own ectasia, the sense that they can exert control over others only through the mediation of de-tached objects which represent parts of their corporeality (including their female relatives given in marriage, who represent their own "blood"),[6] a dilation (and attenuation) of their body space through its extension by metonymic wealth items.

But this ectasia allows in the end a more comprehensive mirroring resynthesis of the body, and is just a special case of a more encompass-ing dialectic of objectification and reunification through which the Foi distribute inscriptive agency to themselves in varying degrees. They synthesize their territory, their geographic world in a similar fashion; inscriptive powers are attributed to bodily exuviae, particularly in their origin myths, as the following version of the *kara'o* origin myth suggests:

THE ORIGIN OF KARA'O

There once lived two women named Sosame and Verome. They came from a swamp named Pasa'afu which is located near the border of Lower Foi and Kewa territory to the southeast. They travelled to Kaffa, south of Pimaga, until they arrived at the Upper Mubi. Travelling upstream on foot, they arrived at Ganudobabo, a small stream in Herebo territory. They kept traveling upstream into Hegeso territory until they reached Segemi. There they crossed the river to the north bank and followed it downstream back the way they had come. They crossed the Baru River and arrived at a place named Sererabe. From there they followed the base of Mt. Vivi in Herebo territory and went to Masera'afu and Tugifu in that area. One of the women died at Sebebufu in Herebo territory and the other died at Faibufu which is owned by Hegeso.

While the women traveled, they wore no string skirts but rather fastened the leaves of *kafane* ferns around their waists as pubic coverings, like widows do. They were both menstruating and in the places they traveled, their menstrual blood dropped to the ground. From it, the first *kara'o* trees sprung up, and the swamps they passed through have *kara'o* trees in them now next to the sago palms. In the two swamps at which the two women died, Sebebu and Faibu, there are today many *kara'o* trees. (Weiner 1988:65)

What one is inclined to pass off as trivial in this version—that the women originate from the downstream direction, and then reverse themselves and move back downstream, at which point the narrator mentions that they are menstruating—is actually critical. Women, associated with death in many ways, linguistically and otherwise, come from the direction of the afterworld, the land of the spirits of the dead. But the wealth item they produce, kara'o, springs up when they start heading back in that direction, as if they were coming from the west, the mythical source of all wealth items for the Foi. Significantly, they both die in this phase of their journey. The intersexual antagonism that is the by-product of the men's and women's switching roles in Sillitoe's version is replaced by a less forcefully articulated implication of death and female widowhood.

One can see these two versions of the kara'o origin myth as presenting alternate symbolic elaborations, that of corporeal embodiment and territorial expansion, respectively. Rather than men inscribing their agency directly on women through the cutting of Verome's vagina and body and the kara'o tree, in the second version Verome and Sosame themselves fertilize the earth with their menstrual blood, multiplying the number of potential uterus-like cavities (the trees themselves). Since the Campnosperma tree is a managed resource, planted and situated through men's agency, the planting and husbanding of kara'o groves becomes equivalent to the act of cutting and tapping the single tree, just as a man "husbands" his wife by depositing his semen in her.

Like a myth itself, which achieves its capacity for analogic expansion as a result of its self-signifying properties, Foi wealth items, like Wiru pearl shells (Clark 1991), are similarly embodied: they encapsulate a relationship, as well as being mediators of other relationships. Kara'o embodies the two women's journey from southeast to northwest and the geographical creativity that resulted from it, just as the pearl shell encapsulates the southeasterly flow of water from the Mubi Valley to the sea, against which pearl shells, in anti-entropic fashion, arrive in Foi territory. At the same time as these wealth items are tethered by these simultaneously geographical and cosmological points, they expand a certain image of Foi social relationship back onto that geograph. The antagonism and death that compose Foi intersexual mediation are a movement from downstream to upstream, from southeast to northwest, that is, just as the pearl shell, the foreign object, brings the distant end points of water flow back to its source, as it were: the pearl shell keeps the beginning and end of all flows within Foi territory, within the marriage community. We can virtually reverse the terms of our conventional understanding of exchange in this case: the item is the exchange all by itself, containing within it all the necessary relationships, territorial as well as biopolitical, and their mediation; while the actual swapping of it back and forth in "real life" becomes no more than a highly ritualized (mythologized) playing out of its embodied reciprocity. The (enacted) myth embodies the item.[7]

One aspect of the way we make a self-evident distinction between inside and outside do work in our social theory is by assuming that what is autochthonous and spontaneous is internal, and by contrast, what is foreign and contingent is external. But the Foi view of precious substances reverses this Western folk theory: although *kara'o* is an indigenous item, in the myth it is brought into Foi territory from the outside, while on the other hand, the pearl shell, the exogenous item, is expelled or lost from its origin in the heart of the Foi region. The efficacy of both is appealed to by virtue of their *extrusive* properties, their ability to constitute inside and outside through introjective and projective movements, to create the spaces or folds within which such objects can acquire mediatory capacities. In the second half of this chapter, I want to describe what happens when this body of Foi wealth stories is opened up by the advent of yet another socially and sexually fertile fluid: crude oil.

In early 1988, during my last visit to Hegeso, the extraction of crude oil had just begun on several sites around Lake Kutubu. Most of the sites were actually located in the territory of the neighboring Fasu people, but Foi people from Lake Kutubu were also involved as collateral landowners and employees on the oil rigs, as were men from the Hegeso area, several hours' walk from the nearest rig.

During that trip I heard two stories about how petroleum had come to be located in the Lake Kutubu region. Both are cast unmistakably in the genre which I have previously identified as Foi myth or *tuni* (Weiner 1988). I now want to discuss these two stories as part of the reactions to economic neocolonialism in its early days, before the speculative theories of mythical recreations of this presence are likely to become overshadowed (for us) by the subsequent hard histories of labor migration, village disintegration, disease, and ecological degradation. A myth might have less social force (or less media presence) than a government injunction allowing unrestricted foreign mineral exploration, or an oil spill, but the myth "in its singularity can be far more powerful in elucidating the conditions of social structure than a description or analysis, for the very fact that it is, simply a destiny—a 'falling together' of the details and conditions of social life" (Wagner n.d.:19).

THE ORIGIN OF KARA'O AND PETROLEUM

One time there was a woman from Baru village named Verome. The men of Baru village accused her of adultery and struck her in the side with a cassowary thigh bone spike, like the ones used for splitting pandanus fruits. The woman ran away. She didn't run straight to Mt. Kuabo or Sumi downstream, but rather ran around aimlessly in this area. The blood from her wound fell in various places around this area, and from it *kara'o* trees sprouted. She then followed the Mubi River southeast and went between Mt. Kuabo and Mt. Sumi. She went to Waro swamp, near the current Waro Station. Before she arrived at Waro, she followed the Soro River across into Fasu territory.

In the swamp, she missed her footing and sank below her head. A man tried to pull her up by the arm but only succeeded in grabbing her armband, which slipped off, and the woman sank down. That's why there is oil down at Waro.

So, the petroleum and *kara'o* come from the same source, the woman Verome. The men who struck her were jealous of her, and that's why they attacked her. The oil and *kara'o* stayed here, where Verome remained, it didn't go up to the Highlands or down to Lower Foi, but stayed here in these places.

Now where the oil company has put all their rigs, all the places they are drilling for oil, these are all the places that Verome passed through. At Warotebo, at Dagina and Abu, at Masiba and Wu, there is oil. The people of other places must understand that Verome was a woman of Baru, and since she was the source of the oil, it is in our place.

The owners of these places can be expected to be very possessive of their oil, just as men are possessive of their women. But if the local men continue to be jealous of the oil and fight with each other, the oil will run away just as a woman does, just as Verome did, because the oil is like a woman.

This story is probably a gloss on one or both of the other *kara'o* origin stories, expanding the theme of sexual antagonism by theorizing that it originated in male suspicions of female adultery, another expression of male anxiety over their control of feminine reproductivity. This story was told during one of the many arguments that have been raised concerning the control and ownership of oil-bearing ground. The Foi, in whose territory major reserves have not yet been pinpointed, are jealous of their neighbors, the Fasu, in whose land most extraction is now going on. But each Foi village is casting wary eyes on its neighbors, anticipating the disputes over territorial borders that will be ushered in when the oil company's activities expand into Foi territory. In 1988, when I heard this story recounted during a debate amongst Hegeso and Barutage big-men, people were balancing their own foreseeable economic gains against the obvious advantage of united activity to obtain the best deal from the government and oil company.

Now, by focusing on the equity between *kara'o* and petroleum, another opposed comparison can be made: for *kara'o* is the Foi's primordial valuable that became so when it was first *exported* to foreign groups. *Kara'o* is not ordinarily used in internal ceremonial payments in Foi (never in bridewealth payments, only in mortuary payments, which the Foi ceased making in the 1960s). The one indigenous, autochthonous wealth item the Foi recognize—all others, they say, were originally acquired in trade with outsiders—exists only to be exported, to be exchanged for the real media of local exchange: pigs and shell wealth. Is it farfetched to assume that the Foi are aware that the petroleum plays exactly the same role vis-à-vis the national Papua New Guinea economy? That both *kara'o* and petroleum achieve their value by being highly sought after by foreigners, who will trade other wealth items to obtain it?

The previous story preserves the indigenous cosmology, coats the global politics of oil with its own Foi perception of territorial power and competition. The final story, however, goes to the "heart of the oil shale."

THE ORIGIN OF PETROLEUM AT LAKE KUTUBU

This is how oil came to be in the Lake Kutubu area. A long time ago a white man flew over the lake in an airplane. He leaned out the window to get a better look, but as he did, a gold coin fell out of his pocket and dropped into the lake. Before it reached the bottom, it was swallowed by a long black catfish.

Some time later, a very tall, thin white man came down to the lake on patrol. The Kutubu people sold him some smoked catfish in a fire-blackened bamboo tube. The fish he ate was the one which had swallowed the gold coin. After he ate it, he got very bad diarrhea. He had very bad diarrhea in the lake. The diarrhea settled on the bottom of the lake and permeated the limestone underneath it. Now an airplane arrived and hoisted the white man by winch and flew him back to the Highlands. The sick man couldn't walk, he could only be carried by airplane.

When the white men came back and stuck their pipes into the ground, they found that the diarrhea had turned into oil. Now the white men have come back searching for that gold coin, only it has turned into oil.

There are probably now as many myths of the origin of money in Papua New Guinea as there are pearl shell origin myths; one wonders whether in a mythical analogue of Gresham's law, they will ever eventually drive out the "good" origin stories. In the above striking Foi story, money, the gold coin, is dropped onto the Foi world as a concomitant, accidental or otherwise, of European interest in their world. It is swallowed by the catfish (in the same way, Foi men use their wealth to buy smoked catfish or—the most common use of money in the Foi area—to purchase tinned fish: fish swallows their money).

But of course, when they buy tinned fish, the Foi sense, without really knowing the details, that the white men are taking their money back, for they are ultimately the suppliers of the manufactured tinned fish in Foi trade stores.[8] The white man drops his coin onto the Foi and then, in the form of a fish, swallows their money again. Western money is self-equivalent and not equitable; it resists complementarization in terms of human value or "vital substance," which is how Foi wealth items acquire value. Money has yet to enter ceremonial wealth payments in Foi in more than a token fashion. Money does not commoditize bridewealth among the Foi (as it has in other areas of Papua New Guinea, such as Chimbu and Moresby); rather, Foi bridewealth has dignified the use of money. Through money, the "prestige-luxury" economy does not seep into the Foi "ceremonial" economy, because they have always had a well-separated "export" economy in the kara'o trade.

Thus, the Foi myth of petroleum highlights its parthenogenic origin, appeals to the sense of isolated completeness that is the Western individual and his/her wealth objects. Just as Western notions of the "body corporate" expand our understanding of the human body's integration and oneness, so Foi notions of the local patrilineal clan summarize their notions of the contingency and limited reproductive capacity of the male body. A group of agnatically related men, itself the contingent product of a history of negotiated bridewealth collections and transfers, pool their wealth for the purpose of providing each other's bridewealth requirements and hence must see its accumulated wealth and animal resources continuously drain away by the necessity to acquire wives.

In the confrontation between their own image of the body politic and the Westerner's, the Foi are resynthesizing their own ontogenetic mirror stage. These contrasting images of wealth as metonym (Foi) and meta-phor (West) provide the bridging point between Western notions of the whole, unmediated person, who is alienated in toto by a global political economy, and Melanesian notions of the extroverted, mediated, part-ible "dividual" (Strathern 1988), the person who is decomposed as a result of the way his or her corporeal regenerative substances and pow-ers can be fixed in objects and passed on to others within a system that never totalizes or generalizes exchange beyond the parties involved. The Westerner seeks forever to reintegrate him/herself and only sexu-ally strives to achieve oneness with others; the Melanesian seeks (al-ways unsatisfactorily) to avoid unwanted corporeal (sexual) intrusion by others while at the same time aiming to project his/her own body as widely and comprehensively as possible.

Western law, administration, economic development, nationalism—especially nationalism—all appeal to a collective morality quite op-posed to the local New Guinea ideologies of contingency and influence. In fact, they mirror back onto Papua New Guineans a totalized version of their social life, just as Western administrators originally inscribed districts, provinces, census divisions, ethnic and linguistic groupings onto New Guinea in the first place.

Now I've said that the Foi attempt to exert influence on others through the media of wealth objects which represent their embodied labor and corporeal substance. But earlier, in discussing the mirror stage, I suggested that this dialectic of objectification and encompass-ment works not just at the level of actual human bodily integration but is a feature of every symbolic articulation in Foi social life: wherever there is scope for projection and ectasia, there must by implication be a boundary, a falling back onto itself of that initial extension. To put it another way, any self-closure is assessed as such only against an al-lowed expansion; any scope for projection acquires force only when seen against a countervailing centripetality.

For the Foi, the expansion of a social network through pearl shells comes up against the practical limits of embodied commensality—a function of actual coresidence—and blood kinship. Each Foi village, centering on the men's longhouse, consists of between three and thir-teen local patrilineal groupings, the *amenadoba*, "man line"; three or four closely neighboring villages recognize themselves as a unit and form the practical limits within which over 90 percent of the commu-nity members find spouses. The Foi thus recognize a limit of geographic propinquity on the theoretically unlimited scope of their exogamic ideology.

Appeals to this practical limit are phrased in terms of the communality of food consumption. One of the frequent remarks I heard during heated arguments concerning contributions to bridewealth was one man accusing another: "You spend too much of your shell wealth down at Lake Kutubu buying fish to fill your belly." In the time that I have been visiting the Foi, there has been a vigorous trade between middle Mubi Foi (those that live between Pimaga and Hegeso) and the lake dwellers. At first light every Saturday morning, families could be seen starting out on the three-hour walk down to Gesege village at the southern tip of the lake. There, the lake dwellers, the *gurubumena*, would gather bringing soot-blackened bamboo tubes of roasted fish and game. At this "market," the Mubi men would buy this fish and game for small pearl shells, cowrie shells, and PNG currency.

Insofar as permanent wealth (albeit in small denominations) is being expended on something with no enduring socially reproductive capacity (consumable food), it is denigrated. But the Foi do *not* similarly denigrate such consumption when it takes place between members of the same local community. Men of the middle Mubi area regularly slaughter pigs by the ones and twos, butcher and cook the meat, and then "sell" the meat in pieces to raise shell wealth that they might require for ceremonial payments. This practice is called *aname kobora*. It is considered the responsibility of all men and women in the community to purchase small amounts of cooked meat at this time, and people do so in the knowledge that they too will inevitably depend on others' bringing their shell wealth and money to buy meat on those occasions where they will have to raise the werewithal for a ceremonial payment.

What the rebukes of Foi men at bridewealth ceremonies really amount to is their disgust with men who go *outside* the community to do this. It leaks wealth outside the local community, which is the functional unit of endogamy in Foi, rather than retaining it within, where it will inevitably return to some other community member in the form of bridewealth or compensation payment. In line with the dialectic between bodily ectasia and containment that I have identified as a recursive feature of Foi social articulation, it is no paradox that the Foi wish to encapsulate their wealth within the community to ensure its internal flow, to ensure its socially inscriptive power.

There is this idea of maintaining the *continence* of wealth within a community, in the same way as men are concerned with the continence of women's menstrual blood for somewhat different reasons. The Foi make use of the contrast between viscosity and fluidity to elaborate upon these contrasting fluid vectors. Fluid held in place, like menstrual blood held in the uterus by an accumulation of semen, is thick, viscous; like Green's Type I symbols, it adheres to itself and forms an unreactive

solidity, like a fetus. By contrast, "Type II" fluid allowed to flow unre-
strained to no purpose, like menstrual blood which a woman releases
during her period, blood which has not been "fastened" by an accumulation of semen by copulation, is "watery," and in this form it
readily adheres to other surfaces, like men's tools and clothing, where
it exerts a deleterious effect on their health and vigor (cf. Battaglia 1990).

Anxiety over uncontrollable flow is the way Western and Foi concerns over oil mirror each other. What the Foi now see is that from the
outset, "their" petroleum will inexorably and irreversibly leave their
region, to be returned or recompensed by an as yet unperceived advantage. The oil is being expended (on the orders of the national government) to someone else's benefit. What the Foi see as a broadened loss of
vitality, of surface "social coenaesthesis," of precious bodily fluids leak-
ing away, the Westerner sees in more consumptive, anal terms as loss
of control over alimentation and incorporation. For people like the Foi,
the end product of consumption—those things that are the product of
the anus—lack inscriptive power (unlike semen and bone and blood
and flesh, for example). In fact, shit is an all-inclusive term for those
things produced which have no inscriptive value or cannot carry or sus-
tain a power relation.[9]

When consumption is given inscriptive power, however (as it is in
the West, through the commoditization of food and its aestheticization
through advertising), when, in other words, it is seen to fuel production, rather than being "mere (organic) fuel" itself, then the end product
of consumption, excrement, becomes a socially meaningful process.
(We measure the child's real socialization when it agrees to part with its
excrement and send it on its way into the city's anus, the sewers that are
an underversion of roads, or the suburban septic tank, the underground "mirror larder.") Through the conventionalization of the Oedipal trauma as our Western myth of kinship, the child's control over
its feces is privatized, as a function of its mastery of body and of intention and personal destiny, as it becomes independent of its parents. The
control of money proceeds alongside this process and is in no major
way any different from it (see Freud 1933:100–102).

The petroleum myth establishes the unmistakable association that
Western wealth and consumption have in New Guinea eyes. Our
wealth gets shitted away ultimately, because it is never circulated and
always privately consumed. But the Foi do not fetishize defecation because they don't glorify the oral cavity, that is, they don't fetishize consumption, as Westerners do. In fact, fetishization is possible only where
totalization is a problem, for by our lights, the Foi fetishize every part
of their bodies, inside and out. Their concern with the social effects of

metonymic extension must surely strike us at times as an anxiety over potency, and a mania for bodily ectasia (see, for example, Herdt 1987).

Insofar as the Foi understand what the crude oil is used for—as the raw material for refined petroleum fractions like gasoline and kerosene— they understand these fluids to achieve their effect through internality and consumption: motor vehicles and outboard boat engines consume gasoline as do kerosene lamps. The effect of the *kara'o* is opposite: it is placed on the outside of the body, it is not nutritive but sexual-decorative.

This brings us back to the difference between the Fasu and the Foi, because the presence of crude oil in Fasu territory and its absence (so far) in Foi territory could hardly be more fateful.

It is characteristic of origin myths of the Foi, as well as many other Papuan and Australian peoples such as the Daribi and Yolngu, that features of the landscape and natural environment resulted from an initial, originary event of sexual conflict—an act of adultery, or incest, or sexual shaming. But a more inclusive way of describing this is to say that people like the Foi assign inscriptive effects to productive and reproductive activity, to human procreative acts and substances. Such acts, and the fluids produced in them, inscribe a moral and cosmological landscape, both literally (in myth) and figuratively (in the network of embedded debts in wealth objects that people are born into as a result of such reproductive events).

As I've said, *kara'o* is used as a body decoration by most New Guinea Highlands men and many women. Foi men say that the rich shiny orange-red sheen it imparts makes their bodies sexually alluring to women, especially when it reflects the glint of hand-held bamboo torches during nighttime ceremonial song recitals in the longhouse. Consider, then, the spectacle of men covering their bodies with an explicit form of women's menstrual blood in order to heighten their own sexual attractiveness.

In 1988, I was at Barutage longhouse, Hegeso's closest neighboring settlement, when a group of Fasu men visited to perform their own version of the memorial songs that the Foi also sing on the night of certain ceremonies. On their skins the Fasu men had applied *their* characteristic skin covering: a dead mat black covering, a mixture of oil and charcoal. They could have as easily used old crankcase oil had it been available to achieve the same effect. The unrelieved blackness of their skins and their unsmiling faces were vividly set off by the spray of white cockatoo feathers they wore as a headdress and the white baler shells around their necks.

Now the Fasu were traditionally cannibalistic while the middle Mubi Foi of Barutage village were not. The Fasu also traditionally practiced a form of boys' insemination as did their neighbors across the Hegigio River near Mt. Bosavi, again, in contrast to the Mubi Foi. What the Foi men saw therefore were cannibal men, men who prevented the depletion and outward flow of their semen to such an extent that they strove to retain it for their exclusive use, men whose whole rationale was that of closed cycles of internal consumption, covered in crude black oil, the recovered alimentary residue of the white man. The black oil of the white men covered the black bodies of men who surrounded and framed their faces with a background of white shells and feathers, white wealth items, an endless mirroring and remirroring of body against wealth objects.

In the end, the mirror is provocative for the Westerner only because we stubbornly refuse to see anything in it but ourselves. The mirror, as Lacan well realized, reflects only an outline for the child who is not yet a person. But for Western adults, who learn that signification and not embodiment founds the Western image, the mirroring body drops out of sight. From this point of view, the Foi and Fasu never articulate the Lacanian mirror because for them the body is its own mirror. New Guinea wealth objects acquire their shape against the ground of the bodies of their wearers. But each person also acquires his or her social shape as a result of the flow of wealth objects against which he or she has moved historically. And if New Guinea persons thus mirror themselves, they spontaneously mirror all other persons around them, to whom they continuously reflect an assessment of the efficacy of their social extension, the metonymic dilation of their partible bodies/ wealth items. That is why metonymic extension never becomes mere alienation for the New Guinean, for alienation—of body parts, of labor, of others—results only when the social skin encompassing relations is itself not articulated.

Deleuze and Guattari suggest an expansion of the original Marxian notion of alienation to include alienation from an embodied sociality; this is the manner in which capitalism "decodes" the embodied, territorial flows that constitute "primitive" social process. The "primitive territorial machine" expands a productive scheme located in the body itself. Desiring production takes the form of a sexualized reproduction projected onto the landscape, where the mechanisms of descent, marriage, and land transmission are subsumed within more central protocols regarding the production, transmission, and control of sexually fertile corporeal fluids. Capitalism, however, disembodies labor and production from such a territorialized, historical grounding, and noth-

ing can stand better for the first seeping in of this detachment than petroleum, the deterritorialized fluid that lubricates the atomized fragmented body parts of its mode of production.

Lacan recovered that insight of Freud's which subsequently was lost
sight of: that the nature of the psychoanalytic cure lies in language, and
that both the patient's resurrection of dream and past event, and the
analyst's reconstruction and interpretation of it, are part of the same
anamnesis and hence are essentially *hermeneutic:*

> for Freud it is not a question of biological memory, nor of its
> intuitionist mystification, nor of the paramnesis of the symptom,
> but a question of rememoration, that is, of history—balancing the
> scales in which conjectures about the past cause a fluctuation of
> the promises of the future upon a single fulcrum: that of chrono-
> logical certitude . . . the effect of a full Word is to reorder the past
> contingent events by conferring on them the sense of necessities to
> come . . . (1977a:18)

Lacan also maintains that meaningful memories for a society are not
distinguishable from meaningful memories for the individual. As Wilden puts it, "to have meaning, they must be intentionalized in the *present,* through speech in the individual, through the historical consciousness in the collective" (1968:208). In looking at the Foi's stories about
petroleum, we are not confronting a case of a myth's fixed and imme-
morial message being extended to encompass a novel situation of culture contact; the myth as full-bodied "lasting" word reorders the cosmology which it itself explains, by fragmenting it, as Boas put it, in
order for it to be retotalized. What we as anthropologists thus owe to
Lacan is this insistence that the mirror stage is a *hermeneutic of embodiment*—that linguistic embodiment (in myth) and bodily signification (in
detachable and inscriptive substances and wealth objects) develop historically as well as ontologically as reversible figure and ground of each
other. And this mirror-imaging is as much a cohesion within a language
or culture as an adhering, coenaesthetic creation of contact between cultures. We look at the Foi's and Fasu's techniques of social extrusion and
see our own fragmentation and alienation; they look at our wealth objects and oil and see the embodied metonyms of an economy of human
productive values. But a metonymic culture like the Foi also projects its
own vision of detachment and fragmentation, like pearl shell splinters
that move of their own accord (Weiner 1988), and likewise a vision of
unmediated exchange where metonymy does not exist (as in Anganen
theories of ceremonial exchange [Nihill 1988]), just as a culture of frag-

mentation such as our own is obsessed with the project of coherence and unification on the one hand and a "body without organs"—a totality without internal differentiation or seams—on the other.

Kara'o is the menstrual blood that is always under complete control by men and yet never pollutes them. The *kara'o* myth has appropriated and domesticated the Western concern with petroleum even as that incorporation has altered the terms of their indigenous oil industry. Like wealth items in general, these myths are also themselves "Type III" symbols for the Foi, terms that flow and attract other significances within their orbit, yet maintain their value throughout, coating other terms with value, rather than being eclipsed or preempted by them. They maintain the reproductive vitality of certain core images, particularly among peoples like the Foi and Daribi for whom "origin" consists of a primordial inscriptive movement of ancestral beings through a territory, an originary act of naming and signifying that we are deluded into thinking had a beginning and an end (because we record the myth as having a beginning and an end). And hence it is not accidental that this territorial inscription opens up as the result of an originary sexual act, an inauspicious embodiment that has an unintended expansion as social movement.

It is not just the sexually embodied nature of *kara'o* that is being maintained and extended in the new myths but its related status as *pharmakon*, as poison and cure, as a symbol which in its extension sets the terms for its own retraction, its own causing-to-withdraw, just as the social implications of women's menstrual blood include a withdrawal of male potency and continuity, and just as petroleum and the money it heralds cause an effacement of Foi and Fasu men's extension of power and control. What *kara'o*, blood, petroleum, and all sexual substances (including their lethal inverses, sorcery medicines) have in common is that they are poison only in their un-held-back state—when they are allowed to flow, to make unmediated suture with other substances and other bodies. Held-back blood becomes the fetus, held-back semen a vital healthful adult man. By contrast, the wealth items that encompass and negotiate them, shells, animals, and to a smaller extent money itself, *flow too quickly,* never make suture, never adhere, and so never poison. But this argues for a more generalized economy of significances, an expanded version of Gresham's law which suggests that those kinds of significances not drawn into the gravity well of some local complex, that don't make suture, ultimately flow around and eventually drive out local, grounded, embodied signs.

When the *kara'o* origin story is expanded into that of petroleum, its original terms become altered, decentered; the oil is decanted and its story recanted with every new tapping and collection. The third myth hypothesizes the contingency of petroleum, as men's control of menstrual blood is contingent, and equates the tension between men and women with the colonial tension between a deterritorialized European petrocracy and the local Foi tradition of inscribed wealth and territory. But the last story points to a more ominous future, one hinted at by the blackened Asmat men, their erect penes coated with oil, covered with the shit that is all that is produced from self-closure, either consumptive or sexual. The oil and its money may well swallow the Foi and Fasu as the Fasu once swallowed everyone else. What the *kara'o* stories are to the process of embodied inscription, the petroleum story is to its negation, the elevating of externalized consumption to a desiring production.

8

Afterword:
The Resistance of Myth

The myth "The Lost Drum" traces the progress of the Foi drum from the heart of Foi life, in the gift of a man to his younger brother, which gift is the moment at which the displacing, ecstatic effects of the object create the illusion of stability in the Foi world, to its resting point beyond the human world altogether where it can only vibrate against itself, echoing hollowly the strident ululations and cries of male striving. As if to give some shape to this dimensionless sound, the songs that Foi men sing in the longhouse are always punctuated by the rapid, glottal vibration of the singers' vocal cords. What we find then is that in the heart of the Foi male experience of ceremonial consociation, there is this warning note of detachment, this bull-roarer buzz of stasis and self-cancellation.

The flute, drum, and bull-roarer produce an auditory icon, through the vibratile quality of the sound they make; each of them produces not a single drawn-out note, but a rapid series of notes. As I argued in *The Empty Place* (Weiner 1991a), this renders within sound-space the moving qualities of life process itself, its dependence upon interval, stoppage, and redirection. These instruments produce not only notes, but also the intervals of silence and death that define the notes. The voice of such an instrument is not then a fixed sign of social power. In these Papuan societies, social life is anchored in the moving, not in the inalienable or the immobile. Ultimately, this movement is the heart of discourse itself, the discourse which is the real production of the object.

If the instruments trap the voice of movement, the myths likewise trap the instruments, reclaim them from the acoustemic caducity to which the embodied, imaginary perception consigns them. The myths make appear the objects—the pearl shell, bull-roarer, flute, drum, string bag, tree oil—even though the objects themselves signal a rupture or absence; they cover over the unformed or unperceived parts of persons, and in so doing, they attempt the social act of completion.

But the myth and the object precisely have a differential *relationship to absence:*

> It is the [differential] relationship to absence which accounts for the rather peculiar fact that Freud's grandson found it necessary to substitute for a phantasy relationship to the lack of object (at one level, the breast; at another, the mother's comings and goings) the signifier relationship of speech, at the same time as he employed a substitute (the toy) for the more primordial object. (Wilden 1968: 163–64)

In other words, the spool is the game of the substitute object played within the field of the Imaginary, the specular, scopic field, while the child's word game of *fort/da* plays on the gap created by the loss itself within the register of the Symbolic, of language itself.

We can if we so wish see this same differential relationship depicted in the myth "The Lost Drum," even though it focuses not on the visual appearance but on *the sound-shape of objects* that plays as important a role within the Imaginary for the Foi as vision does for us. In the myth, the sound of the drum disappears, but what the younger brother gives voice to is his demand for water/breast milk. It is significant that the main obviating hinge of the myth should have as one of its effects to make visible the differential placement of the drum within the fields of the Imaginary and the Symbolic. This implies that such a differential is made particularly visible within the field of communal speech, and in the case of the Foi, in their most ostensively interpretational forms of language. Let us then consider the wider implications of the obviational properties of myth.

Obviation and Deferral

Obviation occurs in the narrative of a myth because in the successive and patterned substitution of images for each other, a contextual field is set up which provides the grounding for the retroactive illumination of earlier substitutions. These retroactive motivations build upon each other so that when the final point of obviation is reached in the myth, what is achieved is not a single insight or the revelation of a coded meaning but a sense of the range of interpretations that have been made possible by the myth's dialectical and retroflexive properties.

Wagner referred to as "retroactive implication" (1986:54) the process by which a point of closure within a larger obviation sequence extends back to frame the point which opens that sequence. In Figure 1, point *A* begins the sequence and a temporary or partial closure is achieved at point *C*, which at that point provides a retrospective grounding of the opening substitution *A*. Since there are three basic triads of this sort within the overall ternary structure of the obviation sequence, this partial closure occurs three times and inscribes an internal triangle, $A \rightarrow E \rightarrow C$.

In the example of "The Hornbill Husband" in Chapter 2, the external triangle *BDF* corresponds to the microcosmic pole, the "encompassing mode," the register which relates the events of the myth, while inscribed internally is the macrocosmic sequence of social protocol moving against it, the "encompassed mode." As I suggested, the sequence is precipitated by the idiosyncratic and nonconventional events of the myth. Thus Wagner notes:

> whereas motion in the encompassing mode moves forward and carries the movement of the sequence as a whole, that in the, encompassed mode moves backward in time against it . . . , augmenting the relativity of its perceptions through the implications of future resolutions. Retroactive implication gives the actor a glimpse of the futility and arbitrariness of the undertaking, against which he may redouble his efforts and his commitment. (1986:54–55)

Retroactive implication here bears a striking resemblance to Freud's (1895:356) notion of *Nachträglichkeit*, "deferred action" or retroactive motivation. Freud suggested that sexual experiences that occurred at a very young age were incapable of being understood, owing to the subject's lack of sexual maturity. They are therefore "deferred" until a later date, when, after having become capable of understanding sexual motivation, desire, and its drives, the subject can reconstruct the events as meaningful, and "it is this revision which invests them with significance and even with efficacy or pathogenic force" (LaPlanche and Pontalis 1988:112). A crucial feature of language so conceived is that it includes repression, denial, and forgetting as integral components of its meaning-giving function, without which the perception of temporality would not be possible.[1] The perceived efficacy of past events, in other words, is a function of insights arrived at in the subject's own present.

The capacity for revision and retroactive grounding is itself constitutive of human temporality. But this temporality is itself embodied, made possible by the configuration of the human body's own physical and sensory makeup. As I mentioned in Chapter 1, Freud, Lacan, and Wagner all make a key issue out of the long period of postpartum physical immaturity of humans. The drives exercise themselves within the specular bounds of the body image, where the outline of the body emerges within the field of objects of desire. But it remains for the later acquisition of language, the symbolic capacity, to fix the history of these drives within the narrative of the subject, a narrative that retains and makes visible the other that is its source.

Nor can we refuse to consider that such retroactive motivation is at work in the excavations of subjectivity that we anthropologists label the "analysis of culture" or "cultural symbolism" and the forms in which we usually locate it—myth and ritual. While it is true that there is great variation in gross scale of time in the examples I have referred to—the narration of a myth, the performance of a ritual, the early years of a person's life—it is precisely Wagner's observation that in terms of the way humans construct and perceive interval and causality, obviation, deferral, and retroactive motivation occupy their own time: "What matters in the working out of a sequence, or in the transformation from one sequence to another, is a matter of relationship among points— opposition, mediation, cancellation—rather than arbitrary interval" (1986:81).

To phrase it in the most paradoxical way possible, history also takes place in its own time. History, Lacan said, is not about past events. History is about how a subject views and reconstructs the past and brings this perceived pattern of events into a relation with a current state of affairs (1991a:12). And this process can be studied at the level of a single individual subject or the shared subjectivity of a community of language speakers. The meanings generated in either case are not of different scales; they are perceived as different because they are articulated through different discursive modalities.

What we must realize is that the drives ultimately place their imprint upon all of the body's functions—especially the oral ones upon which it first exercises its form-producing power—and if we then say that consumption and speech have become sexualized, we must speak of that sexuation not in narrowly genital terms but by way of broader processes of splitting, loss, introjection, and extrojection that themselves shape the genital form of sexuality.

Transference and the Resistance of Ritual

Although at times only indirectly, in this book I have made at least two arguments for why I think psychoanalysis and psychoanalytic principles are fundamental to any social science including anthropology. First of all, I do not think it is a coincidence that Freud built his image of the human psyche on what could be called the specimen myth of Western culture—that of Oedipus the King, wherein the whole human drama of temporality, denial, concealment, revelation, and retroactive motivation is depicted. That Freud should resort to this essentially anthropological and cultural analysis indicated that he did not dissociate the mechanisms by which the psyche was formed from those involved in the making visible of cultural symbolism in general. In *The Question of Lay Analysis,* Freud included the following disciplines in what he conceived of as a faculty of psychoanalysis: "the history of civilization, mythology, the psychology of religions, literary history, and literary criticism" (1926:246). But this is not to repeat the mistake of conventional psychological anthropology and view a myth as a collective version of an individual neurosis. Rather, it is to reaffirm the dialectic that Ricoeur identified between analytic and genetic interpretation (see Chapter 1). The former contrast asserts the self-evidence of the distinction between the individual and his/her relations. Ricoeur, on the other hand, makes the contrast between psyche and culture a product of the differential proportions that meaning and interpretation take in social life.

Second, and more specifically, because of Freud's and Lacan's understanding of the centrality of language, and their identification of language as the constituting mechanism of the unconscious, I view the psychoanalytic notions of repression and denial as intrinsic consequences of the metaphoric and metonymic dimensions of language itself in its entirety. And because this language is at once the tool and the object of study, we return to the characterization with which I opened in Chapter 1: both psychoanalysis and anthropology become possible when the analytical model becomes or takes over the thing being modeled. To further elaborate upon this parallel, I must once again consider the technique of both psychoanalysis and anthropology.

Let us recall the theme of one of Freud's most powerful papers on technique, "Remembering, Repeating, and Working Through": what cannot be remembered is repeated in behavior (Lacan 1977b:129). Freud's theory, as I have just noted, was that certain childhood experiences of a traumatic nature are *repressed;* they are consigned to a region of subjectivity that as we know Freud called the unconscious. Once there, they are insulated from language and discourse. But they are not insulated from representation and symbolism *tout court.* They resurface during the life of the subject in disguised form, in dreams, slips of the tongue, and so forth. Most important, their presence is marked in the subject by what he/she *cannot remember.*

What cannot be remembered is repeated in behavior. The subject reproduces the force of the action which accounted for the memory by repeatedly *acting it out.* And he/she does so most explicitly in the analytical situation, and with the analyst as object of the action. So Freud observed: "the patient does not say that he remembers that he used to be defiant and critical towards his parents' authority; instead, he behaves that way to the doctor" (1914:150). Or a woman does not admit that she harbored sexual feelings toward the father; instead, she finds herself falling in love with the analyst. Freud said the following, and there is no other passage in twentieth-century social theorizing which so powerfully illuminates the limits of language: "When one has announced the fundamental rule of psycho-analysis to a patient with an eventful life-history and a long story of illness and has then asked him to say what occurs to his mind, one expects him to pour out a flood of information; but often the first thing that happens is that he has nothing to say . . ." (1914:150). Let us not fail to notice that Freud, like Heidegger, accords a central and important role to silence in characterizing human language. And when we consider what it is we elicit and demand from our informants, is it not true that we rarely know how to leave room for the silence of the repressed and the foreclosed? That in the methodology of the current psychological anthropology the work of repression is made to have the same integrating, representational function that the collective unconscious once had for cultural anthropology?

"Above all, the patient will *begin* his treatment with a repetition of this kind . . . As long as the patient is in the treatment he cannot escape from this compulsion to repeat; and in the end we understand that this is his way of remembering" (Freud 1914:150).

What cannot be said must be acted out. Hence, what is in behavior is not the same thing as what is in language; in fact, what is in behavior competes with or negates what is in language, and what is in language forecloses or repudiates what is in behavior. But it is in the fact of this negation, foreclosure, or repudiation that the possibility of meaning lies, the possibility of the meaningful resolution or interpretation of that repudiation through language. In other words we are led to conclude: *What is seen to lie beyond language must be included in a description of it.* What is negated by language, and what language negates, is part of language. The repetition, the acting out, is made necessary by language's repressive possibilities; it is a function of language, and does not originate or become possible outside it. Ritual, as the anthropological example par excellence of acting out, is a part of language, not as another form of it, but as the articulation of its defining limits, as the repetition which is the beyond of language.

Transference is just a piece of repetition, Freud goes on to say. The analyst wants to encourage such transference, to get the patient to act out such memories, and to aid the patient in transferring the actions themselves to the realm of discourse so that the patient can understand them. But what happens when this is attempted? The patient *resists.* He/she resists the transference. And what is more, "the greater the resistance, the more extensively will acting out (repetition) replace remembering." The stronger the resemblance of the situation to the repressed incident, the more strongly will resistance occur—the more strongly will the subject assert the gaps in discourse.

The general conclusion we draw from this for social science is the following: any interpretive framework must contain within itself some mechanism for its own limitation.[2] For the Foi at least and people like them the process of interpretation is more a narrowing down of the expansive tendencies of trope than an exercise in proliferating alternative readings. The use of terms that refer to concealment, cutting off, covering over, and so forth in the mythic, ritual, and magical languages of the Foi and other myth tellers I have considered attests as much to this restrictive power of trope as to its capacity to enhance meaning and multiply possible glosses. And according to Lacan, this is what Freud tells us to make of the analytic encounter: to annul "the times for understanding in favour of the *moments of concluding* which precipitate the meditation of the subject towards deciding the sense to attach to the original event" (Lacan 1977a:48). The resulting *gaps* in discourse between these discursive punctuations come to model it in at least as important a manner as do the elements which the gaps separate. Furthermore, only by recognizing the gaps will we understand that our theory must always remain incomplete. To construct a complete theory is a formidable accomplishment, but in the completion, the closure of the theory comes a shrinkage, a miniaturization of its effect. To leave a theory incomplete, to leave in it the space to polarize itself against any part of the world one cares to point it, to preserve its greater potential over the thing measured, that is the interpretive task. And we thus return to the caducity with which we began, the acts of detachment which make possible the anticipation of completion.

Desistance and Caducity

On the very first page of the introduction to *Shooting the Sun,* Bernard Juillerat sets out the problem to which he directs his and the contributors' attention: "Of all the productions that human genius and the unconscious have been pleased to present to the observer, often in figurative language, ritual and myth have perhaps proved to be the most *resistant to interpretation*" (1992:1, my emphasis). The first thing that happens, Juillerat observes, is that the myth *has nothing to say* to us. But I hope we can now see this not as some accidental property of symbolism, some complexity that representation has by itself, but rather as the most basic property of any analytic discourse. The analyst or the anthropologist interprets the discourse of the alter not by extending or enlarging its field of associations, but through the opposite: by narrowing down its inherent tendency toward proliferation. And from the opposite perspective, the route of analysis, whether psychoanalytic or anthropological, is always made visible by something that resists, something that cuts off the continuity of conscious meaning and makes it appear incomplete and hence incomprehensible (see Felman 1987: 108). In the same vein, Lacan says that

> one of the things we must guard most against is to understand too much, to understand more than what is in the discourse of the subject. To interpret and to imagine one understands are not at all the same things. (1991a:73)

The analyst/ethnographer interrupts the discourse of the patient by punctuating it. The analyst provides the contours of the interpretive vantage point. He/she controls the way the patient's story will be resolved (see Wilden 1968:74; Lacan 1977a). And this is what I feel is one sense of the phenomenon that Wagner labels obviation: the effect of the analyst, the moment of transference and countertransference between the language of the informant and that of the anthropologist.

What cannot be remembered—that is, what is not sayable—is repeated in behavior. It is *repeated,* and repeatable, and it is also *behavior,* that is, it takes place within the field of specularized body image—or, in New Guinea, the *acoustemic* body image. We have here in Lacanian terms the precise relationship between myth and ritual as we confront it in the Yafar, Umeda, Marind-anim, Foi, and Gimi cases—but elsewhere as well: for example, in the Amazonian *He* (Hugh-Jones 1978), the Australian Djanggawul and Kunapipi (Berndt 1951, 1952), and similar situations where a determinate but nonfunctional relationship exists between discourse and what discourse cannot reveal.

The Marind-anim offered the following as a gloss on the story of Sosom: "*Sosom* is still in the bullroarer he presented to man, it being his voice" (van Baal 1966:486). The object is the form the myth takes *for the Marind,* just as the *dema* are not ancestor creator beings as such but the way they appear in certain notable features of the landscape and through myth. As Manenti concludes in his chapter of *Shooting the Sun,* the ritual belongs to the plane of the Imaginary; to the plane of projection, to where caducity is played out through a series of drives and their objects. The myth is this image whose dehiscence is effected through language, and hence can be said to belong to the Symbolic register, to that which is made partial and hence introjectable. We are struck by how tangential much of the subject matter of these myths is to the portions of ritual to which they are attached, as if the myths were a distorted projection within the field of speech of an essentially unsayable image. In no sense do the myths always explain the origin or meaning of the ritual or any part of it. And if they do, such explanations are external to the imagery of the myth; they cover over the relationship between myth and ritual, they do not represent it. What is *shown* in ritual cannot be hidden or negated; it is subject only to the distortions and refractions of the specular or the acoustemic. In the Yangis, the image of sago growth is shown in its different guises and different masks, and at every point it equates the body part, the whole body, and the container. What is *said* in myth can be and always is hidden; the narrative form the myths take prevents us from seeing them as a mere effusion of the visual representation of ritual within the plane of language.

The depiction of Aphrodite and her shell was commonly found on Grecian burial urns, and in the later Roman Empire shell images were associated with funerary artifacts of all kinds. Jurgis Baltrusaïtis recalls that "as late as the Carolingian epoch, burial grounds often contained snail shells—an allegory of a grave in which man will awaken." What ritual does is to make of language itself a caducity—the *cadeuseus*, the messenger's wand that often commanded the death of the messenger, or, in one of its New Guinea manifestations, the Maring *rumbim*, the cordyline sprig which is passed between groups who have taken each other's lives (Rappaport 1984:148 ff.). Such a message, then, is not a token of the vitality of meaning, its spontaneous efflorescing properties, but the embodiment of a property much more fundamental to it: "the caducity of language, in virtue of which every effusion of the human spirit is lodged in a body of death," as Mark Pattison once put it (1879: 199). The signifier drops away, dies at the moment of its own significatory embryosis. And as a final note, I can do no better than invoke Wittgenstein's famous image of explanatory caducity: The propositions of any social science are of value to us only as they give us some perspective on our interlocutors. Once they have done so, they are like ladders that should fall away after they have been climbed.

Notes

References

Index

Notes

Introduction: The Object(s) of Myth

1. "The antithesis between subjective and objective does not exist at first. It only comes into being from the fact that thinking possesses the capacity to bring before the mind once more something that has once been perceived, by reproducing it as a presentation without the external object having still to be there. The first and immediate aim, therefore, of reality-testing is, not to *find* an object in real perception which corresponds to the one presented, but to *refind* such an object, to convince oneself that it is still there" (Freud 1925:237–38).

2. See Mimica 1988 for an eludication of part-whole relations in the Iqwaye (Yagwoia) counting system.

Chapter 1. The Little Other Myth

1. Robert Paul acknowledges this when he says simply that "the essence of psychoanalysis is its method . . ." (1987:84).

2. "It appears incontestable," Lacan wrote in his famous Rome Discourse, "that the conception of psychoanalysis in the United States has inclined toward the adaptation of the individual to the social environment, toward the quest for patterns of conduct, and toward all the objectification implied in the notion of 'human relations'" (Wilden 1968:7).

3. See Wilden (1968:174) for a similar appeal to intrasubjectivity.

4. Including, as Lévi-Strauss first made clear in *The Savage Mind* (1966), temporal and spatial sequences, the idea of species as an operation of perception rather than a physical feature of the Classified World.

5. "We know by now perhaps a great deal—almost more than we can encompass—about what we call the body, without having seriously thought about what *bodying* is. It is something more and different from merely "carrying a body around with one"; it is that in which everything that we ascertain in the processes and appearances in the body of a living thing first receives its own process-character" (Heidegger 1982:79).

6. In Merleau-Ponty's words: "the libido is not an instinct, that is, an activity naturally directed towards definite ends, it is the general power, which the psychosomatic subject enjoys, of taking root in different settings . . . of gaining structures of conduct. It is what causes a man to have a history. Insofar as a

man's sexual history provides a key to his life, it is because in his sexuality is projected his manner of being towards the world, that is, towards time and other men" (1962:158). And Ricoeur similarly notes: "between sexual behaviour and total behaviour there can only be a relationship of style, or, to put it another way, a relationship of homology. Sexuality is a particular manner of living, a total engagement towards reality" (1970:383).

7. In a Foi myth (Weiner 1985), a woman murders her co-wife and buries the body in a bush-fowl nest. When the husband discovers the crime, he forces the woman to consume the dead victim. Her body swells up and eventually bursts. Out of the fragments originate the first pigs.

Chapter 2. Convention and Motivation in Foi Myth

1. " 'How am I to obey a rule?'—if this is not a question about causes, then it is about the justification for my following the rule the way I do.

"If I have exhausted the justifications I have reached bedrock, and my spade is turned. Then I am inclined to say: 'This is simply what I do'" (Wittgenstein 1953:§217; see also Weiner 1992).

2. Ricoeur says: "Is not the history of the libidinal object, through the various stages of the libido, just such an explication by means of successive retro-references?" (1970:381).

3. The problem is illustrated by the story of a group of long-term prisoners, who knew each other's jokes so well that they numbered them for convenience and instead of relating the joke just called out the numbers: "52," "31," and so on. A new arrival observes his fellow inmates laughing at the mention of numbers and has a stab himself: he calls out "28" but is met only with stony silence. One of the old-timers explains to him, "You just don't know how to tell a joke."

4. Wittgenstein (1953:§225) said that the idea of "the same" was inextricably linked to the notion of "a rule."

5. See Lacan (1977b); Freud (1920:63). Bolinger (1965) explores the implications of repetition on what Chomsky refers to as the basic creativity of speech.

6. These questions have been explored with respect to Western theories of language and meaning by Derrida (1976, 1982).

7. This is what Heidegger (1962) meant by *Vorhabe*, the "fore-having" or anticipation of meaning (see also Rosen 1991). Marilyn Strathern also refers to the "anticipation of completeness" in the context of Melanesian ceremonial exchange (1991a).

8. Schodde and Hitchcock (1968:57) report that "yabaiyu" was the Kutubuan name given to them for the black-headed butcherbird. Like other *Cracticidae*, it subsists on insects and small animals and not fruit, so can be considered a "hawk."

9. See Gillian Gillison's comments on tree imagery among the Gimi of Papua New Guinea: "Trees are phallic projections which not only have 'heads' that feed birds . . . but they also have hollow trunks inside which nest 'female' marsupials" (1980:170).

10. Another Foi myth describes how the hornbill and cassowary, who were

cross-cousins to each other, once inhabited each other's realms: the cassowary flew in the air and the hornbill inhabited the ground. They agreed to switch places and the hornbill now flies through the air and the cassowary is a ground dweller.

11.   It is clear that the theory of symbolic obviation shares much in common with Derrida's (1978, 1982) notions of original *différance*, particularly as he interprets Freud's early theories of neuronic differentiation and originary "breaching" of neuronic pathways.

12.   Schwimmer (1974) suggests that there is a difference in Orokaiva between "metaphoric" gifts, about which we are told in myths and which establish an equivalence between the gift and the recipient, and "metonymic" gifts, in which the social relations between the exchangers are not changed by the gift; in short, between equivalences taking place within a surrounding mythic frame, and those that index normative social structure. But this would be to make an arbitrary division between discursive and nondiscursive effects of signifying objects not wholly substantiated. What betel nut and coconut mark out for the Orokaiva, for example, is not metaphoricity or metonymy in and of themselves, but a certain way in which gender roles are created in relation to symbolic discourse.

Chapter 3. The Space and Time of Sexuality

1.   *Waridj* is the kinship term designated MMBSS, or classificatory brother (female speaking).

2.   Other examples of movement through space iconically rendered in discursive form include: the detotalization of animal bodies as the North American Osage chiefs "walk the path of life" (La Flesche 1917); the mourning epic sung by the Rotinese of Eastern Indonesia (Fox 1988), which makes a journey of a person's life course; and the mourning laments of the Foi of Papua New Guinea which I have described elsewhere (Weiner 1991).

3.   "The consciousness of my existence is at the same time an immediate consciousness of the existence of other things outside me" (Kant 1990:B276).

4.   This translation of Muller and Richardson's, which I prefer, diverges significantly from that given in Alan Sheridan's English translation of *Écrits*, which reads as follows: "If linguistics enables us to see the signifier as the determinant of the signified, analysis reveals the truth of this relation by making 'holes' in the meaning of the determinants of its discourse" (Lacan 1977a:299).

5.   This is a stylized sequence. The man cries out "Men! men! men!" as if enemy warriors were about to attack (i.e., "Men are coming! Men are coming!"). This is supposed to awaken sleeping men so that they can come to the defense of the house.

6.   In the mythology of the Marind-anim (van Baal 1966), Uaba and Ualiwamb are male and female creator beings or *dema* who become locked in copulation. Crotons are planted around the house where this occurred. As a result, crotons are planted around all the *dema* ritual houses in Marind-anim ceremonies (see next chapter).

7. As Derrida warns in his essay "Differance": "The structure of delay . . . in effect forbids that one make of temporalization (*nachträglichkeit*) a simple dialectical complication of the living present as an originary and unceasing synthesis . . . of retentional traces and protensional openings" (1982:21).

Chapter 4. The Hunger People

1. As we saw in the preceding chapter, the Foi make explicit connection between flowers, pearl shells, and sexual intercourse.

2. The Tahitian chestnut, which needs to be cooked before it can be eaten, unlike the coconut.

3. See also the Kiwai myth (Landtman 1917:119–21), where after eating vegetables a man's penis becomes filled with vegetable food. When he later attempts to have sexual intercourse, he ejaculates the vegetables, which then form the first garden.

4. This version of the *kambara* activities was given by Wirz (1922–25[II]: 68).

Chapter 5. The Lost Drum

1. These skirts, called *kuisiribu,* resemble a woman's string skirt, which itself is like a "string bag" for the vagina and uterus. A man's skirt is ankle-length, just as the drum is long, while the woman's covers only her pubic area.

2. See Weiner 1991a: The drum recites the names of different kinds of geographical water, in the manner of a Foi memorial song poem which characteristically links the life course of a deceased man with the places he inhabited. These places are usually located in the hunting territory of the Foi. Hence, the drum and the breast collide as antithetical objects: hunting and domesticity, and the woman's insertion of the breast milk into the bamboo tube, cancel the hunting imagery evoked by the drum's voice. That is, the woman's phallus, her breast, is not detached, yet it causes the brother's phallus to become detached from him.

Chapter 6. The Stolen String Bag

1. A point Gregory Bateson (1958) made central to his concept of schismogenesis.

Chapter 7. The Origin of Petroleum at Lake Kutubu

1. I am indebted to Donald S. Gardner for this phrase.

2. See for example Battaglia 1990; Jorgensen 1986; A. Weiner 1991.

3. The Australians used them as a medium of barter with local people and as a method of payment for temporary laborers.

4. The neural pathways to the limbs do not become fully sheathed in myelin until the second year.

5. Obviously, the advent of the mirror stage is not literally dependent upon the presence of mirrors for the child to look into, or even of a natural reflecting

surface like still water, or the contemplation of one's shadow. The recognition of one's reflection in the mirror is just a shorthand for the stage which begins when the child recognizes the scope of its own bodily lineaments in the presence and movements of other bodies.

6. In more than one interior Papua New Guinea society, men are reported as saying, "If I, instead of my sister, had been born with a womb, then her children would have been my own" as an explanation of why they have claims on their sisters' children.

7. The fiction that the exchange creates the practical bonds of interpersonal kinship and political/marital alliance is itself a collusion on the part of the anthropologist and informant to give a positivist, economic grounding to what is at best a communal theater in which most often the exchanges bring out into the open what everyone already knows, rather than being spontaneously creative. But by a Freudian act of negation, such a fiction makes exchange do all the creative work in society, seeing it as the Lévi-Straussian, Rousseauian transition to originary sociality.

8. The fact that some Foi know that the tinned fish is produced by Japanese factory ships operating virtually in Papua New Guinea waters does not diminish this image, as Japanese are just another variety of European, a conclusion justified, if anything, by the fact that Australians and Japanese were once enemies and fought with each other.

9. Marilyn Strathern reminds me that the Mt. Hagen people used to think that what was wealth for them was shit for Europeans, and vice versa: what they didn't value at all (i.e., food) was paid for with wealth by Europeans.

Chapter 8. Afterword: The Resistance of Myth

1. "The general precondition of repression is thus clearly deemed to be in the 'delaying of puberty' which is characteristic, according to Freud, of human sexuality: 'Every adolescent individual has memory-traces which can only be understood with the emergence of sexual feelings of his own' [*SE* 1:356]. '*The retardation of puberty makes possible posthumous primary processes*' [*SE* 1:359]" (LaPlanche and Pontalis 1988:113).

2. Crapanzano thus says that: "All hermeneutical systems are threatened with an interpretive swirl and must provide ideologically supported conventions that arrest it. Such conventions . . . require a forgetting" (1992:121).

References

Austin, J. L. 1975. *How to Do Things with Words*. Cambridge: Harvard University Press.

Bachelard, G. 1969. *The Poetics of Space*. Boston: Beacon Press.

Baltrusaïtis, J. 1977. *Anamorphic Art*. Cambridge, Eng.: Chadwyck-Healy.

Bateson, G. 1958. *Naven*. Stanford: Stanford University Press.

Battaglia, D. 1990. *On the Bones of the Serpent*. Chicago: University of Chicago Press.

Beehler, B., T. Pratt, and D. Zimmerman. 1986. *Birds of New Guinea*. Princeton: Princeton University Press.

Benveniste, E. 1971. *Problems in General Linguistics*. Coral Gables, Fla.: University of Miami Press.

Benvenuto, B., and R. Kennedy. 1986. *The Works of Jacques Lacan: An Introduction*. New York: St. Martin's Press.

Berndt, R. 1951. *Kunapipi*. Melbourne: Cheshire.

Berndt, R. 1952. *Djanggawul*. Melbourne: Cheshire.

Berndt, R. 1976. *Love Songs of Arnhem Land*. Chicago: University of Chicago Press.

Bolinger, D. 1965. *Forms of English*. Tokyo: Hokuou Publishing Co.

Bourdieu, P. 1977. *Outline of a Theory of Practice*. Cambridge: Cambridge University Press.

Bowie, M. 1991. *Lacan*. London: Fontana.

Cassirer, E. 1955. *The Philosophy of Symbolic Forms*. Vol. 1: *Language*. New Haven: Yale University Press.

Clark, J. 1991. "Pearlshell Symbolism in Highlands Papua New Guinea, with Particular Reference to the Wiru People of Southern Highlands Province." *Oceania* 61:309–39.

Crapanzano, V. 1992. *Hermes' Dilemma and Hamlet's Desire*. Cambridge: Harvard University Press.

Dali, S. 1990. *Diary of a Genius*. London: Hutchinson.

Deleuze, G., and F. Guattari. 1983. *Anti-Oedipus*. London: Athlone Press.

Derrida, J. 1976. *Of Grammatology*. Baltimore: Johns Hopkins University Press.

Derrida, J. 1978. *Writing and Difference*. Chicago: University of Chicago Press.

Derrida, J. 1981. *Dissemination*. London: Athlone Press.

Derrida, J. 1982. *Margins of Philosophy*. London: Harvester.

Eco, U. 1986. *Semiotics and the Philosophy of Language.* Bloomington: Indiana University Press.

Ernst, T. 1979. "Myth, Ritual, and Population among the Marind-anim." *Social Analysis* 1:34–53.

Felman, S. 1987. *Jacques Lacan and the Adventure of Insight.* Cambridge: Harvard University Press.

Forge, A. 1966. "Art and Environment in the Sepik." *Proceedings of the Royal Anthropological Institute* 1965:23–31.

Forrester, J. 1990. *The Seductions of Psychoanalysis.* Cambridge: Cambridge University Press.

Fox, J. 1988. "Manu Kama's Road, Tepa Nilu's Path: Theme, Narrative, and Formula in Rotinese Ritual Language." In J. Fox, ed., *To Speak in Pairs: Essays on the Ritual Languages of Eastern Indonesia.* Cambridge: Cambridge University Press.

Freud, S. 1895. *Project for a Scientific Psychology. Standard Edition of the Complete Works,* ed. James Strachey. I:283–397. London: Hogarth Press.

Freud, S. 1899. "Screen Memories." *S.E.* III:301–22.

Freud, S. 1910. *Leonardo da Vinci and a Memory of His Childhood. S.E.* XI:59–137.

Freud, S. 1912. "The Dynamics of Transference." *S.E.* XII:98–108.

Freud, S. 1914. "Remembering, Repeating, and Working Through." *S.E.* XII: 145–56.

Freud, S. 1915. "The Unconscious." *S.E.* XIV:159–215.

Freud, S. 1917. "Mourning and Melancholia." *S.E.* XIV:237–58.

Freud, S. 1920. *Beyond the Pleasure Principle. S.E.* XVIII:3–64.

Freud, S. 1923. *The Ego and the Id. S.E.* XIX:3–66.

Freud, S. 1925. "Negation." *S.E.* XIX:234–39.

Freud, S. 1926. *The Question of Lay Analysis. S.E.* XX:179–258.

Freud, S. 1933. *New Introductory Lectures in Psycho-analysis. S.E.* XXII:3–182.

Friedrich, P. 1979. *Language, Context, and the Imagination: Essays.* Stanford: Stanford University Press.

Gell, A. 1975. *Metamorphosis of the Cassowaries.* London: Athlone Press.

Gell, A. 1992. *The Anthropology of Time: Cultural Constructions of Temporal Maps and Images.* London: Berg.

Gillison, G. 1980. "Images of Nature in Gimi Thought." In C. MacCormack and M. Strathern, eds., *Nature, Culture and Gender.* Cambridge: Cambridge University Press.

Gillison, G. 1983. "Cannibalism among Women in the Eastern Highlands of Papua New Guinea." In P. Brown and D. Tuzin, eds., *The Ethnography of Cannibalism.* Washington: Society for Psychological Anthropology.

Gillison, G. 1993. *Between Culture and Fantasy: A New Guinea Highlands Mythology.* Chicago: University of Chicago Press.

Gregory, C. 1982. *Gifts and Commodities.* London: Academic Press.

Grottanelli, V. L. 1951. "On the 'Mysterious' *Baratu* Clubs from Central New Guinea." *Man* 51, no. 185.

Hanks, W. 1990. *Referential Practice: Language and Lived Space among the Maya.* Chicago: University of Chicago Press.

Heidegger, M. 1962. *Being and Time.* Trans. J. Macquarrie and E. Robinson. SCM Press.

Heidegger, M. 1979. *Nietzsche,* vol. 1: *The Will to Power as Art.* New York: Harper and Collins.

Heidegger, M. 1982. *Nietzsche,* vol. 3: *The Will to Power as Knowledge and Metaphysics.* New York: Harper and Collins.

Heidegger, M. 1990. *Kant and the Problem of Metaphysics.* Trans. Richard Taft. Bloomington: Indiana University Press.

Herdt, G. 1984a. "Ritualized Homosexual Behaviour in the Male Cults of Melanesia, 1862–1983: An Introduction." In G. Herdt, ed., *Ritualized Homosexuality in Melanesia.* Berkeley: University of California Press.

Herdt, G. 1984b. "Semen Transfers in Sambia Culture." In Herdt, *Ritualized Homosexuality.*

Herdt, G. 1987. *The Sambia: Ritual and Gender in New Guinea.* New York: Holt, Rinehart, and Winston.

Hugh-Jones, S. 1978. *The Palm and the Pleiades.* Cambridge: Cambridge University Press.

Hylkema, S. 1974. *Mannen in het draagnet.* Verhandelingen van het Koninklijk Instituut voor taal-, land-, en volkenkunde #67. The Hague: Martinus Nijhoff.

Jones, E. 1950. "Early Development of Female Sexuality." In *Papers on Psychoanalysis.* London: Bailliere, Tindall, and Cox.

Jorgensen, D., ed. 1986. *Concepts of Conception: Procreation Ideologies of Papua New Guinea. Mankind* special issue, vol. 14, no. 1.

Juillerat, B., ed. 1992. *Shooting the Sun: Ritual and Meaning in West Sepik.* Washington: Smithsonian Institute Press.

Kant, I. 1990. *Critique of Pure Reason.* Trans. Norton Kemp Smith. London: Macmillan.

Kelly, R. 1977. *Etoro Social Structure: A Study in Structural Contradiction.* Ann Arbor: University of Michigan Press.

Klein, M. 1929. "Infantile Anxiety Situations Reflected in a Work of Art and in the Creative Impulse." *International Journal of Psychoanalysis* 10:436–43. Reprinted in J. Mitchell, ed., *The Selected Melanie Klein,* London: Penguin (1986).

Klein, M. 1986. "Notes on Some Schizoid Mechanisms." In J. Mitchell, ed., *The Selected Melanie Klein,* 175–200. London: Penguin.

Knauft, B. 1993. *South Coast New Guinea Cultures.* Cambridge: Cambridge University Press.

Kooijman, S. 1952. "The Function and Significance of Some Ceremonial Clubs of the Marind-anim, Dutch New Guinea." *Man* 52, no. 139.

Lacan, J. 1977a. *Écrits: A Selection.* Trans. Alan Sheridan. London: Routledge.

Lacan, J. 1977b. *The Four Fundamental Concepts of Psychoanalysis (Seminar Book XI).* Ed. J.-A. Miller. Trans. Alan Sheridan. London: Penguin Books.

Lacan, J. 1991a. *Seminar Book I: Freud's Papers on Technique.* Ed. J.-A. Miller. Trans. John Forrester. New York: Norton.

Lacan, J. 1991b. *Seminar Book II: The Ego in Freud's Theory and in the Technique of Psychoanalysis.* Ed. J.-A. Miller. Trans. Sylvana Tomaselli. New York: Norton.

Lacan, J. 1992. *Seminar Book VII: The Ethics of Psychoanalysis*. Ed. J.-A. Miller. Trans. Dennis Porter. London: Routledge.

Lacoue-Labarthe, P. 1990. *Heidegger, Art and Politics*. Oxford: Basil Blackwell.

LaFlesche, F. 1917. "The Osage Tribe: The Rite of Vigil." *Annual Report of the Bureau of American Ethnology* 39:31–630.

Landtman, G. 1917. *Folktales of the Kiwai Papuans*. Acta Societatis Scientiarum Fennicae 47. Helsinki: Printing Office of the Finnish Society of Literature.

LaPlanche, J., and S. Leclaire. 1972. "The Unconscious: A Psychoanalytic Study." *Yale French Studies* 48:118–202.

LaPlanche, J., and J.-B. Pontalis. 1988. *The Language of Psychoanalysis*. London: Karnac Books and the Institute of Psychoanalysis.

Lawrence, P. 1956. *Road Belong Cargo*. Manchester: Manchester University Press.

LeRoy, J. 1985. *Kewa Tales*. Vancouver: University of British Columbia Press.

Lévi-Strauss, C. 1963. *Structural Anthropology*. New York: Basic Books.

Lévi-Strauss, C. 1966. *The Savage Mind*. Chicago: University of Chicago Press.

Lévi-Strauss, C. 1978. *The Origin of Table Manners (Mythologiques*, vol. 3*)*. New York: Harper and Row.

Macey, D. 1988. *Lacan in Contexts*. London: Verso.

Meggitt, M. 1976. "A Duplicity of Demons: Sexual and Familial Roles Expressed in Western Enga Stories." In P. Brown and G. Buchbinder, eds., *Man and Woman in the New Guinea Highlands*. American Anthropological Association Special Publication no. 8.

Meigs, A. 1984. *Food, Sex and Pollution: A New Guinea Religion*. New Brunswick: Rutgers University Press.

Merian, F., and A. Rumsey. 1991. *Ku Waru: Language and Segmentary Politics in the Western Nebilyer Valley, Papua New Guinea*. Cambridge: Cambridge University Press.

Merleau-Ponty, M. 1962. *Phenomenology of Perception*. London: RKP.

Mimica, J. 1981. "Omalyce: An Ethnography of the Ikwaye view of the Cosmos." Ph.D. thesis. Australian National University.

Mimica, J. 1988. *Intimations of Infinity*. London: Berg.

Muller, J. and W. Richardson. 1982. *Lacan and Language: A Reader's Guide to Écrits*. New York: International Universities Press.

Nancy, J.-L., and P. Lacoue-Labarthe. 1992. *The Title of the Letter: A Reading of Lacan*. Trans. F. Raffoul and D. Pettigrew. Albany, NY: State University of New York Press.

Nihill, M. 1988. "'Worlds at War with Themselves': Notions of the Anti-Society in Anganen Ceremonial Exchange." *Oceania* 58, no. 4:255–74.

Parmentier, R. 1990. "Tropical Semiotics: Global, Local, and Discursive Contexts of Symbolic Obviation." *Semiotica* 79, nos. 1/2:167–95.

Pattison, M. 1879. *Milton*. London: Macmillan.

Paul, R. 1987. "The Question of Applied Psychoanalysis and the Interpretation of Cultural Symbolism." *Ethos* 15, no. 1:82–103.

Rappaport, R. 1984. *Pigs for the Ancestors*. New Haven: Yale University Press.

Ricoeur, P. 1970. *Freud and Philosophy*. New Haven: Yale University Press.

Ricoeur, P. 1981. *Hermeneutics and the Human Sciences.* Ed. and trans. John B. Thompson. Cambridge: Cambridge University Press.

Rodman, M. 1994. "Empowering Place: Multilocality and Multivocality." *American Anthropologist* 94, no. 3:640–56.

Rosen, S. 1991. "Squaring the Hermeneutic Circle." *Review of Metaphysics* 44: 707–28.

Schodde, R., and W. Hitchcock. 1968. "Report on the Birds of the Lake Kutubu Area, Territory of Papua and New Guinea." *Contributions to Papuasian Ornithology* 1 (Division of Wildlife Research Technical Paper no. 13). Melbourne: CSIRO.

Schwimmer, E. 1974. "Objects of Mediation: Myth and Praxis." In I. Rossi, ed., *The Unconscious in Culture.* New York: E. P. Dutton.

Sherzer, J. 1990. *Verbal Art in San Blas: Kuna Culture through Its Discourse.* Cambridge: Cambridge University Press.

Sillitoe, P. 1979. "Cosmetics from Trees: An Underrated Trade in Papua New Guinea." *Australian Natural History* 19, no. 9:292–97.

Sørum, A. 1984. "Growth and Decay: Bedamini Notions of Sexuality." In G. Herdt, ed., *Ritualized Homosexuality in Melanesia.* Berkeley: University of California Press.

Spiro, M. 1951. "Culture and Personality: The Natural History of a False Dichotomy." *Psychiatry* 14:19–46.

Strathern, A. 1968. *The Rope of Moka.* Cambridge: Cambridge University Press.

Strathern, M. 1980. "Culture in a Net Bag: The Manufacture of a Sub-Discipline in Anthropology." *Man* 16:665–88.

Strathern, M. 1988. *The Gender of the Gift.* Berkeley: University of California Press.

Strathern, M. 1991a. *Partial Connections.* Savage, MD: Rowman and Littlefield.

Strathern, M. 1991b. "One Man and Many Men." In M. Godelier and M. Strathern, eds., *Big Men and Great Men.* Cambridge: Cambridge University Press.

Strathern, M. 1993. "The Uses of Knowledge." Paper presented at the plenary session of the ASA IV Decennial Conference, 30 July, Oxford University.

Tuzin, D. 1978. "Sex and Meat-Eating in Ilahita: A Symbolic Study." *Canberra Anthropology* 1, no. 3:82–93.

Van Baal, J. 1963. "The Cult of the Bull-Roarer in Australia and Southern New Guinea." *Bijdragen tot de taal-, land- en volkenkunde* 119:201–14.

Van Baal, J. 1966. *Dema: Description and Analysis of Marind-anim Culture (South New Guinea).* The Hague: Martinus Nijhoff.

Van Baal, J. 1984. "The Dialectics of Sex in Marind-anim Culture." In G. Herdt, ed., *Ritualized Homosexuality in Melanesia.* Berkeley: University of California Press.

Van Buren, J. 1989. *The Modernist Madonna: Semiotics of the Maternal Metaphor.* Bloomington: Indiana University Press.

Wagner, R. 1967. *The Curse of Souw.* Chicago: University of Chicago Press.

Wagner, R. 1972. *Habu.* Chicago: University of Chicago Press.

Wagner, R. 1977. "'Speaking for Others': Power and Identity as Factors in Daribi Mediumistic Hysteria." *Journal de la Société des Océanistes* 56–57:145–52.

Wagner, R. 1978. *Lethal Speech*. Ithaca: Cornell University Press.

Wagner, R. 1981. *The Invention of Culture*. Chicago: University of Chicago Press.

Wagner, R. 1986. *Symbols That Stand for Themselves*. Chicago: University of Chicago Press.

Wagner, R. Foreword. In Weiner 1988.

Wagner, R. 1991. "The Fractal Person." In M. Godelier and M. Strathern, eds., *Big-Men and Great Men*. Cambridge: Cambridge University Press.

Wagner, R. n.d. "Making Sense of the White Man: Two Barok Tales." Manuscript in author's possession.

Weiner, A. 1991. *Inalienable Possessions*. Berkeley: University of California Press.

Weiner, J. 1984. "Sunset and Flowers: The Sexual Dimension of Foi Spatial Orientation." *Journal of Anthropological Research* 40, no. 4:577–88.

Weiner, J. 1985. "The Treachery of Co-Wives: The Mythical Origin of Mediating Food Items in Foi." *Journal de la Société des Océanistes* 41, no. 80:39–50.

Weiner, J. 1988. *The Heart of the Pearl Shell*. Berkeley: University of California Press.

Weiner, J. 1991a. *The Empty Place*. Bloomington: Indiana University Press.

Weiner, J. 1991b. "Reply to Jan Pouwer." *Bijdragen tot de taal-, land- en volkenkunde* 147, no. 4:509–10.

Weiner, J. 1992. "Against the Motion (II)." *Group for Debate in Anthropological Theory*, no. 4: *Language Is the Essence of Culture*, ed. Tim Ingold. Manchester: Department of Social Anthropology, University of Manchester.

Wilden, A. 1968. "Lacan and the Discourse of the Other." In *Speech and Language in Psychoanalysis*. Baltimore: Johns Hopkins University Press.

Williams, F. E. 1936. *Papuans of the Trans-Fly*. Oxford: Clarendon Press.

Williams, F. E. 1977. "Natives of Lake Kutubu, Papua." In *The Vailala Madness and Other Essays*, ed. Erik Schwimmer. Honolulu: University of Hawaii Press.

Wirz, P. 1922–25. Die Marind-anim von Hollandische-Sud-Neu-Guinea, I–IV. 2 vols. Abhandlungen aus dem Gebiet der Auslandkunde, Band 10 und 16 (Reihe B, Band 6 und 9). Hamburg: Hamburgische Universitat.

Witherspoon, G. 1977. *Language and Art in the Navajo Universe*. Ann Arbor: University of Michigan Press.

Wittgenstein, L. 1953. *Philosophical Investigations*. Oxford: Basil Blackwell.

Index

New Directions in Anthropological Writing
History, Poetics, Cultural Criticism

GEORGE E. MARCUS
Rice University
JAMES CLIFFORD
University of California, Santa Cruz

GENERAL EDITORS

Magical Arrows: The Maori, the Greeks, and the Folklore of the Universe
GREGORY SCHREMPP

After Freedom: A Cultural Study in the Deep South
HORTENSE POWDERMAKER
With an introductory essay by Brackette F. Williams and Drexel G. Woodson

Dancing with the Devil: Society and Cultural Poetics in Mexican-American South Texas
JOSÉ E. LIMÓN

To Remember the Faces of the Dead: The Plenitude of Memory in Southwestern New Britain
THOMAS MASCHIO

Sanumá Memories: A Yanomami Ethnography in Times of Crisis
ALCIDA RITA RAMOS

Fragments of Death, Fables of Identity: An Athenian Anthropography
NENI PANOURGIÁ

The Lost Drum: The Myth of Sexuality in Papua New Guinea and Beyond
JAMES F. WEINER